ADVANCED SQL
FUNCTIONS IN
ORACLE® 10g

Richard Walsh Earp
Sikha Saha Bagui

Wordware Publishing, Inc.

Library of Congress Cataloging-in-Publication Data

Earp, Richard, 1940-
    Advanced SQL functions in Oracle 10g / by Richard Walsh Earp
    and Sikha Saha Bagui.
      p. cm.
    Includes bibliographical references and index.
    ISBN-13: 978-1-59822-021-6
    ISBN-10: 1-59822-021-7 (pbk.)
    1. SQL (Computer program language)   2. Oracle (Computer file).
    I. Bagui, Sikha, 1964-. II. Title.
    QA76.73.S67E26 2006
    005.13'3--dc22   2005036444
                                         CIP

ISBN-13: 978-1-59822-021-6
ISBN-10: 1-59822-021-7
10 9 8 7 6 5 4 3 2 1
0601

All inquiries for volume purchases of this book should be addressed to Wordware Publishing, Inc., at the above address. Telephone inquiries may be made by calling:

(972) 423-0090

To my wife, Brenda,
and
my children, Beryl, Rich, Gen, and Mary Jo
R.W.E.

To my father, Santosh Saha, and mother, Ranu Saha,
and
my husband, Subhash Bagui,
and
my sons, Sumon and Sudip,
and
my brother, Pradeep, and nieces, Priyashi and Piyali
S.S.B.

Contents

Contents

Contents

Preface

Why This Book?

Oracle® 10*g* has introduced new features into its reper-
toire of SQL instructions that make database queries
more versatile. When programmers use SQL in Oracle,
they inevitably look for easier and new ways to handle
queries. What is needed is a way to introduce SQL
users to the new features of Oracle 10*g* concisely and
systematically so that database programmers can take
full advantage of the newer capabilities. This book
hopes to meet this need by exploring some common
new SQL features. Each chapter includes numerous
working examples, and Oracle users can run these
examples as they read and work through the book.
Also, many books on Oracle 10*g* present the language
syntax alone with no in-depth explanation, analysis, or
examples. In this book, we present not only the syntax
for new features and functions, but also a thorough
clarification and breakdown of the different functions,
along with examples of ways they can and should be
used.

Audience and Coverage

This book is meant to be used by Oracle professionals
as well as students, but it is not a SQL primer. Readers
of this book are expected to have previously used Oracle, SQL*Plus, and, to some extent, PL/SQL. This book
can be used for individual study or reference, in
advanced Oracle training settings, and in advanced

database classes in schools. It is meant for those familiar with SQL programming since most of the topics present not only the syntax, queries, and answers, but also have an analytical programming perspective to them. This book will allow the Oracle user to use SQL in new and exciting ways.

This book contains nine chapters. It begins by reviewing some of the common SQL functions and techniques to help transition into the newer tools of Oracle 10*g*. Chapter 1 reviews common Oracle functions. Chapter 2 covers some common reporting tools in Oracle's SQL*Plus. Chapter 3 introduces and discusses Oracle 10*g*'s analytical functions, and Chapter 4 discusses Oracle 10*g*'s aggregate functions that are used as analytical functions. Chapter 5 looks at the use of analytical functions in reporting — for example, the use of GROUP BY, ROLLUP, and CUBE. Chapter 6 discusses the MODEL or SPREADSHEET predicate in Oracle's SQL. Chapter 7 covers the new regular expressions and string functions. Chapter 8 discusses collections and object-oriented features of Oracle 10*g*. Chapter 9 introduces by example the bridges between SQL and XML, one of the most important topics Oracle professionals are expected to know today.

This book also has two appendices. Appendix A illustrates string functions with examples, and Appendix B gives examples of some important statistical functions available in Oracle 10*g*.

Overall, this book explores advanced new features of SQL in Oracle 10*g* from a programmer's perspective. The book can be considered a starting point for research using some of the advanced topics since the subjects are discussed at length with examples and sample outputs. Query development is approached from a logical standpoint, and in many areas performance implications of the queries are also discussed.

Acknowledgments

Our special thanks to the staff at Wordware Publishing, especially Wes Beckwith, Beth Kohler, Martha McCuller, and Denise McEvoy.

We would also like to thank President John Cavanaugh, Dean Jane Halonen, and Provost Sandra Flake for their inspiration, encouragement, support, and true leadership. We would also like to express our gratitude to Dr. Wes Little on the same endeavor. Our sincere thanks also goes to Dr. Ed Rodgers for his continuing support and encouragement throughout the years. We also appreciate Dr. Leonard Ter Haar, chair of the computer science department, for his advice, guidance, and support, and encouraging us to complete this book. Last, but not least, we would like to thank our fellow faculty members Dr. Jim Bezdek and Dr. Norman Wilde for their continuous support and encouragement.

Introduction

With the advent of new features added to SQL in Oracle 10*g*, we thought that some collection of material related to the newer query mechanisms was in order. Hence, in this book we have gathered some useful new tools into a set of topics for exploiting Oracle 10*g*'s SQL. We have also briefly reviewed some older tools that will help transition to the new material.

This book mainly addresses advanced topics in SQL with a focus on SQL functions for Oracle 10*g*. The functions and methods we cover include the analytical functions, MODEL statements, regular expressions, and object-oriented/collection structures. We also introduce and give examples of the SQL/XML bridges as XML is a newer and common method of transferring data from user to user. We rely heavily on examples, as most SQL programmers can and do adapt examples to other problems quickly.

Prerequisites

Some knowledge of SQL is assumed before beginning this study, as this book is not meant to be a SQL primer. More specifically, some knowledge of Oracle functions is desirable, although some common functions are reviewed in Chapter 1. Functions have been refined and expanded as Oracle versions have evolved, culminating with the latest in Oracle 10*g* — analytical functions, MODEL statements, and regular expressions. Additionally, the collection/object-oriented structures of later versions of Oracle are covered and include some unique functions as well. Many people now use XML to capture and move data; examples of moving data from SQL*Plus to and from XML are also covered.

Some knowledge of spreadsheets is helpful in digesting this material. The analytical functions and MODEL statements provide convenient ways to display and use data in a manner similar to a spreadsheet. While these functions are far more than simply display mechanisms, often reporting/formatting functions are used in conjunction with analytical functions. We review some common reporting functions in Chapter 2.

Our Approach to SQL

In addition to a basic knowledge of SQL, we will call attention to "our way" of developing queries in SQL. The way we develop queries in SQL is often by beginning with a simple command and then building upon it until the answer is found. There are different approaches to building queries in SQL as in any other language. One way is to build for a result using logical, intermediate steps. A second way to build SQL queries is for performance. In a real-world environment with large tables, performance usually becomes an issue on often-run commands. Even in the development of queries, performance issues may arise.

The way this material is approached is less from the performance perspective and more from the logical, developmental viewpoint. Once a result is obtained, if the query is to be rerun, it is most appropriate to tune the query for performance by examining the way it was done and perhaps look for alternatives, e.g., joins versus subqueries.

To develop queries, we will often find a result set and then use that result set to move to the next part of the query. This modular approach has an uncomplicated appeal as well as a way to check and examine intermediate results. If the intermediate result is faulty, then we correct and refine before we move on. One should always be suspicious of intermediate results by asking questions like, "Does this result make sense?", "How can we have that many rows?", or "How many rows did you expect?" When we are satisfied with the result we have produced, we use the result in a virtual table to attain the next level.

For example, consider this query:

```
SELECT class, COUNT(*)
FROM students
GROUP BY class
```

Having studied this result, we might use it in a virtual table for another query. We can wrap our working query in parentheses (hence making it a virtual view) and then query it like this:

```
SELECT MAX(enrollment)
FROM
(SELECT class, COUNT(*) enrollment
FROM students
GROUP BY class)
```

There are, of course, times in real-world applications where the virtual view is so complicated that it needs to become a real view or even a temporary table. We call this virtual table approach "wrap and build."

In writing queries, we often use aliasing. Some might argue that we overuse aliases, but we believe that it makes a query more meaningful, easier to debug, and more available for change in the future. As well, in deference to precedence rules and defaults, when a programmer uses aliases, he is very clear about what the aliases meant when he wrote the query in the first place.

Chapter 1

Common Oracle Functions: A Function Review

Oracle functions operate on "appropriate data" to transform a value to another value. For example, using a simple calculator, we commonly use the square root function to compute the square root of some number. In this case, the square root key on the calculator calls the square root function and the number in the display is transformed into its square root value. In the square root case, "appropriate data" is a positive number. For the sake of defining the scope of this discussion, we also consider the square root key on a calculator as a one-to-one function. By one-to-one we mean that if one positive number is furnished, then one square root results from pressing the square root key — a one-to-one transformation.

If we show the square root function algebraically as SQRT, the resulting number as "Answer," the equal sign as meaning "is assigned to," and the number to be operated on as "original_value," then the function could be written like this:

```
Answer = SQRT(original_value)
```

where *original_value* is a positive number.

In algebra, the allowable values of *original_value* are called the domain of the function, which in this case is the set of non-negative numbers. *Answer* is called the range of the function. *Original_value* in this example is called the argument of the function SQRT. Oftentimes in computer situations, there is also an upper limit on the domain and range, but theoretically, there is no upper limit in algebra. The lower limit on the domain is zero as the square root of negative numbers is undefined unless one ventures into the area of complex numbers, which is beyond the scope of this discussion.

Almost any programming language uses functions similar to those found on calculators. In fact, most programming languages go far beyond the calculator functions.

Oracle's SQL contains a rich variety of functions. We can categorize Oracle's SQL functions into simple SQL functions, numeric functions, statistical functions, string functions, and date functions. In this chapter, we selectively illustrate several functions in each of these categories. We start by discussing simple SQL functions.

Calling Simple SQL Functions

Oracle has a large number of simple functions. Wherever a value is used directly or computed in a SQL statement, a simple SQL function may be used. To illustrate the above square root function, suppose that a table named Measurement contained a series of numeric measured values like this:

Subject	Value
First	35.78
Second	22.22
Third	55.55

We could display the table with this SQL query:

```
SELECT *
FROM measurement
```

Note: We will not use semicolons at the end of SQL statement illustrations; to run these statements in Oracle from the command line, a semicolon must be added. From the editor, a slash (/) is added to execute the statement and no semicolon is used.

We could also generate the same result set with this SQL query:

```
SELECT subject, value
FROM measurement
```

Using the latter query, and adding a square root function to the result set, the SQL query would look like this:

```
SELECT subject, value, SQRT(value)
FROM measurement
```

This would give the following result:

```
SUBJECT        VALUE SQRT(VALUE)
---------- ---------- -----------
First          35.78 5.98163857
Second         22.22  4.7138095
Third          55.55 7.45318724
```

Numeric Functions

In this section we present and discuss several useful numeric functions, which we divide into the following categories: common numerical manipulation functions, near value functions, null value functions, log and exponential functions, ordinary trigonometry functions, and hyperbolic trignometrical functions.

Common Numerical Manipulation Functions

These are functions that are commonly used in numerical manipulations. Examples of common numerical manipulation functions include:

ABS — Returns the absolute value of a number or value.

SQRT — Returns the square root of a number or value.

MOD — Returns the remainder of n/m where both n and m are integers.

SIGN — Returns 1 if the argument is positive; –1 if the argument is negative; and 0 if the argument is negative.

Next we present a discussion on the use of these common numerical manipulation functions. Suppose we had a table that looked like this:

```
DESC function_illustrator
```

Which would give:

Name	Null?	Type
LINENO		NUMBER(2)
VALUE		NUMBER(6,2)

Now, if we typed:

```
SELECT *
FROM function_illustrator
ORDER BY lineno
```

We would get:

LINENO	VALUE
0	9
1	3.44
2	3.88
3	-6.27
4	-6.82
5	0
6	2.5

Now, suppose we use our functions to illustrate the transformation for each value of VALUE:

```
SELECT lineno, value, ABS(value), SIGN(value), MOD(lineno,3)
FROM function_illustrator
ORDER BY lineno
```

We would get:

LINENO	VALUE	ABS(VALUE)	SIGN(VALUE)	MOD(LINENO,3)
0	9	9	1	0
1	3.44	3.44	1	1
2	3.88	3.88	1	2
3	-6.27	6.27	-1	0
4	-6.82	6.82	-1	1
5	0	0	0	2
6	2.5	2.5	1	0

Notice the ABS returns the absolute value of VALUE. SIGN tells us whether the value is positive, negative, or zero. MOD gives us the remainder of LINENO/3. All of the common numerical functions take one argument except MOD, which requires two.

Had we tried to include SQRT in this example our query would look like this:

```
SELECT lineno, value, ABS(value), SQRT(value), SIGN(value),
  MOD(lineno,2)
FROM function_illustrator
```

This would give us:

```
ERROR:
ORA-01428: argument '-6.27' is out of range
no rows selected
```

In this case, the problem is that there are negative numbers in the value field and SQRT will not accept such values in its domain.

Functions can be nested; we can have a function operate on the value produced by another function. To illustrate a nested function we can use the ABS function to ensure that the SQRT function sees only a positive domain. The following query handles both positive and negative numbers:

```
SELECT lineno, value, ABS(value), SQRT(ABS(value))
FROM function_illustrator
ORDER BY lineno
```

This would give us:

LINENO	VALUE	ABS(VALUE)	SQRT(ABS(VALUE))
0	9	9	3
1	3.44	3.44	1.8547237
2	3.88	3.88	1.96977156
3	-6.27	6.27	2.50399681
4	-6.82	6.82	2.61151297
5	0	0	0
6	2.5	2.5	1.58113883

Near Value Functions

These are functions that produce values near what you are looking for. Examples of near value functions include:

CEIL — Returns the ceiling value (next highest integer above a number).

FLOOR — Returns the floor value (next lowest integer below number).

TRUNC — Returns the truncated value (removes decimal part of a number, precision adjustable).

ROUND — Returns the number rounded to nearest value (precision adjustable).

Next we present illustrations and a discussion on the use of these near value functions. The near value functions will round off a value in different ways. To illustrate with the data in Function_illustrator, consider this query:

```
SELECT lineno, value, ROUND(value), TRUNC(value), CEIL(value),
    FLOOR(value)
FROM function_illustrator
```

You will get:

LINENO	VALUE	ROUND(VALUE)	TRUNC(VALUE)	CEIL(VALUE)	FLOOR(VALUE)
0	9	9	9	9	9
1	3.44	3	3	4	3
2	3.88	4	3	4	3
3	-6.27	-6	-6	-6	-7
4	-6.82	-7	-6	-6	-7
5	0	0	0	0	0
6	2.5	3	2	3	2

ROUND will convert a decimal value to the next highest absolute value if the value is 0.5 or greater. Note the way the value is handled if the value of VALUE is negative. "Next highest absolute value" for negative numbers rounds to the negative value of the appropriate absolute value of the negative number; e.g., ROUND(–6.8) = –7.

TRUNC simply removes decimal values.

CEIL returns the next highest integer value regardless of the fraction. In this case, "next highest" refers to the actual higher number whether positive or negative.

FLOOR returns the integer below the number, again regardless of whether positive or negative.

The ROUND and TRUNC functions also may have a second argument to handle precision, which here means the distance to the right of the decimal point.

So, the following query:

```
SELECT lineno, value, ROUND(value,1), TRUNC(value,1)
FROM function_illustrator
```

Will give:

LINENO	VALUE	ROUND(VALUE,1)	TRUNC(VALUE,1)
0	9	9	9
1	3.44	3.4	3.4
2	3.88	3.9	3.8
3	-6.27	-6.3	-6.2
4	-6.82	-6.8	-6.8
5	0	0	0
6	2.5	2.5	2.5

The value 3.88, when viewed from one place to the right of the decimal point, rounds up to 3.9 and truncates to 3.8.

The second argument defaults to 0 as previously illustrated. The following query may be compared with previous versions, which have no second argument:

```
SELECT lineno, value, ROUND(value,0), TRUNC(value,0)
FROM function_illustrator
```

Which will give:

LINENO	VALUE	ROUND(VALUE,0)	TRUNC(VALUE,0)
0	9	9	9
1	3.44	3	3
2	3.88	4	3
3	-6.27	-6	-6
4	-6.82	-7	-6
5	0	0	0
6	2.5	3	2

In addition, the second argument, precision, may be negative, which means displacement to the left of the decimal point, as shown in the following query:

```
SELECT lineno, value, ROUND(value,-1), TRUNC(value,-1)
FROM function_illustrator
```

Which will give:

LINENO	VALUE	ROUND(VALUE,-1)	TRUNC(VALUE,-1)
0	9	10	0
1	3.44	0	0
2	3.88	0	0
3	-6.27	-10	0
4	-6.82	-10	0
5	0	0	0
6	2.5	0	0

In this example, with –1 for the precision argument, values less than 5 will be truncated to 0, and values of 5 or greater will be rounded up to 10.

Null Value Function

This function is used if there are null values. The null value function is:

> NVL — Returns a substitute (some other value) if a value is null.

NVL takes two arguments. The first argument is the field or attribute that you would like to look for the null value in, and the second argument is the value that you want to replace the null value by. For example, in the statement "NVL(value, 10)", we are looking for null values in the "value" column, and would like to replace the null value in the "value" column by 10.

To illustrate the null value function through an example, let's insert another row into our Function_ illustrator table, as follows:

```
INSERT INTO function_illustrator values (7, NULL)
```

Now, if you type:

```
SELECT *
FROM function_illustrator
```

You will get:

LINENO	VALUE
0	9
1	3.44
2	3.88
3	-6.27
4	-6.82
5	0
6	2.5
7	

Note that lineno 7 has a null value. To give a value of 10 to *value* for lineno = 7, type:

```
SELECT lineno, NVL(value, 10)
From function_illustrator
```

You will get:

LINENO	NVL(VALUE,10)
0	9
1	3.44
2	3.88
3	-6.27
4	-6.82
5	0
6	2.5
7	10

Note that a value of 10 has been included for lineno 7. But NVL does not change the actual data in the table. It only allows you to use some number in place of null in the SELECT statement (for example, if you are doing some calculations).

Log and Exponential Functions

SQL's log and exponential functions include:

LN — Returns natural logs, that is, logs with respect to base e.

LOG — Returns base 10 log.

EXP — Returns e raised to a value.

POWER — Returns value raised to some exponential power.

To illustrate these functions, look at the following examples:

Example 1: Using the LN function:

```
SELECT LN(value)
FROM function_illustrator
WHERE lineno = 2
```

This will give:

```
LN(VALUE)
----------
1.35583515
```

Example 2: Using the LOG function:

The LOG function requires two arguments. The first argument is the base of the log, and the second argument is the number that you want to take the log of. In the following example, we are taking the log of 2, base *value*.

```
SELECT LOG(value, 2)
FROM function_illustrator
WHERE lineno = 2
```

This will give:

```
LOG(VALUE,2)
------------
  .511232637
```

As another example, you if want to get the log of 8, base 2, you would type:

```
SELECT LOG(2,8)
FROM function_illustrator
WHERE rownum = 1
```

Giving:

```
 LOG(2,8)
----------
        3
```

Example 3: Using the EXP function:

```
SELECT EXP(value)
FROM function_illustrator
WHERE lineno = 2
```

Gives:

```
EXP(VALUE)
----------
48.4242151
```

Example 4: Using the POWER function:

The POWER function requires two arguments. The first argument is the value that you would like raised to some exponential power, and the second argument is the power (exponent) that you would like the number raised to. See the following example:

```
SELECT POWER(value,2)
FROM function_illustrator
WHERE lineno = 0
```

Which gives:

```
POWER(VALUE,2)
--------------
            81
```

Ordinary Trigonometry Functions

SQL's ordinary trigonometry functions include:

SIN — Returns the sine of a value.

COS — Returns the cosine of a value.

TAN — Returns the tangent of a value.

The SIN, COS, and TAN functions take arguments in radians where,

```
radians = (angle * 2 * 3.1416 / 360)
```

To illustrate the use of the ordinary trigonometric functions, let's suppose we have a table called Trig with the following description:

```
DESC trig
```

Will give:

Name	Null?	Type
VALUE1		NUMBER(3)
VALUE2		NUMBER(3)
VALUE3		NUMBER(3)

And,

```
SELECT *
FROM trig
```

Will give:

VALUE1	VALUE2	VALUE3
30	60	90

Example 1: Using the SIN function to find the sine of 30 degrees:

```
SELECT SIN(value1*2*3.1416/360)
FROM trig
```

Gives:

```
SIN(VALUE1*2*3.1416/360)
------------------------
              .50000106
```

Example 2: Using the COS function to find the cosine of 60 degrees:

```
SELECT COS(value2*2*3.1416/360)
FROM trig
```

Gives:

```
COS(VALUE2*2*3.1416/360)
------------------------
             .499997879
```

Example 3: Using the TAN function to find the tangent of 30 degrees:

```
SELECT TAN(value1*2*3.1416/360)
FROM trig
```

Gives:

```
TAN(VALUE1*2*3.1416/360)
------------------------
              .577351902
```

Hyperbolic Trig Functions

SQL's hyperbolic trigonometric functions include:

SINH — Returns the hyperbolic sine of a value.

COSH — Returns the hyperbolic cosine of a value.

TANH — Returns the hyperbolic tangent of a value.

These hyperbolic trigonometric functions also take arguments in radians where,

```
radians  = (angle * 2 * 3.1416 / 360)
```

We illustrate the use of these hyperbolic functions with examples:

Example 1: Using the SINH function to find the hyperbolic sine of 30 degrees:

```
SELECT SINH(value1*2*3.1416/360)
FROM trig
```

Gives:

```
SINH(VALUE1*2*3.1416/360)
------------------------
               .54785487
```

Example 2: Using the COSH function to find the hyperbolic cosine of 30 degrees:

```
SELECT COSH(value1*2*3.1416/360)
FROM trig
```

Gives:

```
COSH(VALUE1*2*3.1416/360)
-------------------------
               1.14023899
```

Example 3: Using the TANH function to find the hyperbolic tangent of 30 degrees:

```
SELECT TANH(value1*2*3.1416/360)
FROM trig
```

Gives:

```
TANH(VALUE1*2*3.1416/360)
-------------------------
                .48047372
```

In terms of usage, the common numerical manipulation functions (ABS, MOD, SIGN, SQRT), the "near value" functions (CEIL, FLOOR, ROUND, TRUNC), and NVL (an Oracle exclusive null handling function) are used often. An engineer or scientist might use the LOG, POWER, and trig functions.

String Functions

A host of string functions are available in Oracle. *String functions* refer to alphanumeric character strings. Among the most common string functions are INSTR, SUBSTR, REPLACE, and TRIM. Here we present and discuss these string functions. INSTR, SUBSTR, and REPLACE have analogs in Chapter 7, "Regular Expressions: String Searching and Oracle 10*g*."

The INSTR Function

INSTR ("in-string") is a function used to find patterns in strings. By patterns we mean a series of alphanumeric characters. The general syntax of INSTR is:

```
INSTR (string to search, search pattern [, start [,
  occurrence]])
```

The arguments within brackets ([]) are optional. We will illustrate each argument with examples. INSTR returns a location within the string where *search pattern* begins. Here are some examples of the use of the INSTR function:

```
SELECT INSTR('This is a test','is')
FROM dual
```

This will give:

```
INSTR('THISISATEST','IS')
------------------------
            3
```

The first character of *string to search* is numbered 1. Since "is" is the *search pattern*, it is found in *string to search* at position 3. If we had chosen to look for the second occurrence of "is," the query would look like this:

```
SELECT INSTR('This is a test','is',1,2)
FROM dual
```

And the result would be:

```
INSTR('THISISATEST','IS',1,2)
---------------------------
                          6
```

In this case, the second occurrence of "is" is found at position 6 of the string. To find the second occurrence, we have to tell the function where to start; therefore the third argument starts the search in position 1 of *string to search*. If a fourth argument is desired, then the third argument is mandatory.

If *search pattern* is not in the string, the INSTR function returns 0, as shown by the query below:

```
SELECT INSTR('This is a test','abc',1,2)
FROM dual
```

Which would give:

```
INSTR('THISISATEST','ABC',1,2)
----------------------------
                           0
```

The SUBSTR Function

The SUBSTR function returns part of a string. The general syntax of the function is as follows:

```
SUBSTR(original string, begin [,how far])
```

An *original string* is to be dissected beginning at the *begin* character. If no *how far* amount is specified, then the rest of the string from the *begin* point is retrieved. If *begin* is negative, then retrieval occurs from the right-hand side of *original string*. Below is an example:

```
SELECT SUBSTR('My address is 123 Fourth St.',1,12)
FROM dual
```

Which would give:

```
SUBSTR('MYAD
------------
My address i
```

Here, the first 12 characters are returned from *original string*. The first 12 characters are specified since *begin* is 1 and *how far* is 12. Notice that blanks count as characters. Look at the following query:

```
SELECT SUBSTR('My address is 123 Fourth St.',5,12)
From dual
```

This would give:

```
SUBSTR('MYAD
------------
ddress is 12
```

In this case, the retrieval begins at position 5 and again goes for 12 characters.

Here is an example of a retrieval with no third argument, meaning it starts at *begin* and retrieves the rest of the string:

```
SELECT SUBSTR('My address is 123 Fourth St.',6)
FROM dual
```

This would give:

```
SUBSTR('MYADDRESSIS123F
-----------------------
dress is 123 Fourth St.
```

SUBSTR may also retrieve from the right-hand side of *original string*, as shown below:

```
SELECT SUBSTR('My address is 123 Fourth St.',-9,5)
FROM dual
```

This would give:

```
SUBST
-----
ourth
```

The result comes from starting at the right end of the string and counting backward for nine characters, then retrieving five characters from that point.

Often in string handling, SUBSTR and INSTR are used together. For example, if we had a series of names in last name, first name format, e.g., "Harrison, John Edward," and wanted to retrieve first and middle names, we could use the comma and space to find the end of the last name. This is particularly useful since the last name is of unknown length and we rely only on the format of the names for retrieval, as shown below:

```
SELECT SUBSTR('Harrison, John Edward', INSTR('Harrison,
   John Edward',', ')+2)
FROM dual
```

This would give:

```
SUBSTR('HAR
-----------
John Edward
```

The *original string* is "Harrison, John Edward." The *begin* number has been replaced by the INSTR function, which returns the position of the comma and blank space. Since INSTR is using two characters to find the place to begin retrieval, the actual retrieval must begin two characters to the right of that point. If we do not move over two spaces, then we get this:

```
SELECT SUBSTR('Harrison, John Edward', INSTR('Harrison,
  John Edward',', '))
FROM dual
```

This would give:

```
SUBSTR('HARRI
-------------
, John Edward
```

The result includes the comma and space because retrieval starts where the INSTR function indicated the position of *search pattern* occurred.

If the INSTR pattern is not found, then the entire string would be returned, as shown by this query:

```
SELECT SUBSTR('Harrison, John Edward', INSTR('Harrison,
  John Edward','zonk'))
FROM dual
```

This would give:

```
SUBSTR('HARRISON,JOHN
---------------------
Harrison, John Edward
```

which is actually this:

```
SELECT SUBSTR('Harrison, John Edward',0)
FROM dual
```

which would give:

```
SUBSTR('HARRISON,JOHN
--------------------
Harrison, John Edward
```

The REPLACE Function

It is a common situation to not only find a pattern (INSTR) and perhaps extract it (SUBSTR), but then to replace the value(s) found. The REPLACE function has the following general syntax:

```
REPLACE (string, look for, replace with)
```

where all three arguments are necessary. The *look for* string will be replaced with the *replace with* string every time it occurs.

Here is an example:

```
SELECT REPLACE ('This is a test',' is ',' may be ')
FROM dual
```

This gives:

```
REPLACE('THISISATE
------------------
This may be a test
```

Here the *look for* string consists of " is ", including the spaces before and after the word "is." It does not matter if the *look for* and the *replace with* strings are of different lengths. If the spaces are not placed around "is", then the "is" in "This" will be replaced along with the word "is", as shown by the following query:

```
SELECT REPLACE ('This is a test','is',' may be ')
FROM dual
```

This would give:

```
REPLACE('THISISATEST','IS'
--------------------------
Th may be   may be  a test
```

If the *look for* string is not present, then the replacing does not occur, as shown by the following query:

```
SELECT REPLACE ('This is a test','glurg',' may be ')
FROM dual
```

Which would give:

```
REPLACE('THISI
--------------
This is a test
```

The TRIM Function

TRIM is a function that removes characters from the left or right ends of a string or both ends. The TRIM function was added in Oracle 9. Originally, LTRIM and RTRIM were used for trimming characters from the left or right ends of strings. TRIM supercedes both of these.

The general syntax of TRIM is:

```
TRIM ([where] [trim character] FROM subject string)
```

The optional *where* is one of the keywords "leading," "trailing," or "both."

If the optional *trim character* is not present, then blanks will be trimmed. *Trim character* may be any character. The word FROM is necessary only if *where* or *trim character* is present. Here is an example:

```
SELECT TRIM ('  This string has leading and trailing
    spaces        ')
FROM dual
```

Which gives:

```
TRIM('THISSTRINGHASLEADINGANDTRAILINGSPACES
--------------------------------------------
This string has leading and trailing spaces
```

Both the leading and trailing spaces are deleted. This is probably the most common use of the function. We can be more explicit in the use of the function, as shown in the following query:

```
SELECT TRIM (both ' ' from '    String with blanks    ')
FROM dual
```

Which gives:

```
TRIM(BOTH''FROM'ST
------------------
String with blanks
```

In these examples, characters rather than spaces are trimmed:

```
SELECT TRIM('F' from 'Frogs prefer deep water')
FROM dual
```

Which would give:

```
TRIM('F'FROM'FROGSPREF
----------------------
rogs prefer deep water
```

Here are some other examples.

Example 1:

```
SELECT TRIM(leading 'F' from 'Frogs prefer deep water')
FROM dual
```

Which would give:

```
TRIM(LEADING'F'FROM'FR
----------------------
rogs prefer deep water
```

Example 2:

```
SELECT TRIM(trailing 'r' from 'Frogs prefer deep water')
FROM dual
```

Which would give:

```
TRIM(TRAILING'R'FROM'F
----------------------
Frogs prefer deep wate
```

Example 3:

```
SELECT TRIM (both 'z' from 'zzzzz I am asleep zzzzzz')
FROM dual
```

Which would give:

```
TRIM(BOTH'Z'F
-------------
 I am asleep
```

In the last example, note that the blank space was pre-served because it was not trimmed. To get rid of the leading/trailing blank(s) we can nest TRIMs like this:

```
SELECT TRIM(TRIM (both 'z' from 'zzzzz I am asleep zzzzzz'))
FROM dual
```

This would give:

```
TRIM(TRIM(B
-----------
I am asleep
```

Date Functions

Oracle's date functions allow one to manage and handle dates in a far easier manner than if one had to actually create calendar tables or use complex algorithms for date calculations. First we must note that the date data type is not a character format. Columns with date data types contain both date and time. We must format dates to see all of the information contained in a date. If you type:

```
SELECT SYSDATE
FROM dual
```

You will get:

```
SYSDATE
---------
10-SEP-06
```

The format of the TO_CHAR function (i.e., convert to a character string) is full of possibilities. (TO_CHAR is covered in more detail in Chapter 2.) Here is an example:

```
SELECT TO_CHAR(SYSDATE, 'dd Mon, yyyy hh24:mi:ss')
FROM dual
```

This gives:

```
TO_CHAR(SYSDATE,'DDMO
---------------------
10 Sep, 2006 14:04:59
```

This presentation gives us not only the date in "dd Mon yyyy" format, but also gives us the time in 24-hour hours, minutes, and seconds.

We can add months to any date with the ADD_MONTHS function like this:

```
SELECT TO_CHAR(SYSDATE, 'ddMONyyyy') Today,
TO_CHAR(ADD_MONTHS(SYSDATE, 3), 'ddMONyyyy') "+ 3 mon",
TO_CHAR(ADD_MONTHS(SYSDATE, -23), 'ddMONyyyy') "- 23 mon"
FROM dual
```

This will give us:

```
TODAY     + 3 mon   - 23 mon
--------- --------- ---------
10SEP2006 10DEC2006 10OCT2004
```

In this example, note that the ADD_MONTHS function is applied to SYSDATE, a date data type, and then the result is converted to a character string with TO_CHAR.

The LAST_DAY function returns the last day of any month, as shown in the following query:

```
SELECT TO_CHAR(LAST_DAY('23SEP2006'))
FROM dual
```

This gives us:

```
TO_CHAR(L
---------
30-SEP-06
```

This example illustrates that Oracle will convert character dates to date data types implicitly. There is also a TO_DATE function to convert from characters to dates explicitly. It is usually not a good idea to take advantage of implicit conversion, and therefore a more proper version of the above query would look like this:

```
SELECT TO_CHAR(LAST_DAY(TO_DATE('23SEP2006','ddMONyyyy')))
FROM dual
```

This would give us:

```
TO_CHAR(L
---------
30-SEP-06
```

In the following example, we convert the date '23SEP2006' to a date data type, perform a date function on it (LAST_DAY), and then reconvert it to a character data type. We can change the original date format in the TO_CHAR function as well, as shown below:

```
SELECT TO_CHAR(LAST_DAY(TO_DATE('23SEP2006','ddMONyyyy')),
   'Month dd, yyyy')
FROM dual
```

This will give us:

```
TO_CHAR(LAST_DAY(T
------------------
September 30, 2006
```

To find the time difference between two dates, use the MONTHS_BETWEEN function, which returns fractional months. The general format of the function is:

```
MONTHS_BETWEEN(date1, date2)
```

where the result will be *date1 – date2*.

Here is an example:

```
SELECT MONTHS_BETWEEN(TO_DATE('22SEP2006','ddMONyyyy'),
  TO_DATE('13OCT2001','ddMONyyyy')) "Months difference"
FROM dual
```

This gives:

```
Months difference
------------------
        59.2903226
```

Here we explicitly converted our character string dates to date data types before applying the MONTHS_BETWEEN function.

The NEXT_DAY function tells us the date of the day of the week following a particular date, where "day of the week" is expressed as the day written out (like Monday, Tuesday, etc.):

```
SELECT NEXT_DAY(TO_DATE('15SEP2006','DDMONYYYY'),'Monday')
FROM dual
```

This gives:

```
NEXT_DAY(
---------
18-SEP-06
```

The Monday after 15-SEP-06 is 18-SEP-06, which is displayed in the default date format.

Chapter 2

Reporting Tools in Oracle's SQL*Plus

The purpose of this chapter is to present some illustrations that will move us to common ground when using the reporting tools of Oracle's SQL*Plus. As we suggested in the introduction, some knowledge of SQL is assumed before we begin. This chapter should bridge the gap between a general knowledge of SQL and Oracle's SQL*Plus, the operating environment under which SQL runs.

Earlier versions of Oracle contained some formatting functions that could have been used to produce some of the results that we illustrate in this book. In their own right, these reporting functions are quite useful and provide a way to format outputs (result sets) conveniently. Therefore, before we begin exploring "late Oracle" functions, we illustrate some of Oracle's more popular reporting tools. The analytical functions that we introduce in Chapter 3 may be considered by some to be a set of "reporting tools." As we will show, the analytical functions are more than just reporting tools; however, we need to resort to some formatting of the result for it to look good — hence, this chapter.

COLUMN

Often, when generating result sets with queries in Oracle, we get results with odd-looking headings. For example, suppose we had a table called Employee, which looked like this:

```
EMPNO ENAME       HIREDATE  ORIG_SALARY CURR_SALARY REGION
------ ----------- --------- ----------- ----------- ------
   101 John        02-DEC-97       35000       39000 W
   102 Stephanie   22-SEP-98       35000       44000 W
   104 Christina   08-MAR-98       43000       55000 W
   108 David       08-JUL-01       37000       39000 E
   111 Kate        13-APR-00       45000       49000 E
   106 Chloe       19-JAN-96       33000       44000 W
   122 Lindsey     22-MAY-97       40000       52000 E
```

The DESCRIBE command would tell us that types and sizes of the columns looked like this:

```
DESC employee
```

Giving:

```
Name          Null?    Type
------------- -----    -------------
EMPNO                  NUMBER(3)
ENAME                  VARCHAR2(20)
HIREDATE               DATE
ORIG_SALARY            NUMBER(6)
CURR_SALARY            NUMBER(6)
REGION                 VARCHAR2(2)
```

To get the output illustrated above, we used COLUMN formatting. Had we not used COLUMN formatting, we would have seen this:

```
SELECT *
FROM employee
```

Giving:

EMPNO	ENAME	HIREDATE	ORIG_SALARY	CURR_SALARY	RE
101	John	02-DEC-97	35000	39000	W
102	Stephanie	22-SEP-98	35000	44000	W
104	Christina	08-MAR-98	43000	55000	W
108	David	08-JUL-01	37000	39000	E
111	Kate	13-APR-00	45000	49000	E
106	Chloe	19-JAN-96	33000	44000	W
122	Lindsey	22-MAY-97	40000	52000	E

The problem with this output is that the heading sizes default to the size of the column. We can change the way a column displays by using the COLUMN command. The COLUMN command has the syntax:

```
COLUMN column-name FORMAT format-specification
```

where *column-name* is the column heading one wishes to format. The *format-specification* uses a's for text and 9's for numbers, like this:

an — text format for a field width of n

9n — numeric format with no decimals for a field width of numbers of size n

For example, to see the complete column name for REGION, we can execute the COLUMN command prior to executing the SQL statement:

```
COLUMN region FORMAT a6
```

which gives us better looking output:

```
 EMPNO ENAME                 HIREDATE  ORIG_SALARY CURR_SALARY REGION
---------- -------------------- --------- ----------- ----------- ------
       101 John                 02-DEC-97       35000       39000 W
       102 Stephanie            22-SEP-98       35000       44000 W
       104 Christina            08-MAR-98       43000       55000 W
       108 David                08-JUL-01       37000       39000 E
       111 Kate                 13-APR-00       45000       49000 E
       106 Chloe                19-JAN-96       33000       44000 W
       122 Lindsey              22-MAY-97       40000       52000 E
```

In a similar way, we can shorten the ename field because the names are shorter than 20 characters. We can use this COLUMN command:

```
COLUMN ename FORMAT a11
```

which, when running "SELECT * FROM employee" produces:

```
 EMPNO ENAME       HIREDATE  ORIG_SALARY CURR_SALARY REGION
---------- ----------- --------- ----------- ----------- ------
       101 John        02-DEC-97       35000       39000 W
       102 Stephanie   22-SEP-98       35000       44000 W
       104 Christina   08-MAR-98       43000       55000 W
       108 David       08-JUL-01       37000       39000 E
       111 Kate        13-APR-00       45000       49000 E
       106 Chloe       19-JAN-96       33000       44000 W
       122 Lindsey     22-MAY-97       40000       52000 E
```

In the case of alphanumeric columns, if the column is too short to fit the data, it will be displayed on multiple lines. For example, if the COLUMN format for ename were too short, as shown below:

```
COLUMN ename FORMAT a7
```

```
SELECT * FROM employee
```

We'd see this result:

```
EMPNO ENAME   HIREDATE  ORIG_SALARY CURR_SALARY REGION
----- ------- --------- ----------- ----------- ------
  101 John    02-DEC-97       35000       39000 W
  102 Stephan 22-SEP-98       35000       44000 W
      ie
  104 Christi 08-MAR-98       43000       55000 W
      na
  108 David   08-JUL-01       37000       39000 E
  111 Kate    13-APR-00       45000       49000 E
  106 Chloe   19-JAN-96       33000       44000 W
  122 Lindsey 22-MAY-97       40000       52000 E
```

Formatting Numbers

For simple formatting of numbers, we can use $9n$ just as we used an, where n is the width of the output field.

For example, if we format the empno field to make it shorter, we can use:

```
COLUMN empno FORMAT 999
```

and type:

```
SELECT empno, ename
FROM employee
```

which gives this result:

```
EMPNO ENAME
----- ----------
  101 John
  102 Stephanie
  104 Christina
  108 David
  111 Kate
  106 Chloe
  122 Lindsey
```

With numbers, if the format size is less than the heading size, then the field width defaults to be the heading size. This is the case with empno, which is 5. If the column format is too small:

```
COLUMN empno FORMAT 99
SELECT empno, ename
FROM employee
```

We get this result:

```
EMPNO ENAME
----- ----------
  ### John
  ### Stephanie
  ### Christina
  ### David
  ### Kate
  ### Chloe
  ### Lindsey
```

If there are decimals or if commas are desired, the following formats are available:

```
COLUMN orig_salary FORMAT 999,999
COLUMN curr_salary FORMAT 99999.99

SELECT empno, ename,
  orig_salary,
  curr_salary
FROM employee
```

Gives:

```
EMPNO ENAME       ORIG_SALARY CURR_SALARY
----- ----------- ----------- -----------
  101 John             35,000    39000.00
  102 Stephanie        35,000    44000.00
  104 Christina        43,000    55000.00
  108 David            37,000    39000.00
```

```
111 Kate         45,000    49000.00
106 Chloe        33,000    44000.00
122 Lindsey      40,000    52000.00
```

Numbers can also be output with leading zeros or dollar signs if desired. For example, suppose we had a table representing a coffee fund with these data types:

```
COFFEE_FUND
-----------------------
EMPNO       NUMBER(3)
AMOUNT      NUMBER(5,2)

SELECT *
FROM coffee_fund
```

Gives:

```
EMPNO    AMOUNT
-----  ----------
  102     33.25
  104      3.28
  106       .35
  101       .07
```

To avoid having "naked" decimal points you could insert a zero in front of the decimal if the amount were less than one. If a zero is placed in the numeric format, it says, "put a zero here if it would be null." For example:

```
COLUMN amount FORMAT 990.99
SELECT *
FROM coffee_fund
```

produces:

```
EMPNO  AMOUNT
-----  -------
  102   33.25
  104    3.28
  106    0.35
  101    0.07
```

Then,

```
COLUMN amount FORMAT 909.99
SELECT *
FROM coffee_fund
```

produces:

```
EMPNO  AMOUNT
-----  -------
  102   33.25
  104   03.28
  106   00.35
  101   00.07
```

The COLUMN-FORMAT statement "COLUMN amount FORMAT 900.99" produces the same result, as the second zero is superfluous.

We can also add dollar signs to the output. The dollar sign floats up to the first character displayed:

```
COLUMN amount FORMAT $990.99
SELECT *
FROM coffee_fund
```

Gives:

```
EMPNO   AMOUNT
-----   --------
  102   $33.25
  104   $3.28
  106   $0.35
  101   $0.07
```

Scripts

Often, a formatting command is used but is meant for only one executable statement. For example, suppose we formatted the AMOUNT column as above with "COLUMN amount FORMAT $990.99." The format will stay in effect for the entire session unless the column is CLEARed or another "COLUMN amount FORMAT .." is executed. To undo *all* column formatting, the command is:

CLEAR COLUMNS

A problem here may be that CLEAR COLUMNS clears all column formatting, but a universal CLEAR is likely appropriate as the AMOUNT column may well appear in some other table and one might not want the same formatting for both. If the other AMOUNT column contained larger numbers (i.e., greater than 999), then octothorpes (#) would be displayed in the output.

A better way to use formatting is to put the format and the statement in a script. A script is a text file that is stored in the operating system (e.g., Windows) in the C:/Oracle .../bin directory (Windows) and run with a START command. In the text file, we can include the COLUMN format, the statement, and then a CLEAR COLUMNS command. As an example, suppose we have such a script called myscript.txt and it contains the following:

```
COLUMN amount FORMAT $990.99
SELECT empno, amount
FROM coffee_fund
/
CLEAR COLUMNS
```

This script presupposes nothing about the formatting of AMOUNT, and after it is run, the formatting is not persistent. The script is executed like this:

```
START myscript.txt
```

or

```
@myscript.txt
```

from the SQL> command line.

An even better script would contain some SET commands to control feature values. Such a script could look like this:

```
SET echo off
COLUMN amount FORMAT $990.99
SET verify off
SELECT empno, amount
FROM coffee_fund;
CLEAR COLUMNS
SET verify on
SET echo on
```

The "echo" feature displays the command on the screen when executed. To make the script run cleanly, you should routinely turn echo and verify off at the beginning of the script and turn them back on at the end of the script.

Other feature values that may be manipulated in this way are "pagesize," which defaults to 24 and may be insufficient for a particular query, and "feedback," which shows how many records were selected if it exceeds a certain amount.

All of the feature values may be seen using the SHOW ALL command from the command line, and any of the parameters may be changed to suit any particular user.

Formatting Dates

While not specifically a report feature, the formatting of dates is common and related to overall report formatting. The appropriate way to format a date is to use the TO_CHAR function. TO_CHAR takes a date data type and converts it to a character string according to an acceptable format. There are several variations on "acceptable formats," and we will illustrate a few here (we also used TO_CHAR in Chapter 1). First, we show the use of the TO_CHAR function to format a date. The syntax of TO_CHAR is:

```
TO_CHAR(column name in date data type, format)
```

Here is an example of TO_CHAR being used in a SELECT statement:

```
SELECT empno, ename, TO_CHAR(hiredate, 'dd Month yyyy')
FROM employee
```

This gives:

```
    EMPNO ENAME                  TO_CHAR(HIREDATE,
---------- -------------------- ------------------
      101 John                  02 December  1997
      102 Stephanie             22 September 1998
      104 Christina             08 March     1998
      108 David                 08 July      2001
      111 Kate                  13 April     2000
      106 Chloe                 19 January   1996
      122 Lindsey               22 May       1997
```

An alias is required when using TO_CHAR to "pretty up" the output:

```
SELECT empno, ename,
  TO_CHAR(hiredate, 'dd Month yyyy') "Hiredate"
FROM employee
```

Gives:

```
    EMPNO ENAME                  HIREDATE
---------- -------------------- ------------------
      101 John                  02 December  1997
      102 Stephanie             22 September 1998
      104 Christina             08 March     1998
      108 David                 08 July      2001
      111 Kate                  13 April     2000
      106 Chloe                 19 January   1996
      122 Lindsey               22 May       1997
```

The following table illustrates some TO_CHAR date formatting.

Format	Will look like
dd Month yyyy	05 March 2006
dd month YY	05 march 06
dd Mon	05 Mar
dd RM yyyy	05 III 2003

Format	Will look like
Day Mon yyyy	Sunday Mar 2006
Day fmMonth dd, yyyy	Sunday March 5, 2006
Mon ddsp yyyy	Mar five 2006
ddMon yy hh24:mi:ss	05Mar 06 00:00:00

BREAK

Often when looking at a result set it is convenient to "break" the report on some column to produce easy-to-read output. Consider the Employee table result set like this (with columns formatted):

```
SELECT empno, ename, curr_salary, region
FROM employee
ORDER BY region
```

Giving:

```
EMPNO ENAME       CURR_SALARY REGION
----- ----------  ----------- ------
  108 David            39,000 E
  111 Kate             49,000 E
  122 Lindsey          52,000 E
  101 John             39,000 W
  106 Chloe            44,000 W
  102 Stephanie        44,000 W
  104 Christina        55,000 W
```

Now, if we execute the command:

```
BREAK ON region
```

the output is formatted to look like the following, where the regions are displayed once and the output is arranged by region:

```
EMPNO ENAME        CURR_SALARY REGION
----- ---------- ----------- ------
  108 David           39,000 E
  111 Kate            49,000
  122 Lindsey         52,000
  101 John            39,000 W
  106 Chloe           44,000
  102 Stephanie       44,000
  104 Christina       55,000
```

If a blank line is desired between the regions, we can enhance the BREAK command with a skip like this:

```
BREAK ON region skip1
```

to produce:

```
EMPNO ENAME        CURR_SALARY REGION
----- ---------- ----------- ------
  108 David           39,000 E
  111 Kate            49,000
  122 Lindsey         52,000

  101 John            39,000 W
  106 Chloe           44,000
  102 Stephanie       44,000
  104 Christina       55,000
```

It is very important to note that the query contains an ORDER BY clause that mirrors the BREAK command. If the ORDER BY is not there, then the result will indeed break on REGION, but the result will contain random (i.e., unordered) breaks:

```
SELECT empno, ename, curr_salary, region
FROM employee
-- ORDER BY region
```

Giving:

```
EMPNO ENAME      CURR_SALARY REGION
---------- ---------- ----------- ------
       101 John          39,000 W
       102 Stephanie     44,000
       104 Christina     55,000

       108 David         39,000 E
       111 Kate          49,000

       106 Chloe         44,000 W

       122 Lindsey       52,000 E
```

There can be only one BREAK command in a script or in effect at any one time. If there is a second BREAK command in a script or session, the second one will supercede the first.

COMPUTE

The COMPUTE command may be used in conjunction with BREAK to give summary results. COMPUTE allows us to calculate an aggregate value and place the result at the break point. The syntax of COMPUTE is:

```
COMPUTE aggregate(column) ON break-point
```

For example, if we wanted to sum the salaries and report the sums at the break points of the above query, we can execute the following script, which contains the COMPUTE command:

```
SET echo off
COLUMN curr_salary FORMAT $9,999,999
COLUMN ename FORMAT a10
COLUMN region FORMAT a6
```

```
BREAK ON region skip1
COMPUTE sum of curr_salary ON region
SET verify off
SELECT empno, ename, curr_salary, region
FROM employee
ORDER BY region
/
CLEAR BREAKS
CLEAR COMPUTES
CLEAR COLUMNS
SET verify on
SET echo on
```

Giving:

```
    EMPNO ENAME        CURR_SALARY REGION
---------- ----------  ----------- ------
      108 David           $39,000 E
      111 Kate            $49,000
      122 Lindsey         $52,000
                      ----------- ******
                         $140,000 sum

      101 John            $39,000 W
      106 Chloe           $44,000
      102 Stephanie       $44,000
      104 Christina       $55,000
                      ----------- ******
                         $182,000 sum
```

Note the command for clearing BREAKs and COM-
PUTEs toward the end of the script after the SQL
statement. Also note that in the script, the width of the
FORMAT for the curr_salary field has to be larger
than the salary itself because it has to accommodate
the sums. If the field is too small, octothorpes result:

```
...
    111 Kate          $49,000
    122 Lindsey       $52,000
                  ----------- ******
                  ####### sum
...
```

While there can be only one BREAK active at a time, the BREAK may contain more than one ON clause. A common practice is to have the BREAK break not only on some column (which reflects the ORDER BY clause), but also to have the BREAK be in effect for the entire report. Multiple COMPUTEs are also allowable. In the following script, note that the BREAK "on region" has been enhanced to include a second BREAK, "on report," and that the COMPUTE command has also been enhanced to include other data:

```
SET echo off
COLUMN curr_salary FORMAT $9,999,999
COLUMN ename FORMAT a10
COLUMN region FORMAT a7
BREAK ON region skip1 ON report
COMPUTE sum max min of curr_salary ON region
COMPUTE sum of curr_salary ON report
SET verify off
SELECT empno, ename, curr_salary, region
FROM employee
ORDER BY region
/
CLEAR BREAKS
CLEAR COMPUTES
CLEAR COLUMNS
SET verify on
SET echo on
```

Giving:

```
   EMPNO ENAME       CURR_SALARY REGION
---------- ---------- ----------- -------
     108 David           $39,000 E
     111 Kate            $49,000
     122 Lindsey         $52,000
                     ----------- *******
                         $39,000 minimum
                         $52,000 maximum
                        $140,000 sum


     101 John            $39,000 W
     106 Chloe           $44,000
     102 Stephanie       $44,000
     104 Christina       $55,000
                     ----------- *******
                         $39,000 minimum
                         $55,000 maximum
                        $182,000 sum


                     -----------
sum                     $322,000
```

In this script, the size of the REGION column had to be expanded to 7 to include the words "maximum" and "minimum" because they appear in that column.

Remarks in Scripts

All scripts should contain minimal remarks to document the writer, the date, and the purpose of the report. Remarks are called "comments" in other languages. Remarks are allowable anywhere in the script except for within the SELECT statement. In the SELECT statement, normal comments may be used (/* comment */ or two dashes at the end of a single line).

Here is the above script with some remarks, indicated by REM:

```
SET echo off
REM R. Earp - February 13, 2006
REM modified Feb. 14, 2006
REM Script for employee's current salary report
COLUMN curr_salary FORMAT $9,999,999
COLUMN ename FORMAT a10
COLUMN region FORMAT a7
BREAK ON region skip1 ON report
REM 2 breaks - one on region, one on report
COMPUTE sum max min of curr_salary ON region
COMPUTE sum of curr_salary ON report
REM a compute for each BREAK
SET verify off
SELECT empno, ename, curr_salary, region
FROM employee
ORDER BY region
/
REM clean up parameters set before the SELECT
CLEAR BREAKS
CLEAR COMPUTES
CLEAR COLUMNS
SET verify on
SET echo on
```

TTITLE and BTITLE

As a final touch one, may add top and bottom titles to a report that is in a script. The TTITLE (top title) and BTITLE (bottom title) commands have this syntax:

```
TTITLE option text OFF/ON
```

where *option* refers to the placement of the title:

```
COLUMN n (start in some column, n)
SKIP m (skip m blank lines)
TAB x (tab x positions)
LEFT/CENTER/RIGHT (default is LEFT)
```

The same holds for BTITLE. The titles, line sizes, and page sizes (for bottom titles) need to be coordinated to make the report look attractive. In addition, page numbers may be added with the extension:

```
option text format 999 sql.pno
```

(Note that the number of 9's in the format depends on the size of the report.)
   Here is an example:

```
SET echo off
REM R. Earp - February 13, 2006
REM modified Feb. 14, 2006
REM Script for employee's current salary report
COLUMN curr_salary FORMAT $9,999,999
COLUMN ename FORMAT a10
TTITLE LEFT 'Current Salary Report #######################'
    SKIP 1
BTITLE LEFT 'End of report *********************'   ' Page #'
    format 99 sql.pno
SET linesize 50
SET pagesize 25
COLUMN region FORMAT a7
BREAK ON region skip1 ON report
REM 2 breaks - one on region, one on report
COMPUTE sum max min of curr_salary ON region
COMPUTE sum of curr_salary ON report
REM a compute for each BREAK
SET feedback off
SET verify off
SELECT empno, ename, curr_salary, region
FROM employee
```

```
ORDER BY region
/
REM clean up parameters set before the SELECT
CLEAR BREAKS
CLEAR COMPUTES
CLEAR COLUMNS
BTITLE OFF
TTITLE OFF
SET verify on
SET feedback on
SET echo on
```

Giving:

```
Current Salary Report ########################
    EMPNO ENAME         CURR_SALARY REGION
---------- ---------- ----------- -------
      108 David            $39,000 E
      111 Kate             $49,000
      122 Lindsey          $52,000
                       ----------- *******
                           $39,000 minimum
                           $52,000 maximum
                          $140,000 sum


      101 John             $39,000 W
      106 Chloe            $44,000
      102 Stephanie        $44,000
      104 Christina        $55,000
                       ----------- *******
                           $39,000 minimum
                           $55,000 maximum
                          $182,000 sum


                       -----------
sum                       $322,000

End of report ********************* Page #   1
```

As before, it is good form to turn off BTITLE and
TTITLE lest they persist and foul another application.

There are many reporting tools available in the marketplace that are easier to use and give much more elaborate results than the Oracle reporting tools; however, these introductory examples were presented less to encourage reports than to show the commands that may be used separately or together to aid in reporting situations. Probably the most common command is the COLUMN command, but the others may also prove to be quite useful.

References

A good reference on the web is titled "SQL*Plus User's Guide and Reference." It may be found under "Oracle9i Database Online Documentation, Release 2 (9.2)" for SQL*Plus commands at http://web.njit.edu/info/limpid/DOC/index.htm. (Copyright © 2002, Oracle Corporation, Redwood Shores, CA.)

Chapter 3

The Analytical Functions in Oracle (Analytical Functions I)

What Are Analytical Functions?

Analytical functions were introduced into Oracle SQL in version 8.1.6. On the surface, one could say that analytical functions provide a way to enhance the result set of queries. As we will see, analytical functions do more, in that they allow us to pursue queries that would require multiple intermediate objects (like views, temporary tables, etc.). Oracle calls these functions "reporting" or "windowing" functions. We will use the term "analytical function" throughout this chapter and explain the difference between reporting and windowing features as we come to them. Oracle characterizes the functions as part of a Decision Support System (DSS).

Why use an analytical function? There are two compelling reasons. First, as we will demonstrate, they usually present a simple solution to a more complex querying problem. Most of the results we get can be had with workaround solutions. However, the workaround solution is often clumsy, long, and hard to follow. A second reason for learning how to use these functions is that since the analytical function is "built in" to Oracle, the Optimizer can optimize the function for performance more easily than with a cumbersome workaround.

The analytical functions fall into categories: ranking, aggregate, row comparison, and statistical. We will investigate each of these in turn. The format of the analytical function will be new to some Oracle SQL writers. An example of such a function in a result set would be this:

```
SELECT RANK() OVER(ORDER BY product)
FROM inventory
```

The function has this syntax:

```
function(<arguments>) OVER(<analytic clause>)
```

The *<arguments>* part may be empty, as it is in the above example: "RANK()." The *<analytic clause>* part of the function will contain an ordering, partitioning, or windowing clause. The ordering clause is illustrated in the above example: "OVER(ORDER BY product)." We will cover the other choices in more detail presently.

We use the ORDER BY clause in ordinary SQL to order a result set based on some attribute(s). An analytical function that uses an ordering may also partition the result set based on some attribute value. The analytical functions may provide useful counts and rankings and may provide offset columns much like spreadsheets.

These analytic clauses in analytical functions are most easily explained by way of examples, so let's begin with the row numbering and ranking functions.

The Row-numbering and Ranking Functions

There is a family of analytical functions that allows us to show rankings and row numbering in a direct and simple way. The functions we will cover here are: ROW_NUMBER, RANK, and DENSE_RANK. PERCENT_RANK, CUME_DIST, and NTILE are discussed later in this chapter.

Our first example illustrates the use of row numbering with an analytical function called ROW_NUMBER. The Oracle function ROWNUM has been around much longer than the analytical function ROW_NUMBER, and is not at all the same. ROWNUM is a pseudo-column and is computed as rows are retrieved. Since ROWNUM is computed as rows are retrieved, it is somewhat limited. Some examples will clarify this.

Consider this Employee table:

EMPNO	ENAME	HIREDATE	ORIG_SALARY	CURR_SALARY	REGION
101	John	02-DEC-97	35000	39000	W
102	Stephanie	22-SEP-98	35000	44000	W
104	Christina	08-MAR-98	43000	55000	W
108	David	08-JUL-01	37000	39000	E
111	Katie	13-APR-00	45000	49000	E
106	Chloe	19-JAN-96	33000	44000	W
122	Lindsey	22-MAY-97	40000	52000	E

where the following attributes are used:

Name	Type	Meaning
EMPNO	NUMBER(3)	Employee identification #
ENAME	VARCHAR2(20)	Employee name
HIREDATE	DATE	Date employee hired
ORIG_SALARY	NUMBER(6)	Original salary
CURR_SALARY	NUMBER(6)	Current salary
REGION	VARCHAR2(2)	Region where employed

A first modification of the result set display might be to order the table on the employee's original salary (*orig_salary*):

```
SELECT * FROM employee
ORDER BY orig_salary
```

which gives this:

EMPNO	ENAME	HIREDATE	ORIG_SALARY	CURR_SALARY	REGION
106	Chloe	19-JAN-96	33000	44000	W
101	John	02-DEC-97	35000	39000	W
102	Stephanie	22-SEP-98	35000	44000	W
108	David	08-JUL-01	37000	39000	E
122	Lindsey	22-MAY-97	40000	52000	E
104	Christina	08-MAR-98	43000	55000	W
111	Katie	13-APR-00	45000	49000	E

Having seen this listing, one might choose to focus a bit on original salary and number the rows (i.e., rank order them) using the ROWNUM function. A first attempt at ordering and row-numbering type ranking directly could result in something like this:

```
SELECT empno, ename, orig_salary, ROWNUM
FROM employee ORDER BY orig_salary
```

Giving:

```
  EMPNO ENAME                     ORIG_SALARY     ROWNUM
---------- --------------------- ------------ ----------
    106 Chloe                           33000          6
    101 John                            35000          1
    102 Stephanie                       35000          2
    108 David                           37000          4
    122 Lindsey                         40000          7
    104 Christina                       43000          3
    111 Katie                           45000          5
```

The problem here is that the ROWNUM numbering takes place before the ordering, i.e., as the rows are retrieved. Chloe would have come out on the sixth row without ordering. Why the sixth row? The reason is because there is no way to predetermine where Chloe's row actually resides in the database. The problem with the query is that ROWNUM operates before the ORDER BY sorting is executed. While this type of display could be useful, it likely is not because relational databases do not order rows internally and the order of the result set has to be controlled by the person doing the query.

As a side issue, if data were added to the table, Chloe's sixth row status could change because relational databases do not preserve row orderings. New data in the database might be placed before or after Chloe.

To more correctly depict the rank of the salaries, one could gather information in a query and then put that result set into a virtual table. Such a solution could look like this:

```
SELECT empno "Emp #", ename "Name", orig_salary "Salary",
  ROWNUM rank
FROM
  (SELECT empno, ename, orig_salary
  FROM employee ORDER BY orig_salary)
```

Giving:

Emp #	Name	Salary	RANK
106	Chloe	33000	1
101	John	35000	2
102	Stephanie	35000	3
108	David	37000	4
122	Lindsey	40000	5
104	Christina	43000	6
111	Katie	45000	7

Now this solution correctly depicts an ordering based on the order of the result set. However, when users see this ordering, they might think we have produced a ranking, but this is not quite the same thing. There is a tie in salary between John and Stephanie. Since there is a tie, the correct statistical rank for John and Stephanie would be 2.5 — the average of the tied ranks. Oracle's analytical functions approximate this "averaging rank" in what is called a "top-n" solution, where n is the number of "top" salaries one is seeking. "Top" can be "from the top" or "from the bottom," depending on how one looks at the ordering of the listing. For example, reversing the order to be salary top down, the top seven salaries are found with this query (still ignoring the tie problem):

```
SELECT empno "Emp #", ename "Name", orig_salary "Salary",
  ROWNUM rank
FROM
  (SELECT empno, ename, orig_salary
FROM employee ORDER BY orig_salary desc)
```

which gives:

```
Emp # Name                   Salary      RANK
---------- -------------------- ---------- ----------
      111 Katie                 45000         1
      104 Christina             43000         2
      122 Lindsey               40000         3
      108 David                 37000         4
      101 John                  35000         5
      102 Stephanie             35000         6
      106 Chloe                 33000         7
```

How can you deal with the tie problem? Without analytical functions you must resort to a workaround of
some kind. For example, you could again wrap this
result set in parentheses and look for distinct values of
salary by doing a self-join comparison. You could also
use PL/SQL. However, each of these workarounds is
awkward and messy compared to the ease with which
the analytical functions provide a solution.

There are three ranking-type analytical functions
that deal with just such a problem as this: ROW_
NUMBER, RANK, and DENSE_RANK. We will first
use ROW_NUMBER as an orientation in the use of
analytical functions and then solve the tie problem in
ranking. First, recall that the format of an analytical
function is this:

```
function() OVER(<analytic clause>)
```

where *<analytic clause>* contains ordering, partitioning, windowing, or some combination.

As an example, the ROW_NUMBER function with
an ordering on salary in descending order looks like
this:

```
SELECT empno, ename, orig_salary,
  ROW_NUMBER() OVER(ORDER BY orig_salary desc) toprank
FROM employee
```

Giving:

EMPNO	ENAME	ORIG_SALARY	TOPRANK
111	Katie	45000	1
104	Christina	43000	2
122	Lindsey	40000	3
108	David	37000	4
101	John	35000	5
102	Stephanie	35000	6
106	Chloe	33000	7

The use of the analytical function does not solve the tie problem; however, the function does produce the ordering of the rows without the clumsy workaround of the virtual table.

Analytical functions will generate an ordering by themselves. Although the analytical function is quite useful, we have to be careful of the ordering of the final result. For this reason, it is good form to include a final ordering of the result set with an ORDER BY at the end of the query like this:

```
SELECT empno, ename, orig_salary,
  ROW_NUMBER() OVER(ORDER BY orig_salary desc) toprank
FROM employee
ORDER BY orig_salary desc
```

Although the final ORDER BY looks redundant, it is often added because as the query grows, more analytical functions may be added to the result set and other orderings may be desired. The final ORDER BY ensures the ordering of the final display. There will be cases where the final ORDER BY is unnecessary to obtain a result (actually it is unnecessary in the above query); however, we use the final ORDER BY for consistency.

To illustrate a different ordering with the use of analytical functions, after having generated a result set with a row number "attached," the result set can be easily reordered on some attribute other than that which was row numbered, like this:

```
SELECT empno, ename, orig_salary,
   ROW_NUMBER() OVER(ORDER BY orig_salary desc) toprank
FROM employee
ORDER BY ename
```

Giving:

EMPNO	ENAME	ORIG_SALARY	TOPRANK
101	John	35000	5
106	Chloe	33000	7
104	Christina	43000	2
108	David	37000	4
111	Katie	45000	1
122	Lindsey	40000	3
102	Stephanie	35000	6

In this case, the reordering happens to give the same result as the following query without analytical functions:

```
SELECT empno, ename, os Salary, ROWNUM Toprank
FROM
   (SELECT empno, ename, orig_salary os
   FROM employee
   ORDER BY orig_salary desc)
ORDER BY ename
```

Giving:

EMPNO	ENAME	SALARY	TOPRANK
101	John	35000	5
106	Chloe	33000	7
104	Christina	43000	2
108	David	37000	4
111	Katie	45000	1
122	Lindsey	40000	3
102	Stephanie	35000	6

Now, to return to the ranking as opposed to a row-numbering problem (the problem of ties), we can use the RANK or DENSE_RANK analytical functions in a way similar to the ROW_NUMBER function. The RANK function will not only produce the row numbering but will skip a rank if there is a tie. It will more correctly rank the ties the same. Here is our example:

```
SELECT empno, ename, orig_salary,
   RANK() OVER(ORDER BY orig_salary desc) toprank
FROM employee
```

Giving:

EMPNO	ENAME	ORIG_SALARY	TOPRANK
111	Katie	45000	1
104	Christina	43000	2
122	Lindsey	40000	3
108	David	37000	4
101	John	35000	5
102	Stephanie	35000	5
106	Chloe	33000	7

The DENSE_RANK function acts similarly, but instead of ranking the tied rows and moving up to the next rank beyond the tie, DENSE_RANK will not skip up to the next rank level:

```
SELECT empno, ename, orig_salary,
  DENSE_RANK() OVER(ORDER BY orig_salary desc) toprank
FROM employee
```

Giving:

EMPNO	ENAME	ORIG_SALARY	TOPRANK
111	Katie	45000	1
104	Christina	43000	2
122	Lindsey	40000	3
108	David	37000	4
101	John	35000	5
102	Stephanie	35000	5
106	Chloe	33000	6

Both RANK and DENSE_RANK handle ties, but in a slightly different way. Choose whichever way is appropriate for the result.

A top-n solution is now easily accomplished with a WHERE clause in the statement. For example, if we wanted to see the top five original salaries, we would use this query:

```
SELECT *
FROM
(SELECT empno, ename, orig_salary,
  DENSE_RANK() OVER(ORDER BY orig_salary desc) toprank
FROM employee)
WHERE toprank <= 5
```

Giving:

EMPNO	ENAME	ORIG_SALARY	TOPRANK
111	Katie	45000	1
104	Christina	43000	2
122	Lindsey	40000	3
108	David	37000	4
101	John	35000	5
102	Stephanie	35000	5

Notice that the direct application of a WHERE clause in the query is not allowed:

```
SELECT empno, ename, orig_salary,
  DENSE_RANK() OVER(ORDER BY orig_salary desc) toprank
FROM employee
WHERE DENSE_RANK() OVER(ORDER BY orig_salary desc) <= 5
```

Gives:

```
WHERE DENSE_RANK() OVER(ORDER BY orig_salary desc) <= 5
      *
ERROR at line 4:
ORA-30483: window  functions are not allowed here
```

And,

```
SELECT empno, ename, orig_salary,
  DENSE_RANK() OVER(ORDER BY orig_salary desc) toprank
FROM employee
WHERE toprank <= 5
```

Gives:

```
WHERE toprank <= 5
      *
ERROR at line 4:
ORA-00904: "TOPRANK": invalid identifier
```

We therefore have to alias the rank and use the alias in the ORDER BY.

The Order in Which the Analytical Function Is Processed in the SQL Statement

There is an order in which the parts of a SQL statement are processed. For example, a statement that contains:

```
SELECT
FROM x
WHERE
```

is executed by the database engine by scanning a table, x, and retrieving rows when the WHERE clause is true. WHERE is often called a "row filter." The SELECT .. FROM .. WHERE may contain joins and GROUP BY as well as WHERE. If there were GROUPING and HAVING clauses, then the criteria in HAVING would be applied after the result of the SELECT .. WHERE is completed. HAVING is often called an "after filter" because it is done after the other parts of the query are completed — after the initial retrieval (which might include joins), after the WHERE, and after the GROUP BY is executed.

If there is ordering in the statement (ORDER BY), the ordering is done last, after the result set has been established from SELECT .. FROM .. WHERE .. HAVING.

Now, in which part of the execution process is the analytical function performed? It is performed just before the ORDER BY. All grouping, joins, WHERE clauses, and HAVING clauses will have already been applied. Following are some examples.

A SELECT with Just a FROM Clause

```
SELECT empno, ename, orig_salary
FROM employee
```

Gives:

```
    EMPNO ENAME                 ORIG_SALARY
---------- --------------------- -----------
      101 John                        35000
      102 Stephanie                   35000
      104 Christina                   43000
      108 David                       37000
      111 Katie                       45000
      106 Chloe                       33000
      122 Lindsey                     40000
```

A SELECT with Ordering

Note that the ordering is applied to the result set after the result is established:

```
SELECT empno, ename, orig_salary
FROM employee
ORDER BY orig_salary
```

Gives:

```
    EMPNO ENAME                 ORIG_SALARY
---------- --------------------- -----------
      106 Chloe                       33000
      101 John                        35000
      102 Stephanie                   35000
      108 David                       37000
      122 Lindsey                     40000
      104 Christina                   43000
      111 Katie                       45000
```

A WHERE Clause Is Added to the Statement

Notice that the WHERE has excluded rows before the final ordering:

```
SELECT empno, ename, orig_salary
FROM employee
WHERE orig_salary < 43000
ORDER BY orig_salary
```

Gives:

```
    EMPNO ENAME                    ORIG_SALARY
---------- -------------------- -----------
      106 Chloe                        33000
      101 John                         35000
      102 Stephanie                    35000
      108 David                        37000
      122 Lindsey                      40000
```

Notice that ORDER BY is applied last — after the SELECT .. FROM .. WHERE.

An Analytical Function Is Added to the Statement

Note here that the WHERE is applied before the RANK().

```
SELECT empno, ename, orig_salary,
  RANK() OVER(ORDER BY orig_salary) rankorder
FROM employee
WHERE orig_salary < 43000
ORDER BY orig_salary
```

Gives:

EMPNO	ENAME	ORIG_SALARY	RANKORDER
106	Chloe	33000	1
101	John	35000	2
102	Stephanie	35000	2
108	David	37000	4
122	Lindsey	40000	5

A Join Is Added to the Statement

What will happen to the order of execution if a join is included in the statement? We will add another table to the statement, then perform a join and see what happens. Suppose we have a table called Job with this description:

Name	Null?	Type
EMPNO		NUMBER(3)
JOBTITLE		VARCHAR2(20)

and this data:

EMPNO	JOBTITLE
101	Chemist
102	Accountant
102	Mediator
111	Musician
122	Director Personnel
122	Mediator
108	Mediator
106	Computer Programmer
104	Head Mediator

Now, we'll perform a join with and without the analytical function.

The Join Without the Analytical Function

Just adding the join to the query shows that the join is performed with the other WHERE conditions:

```
SELECT e.empno, e.ename, j.jobtitle, e.orig_salary
FROM employee e, job j
WHERE e.orig_salary < 43000
  AND e.empno = j.empno
```

Gives:

EMPNO	ENAME	JOBTITLE	ORIG_SALARY
101	John	Chemist	35000
102	Stephanie	Accountant	35000
102	Stephanie	Mediator	35000
106	Chloe	Computer Programmer	33000
108	David	Mediator	37000
122	Lindsey	Director Personnel	40000
122	Lindsey	Mediator	40000

Here, the WHERE is used to filter all salaries that are less than 43000 *and*, because we are using a join (actually an equi-join), the WHERE provides the equality condition for the equi-join.

Adding Ordering to a Joined Result

If an ordering is applied to the statement at this point, it occurs after the WHERE has been executed:

```
SELECT e.empno, e.ename, j.jobtitle, e.orig_salary
FROM employee e, job j
WHERE e.orig_salary < 43000
  AND e.empno = j.empno
ORDER BY orig_salary desc
```

Gives:

EMPNO	ENAME	JOBTITLE	ORIG_SALARY
122	Lindsey	Director Personnel	40000
122	Lindsey	Mediator	40000
108	David	Mediator	37000
101	John	Chemist	35000
102	Stephanie	Accountant	35000
102	Stephanie	Mediator	35000
106	Chloe	Computer Programmer	33000

Note that the same number and content of rows is in the result set, and the ordering was applied after the WHERE clause.

Adding an Analytical Function to a Query that Contains a Join (and Other WHERE Conditions)

In this query, we add the analytical function to the previous statement to see where the analytical function is performed relative to the WHERE.

```
SELECT e.empno, e.ename, j.jobtitle, e.orig_salary,
  RANK() OVER(ORDER BY e.orig_salary desc) rankorder
FROM employee e, job j
WHERE e.orig_salary < 43000
  AND e.empno = j.empno
ORDER BY orig_salary desc
```

Gives:

EMPNO	ENAME	JOBTITLE	ORIG_SALARY	RANKORDER
122	Lindsey	Director Personnel	40000	1
122	Lindsey	Mediator	40000	1
108	David	Mediator	37000	3
101	John	Chemist	35000	4
102	Stephanie	Accountant	35000	4
102	Stephanie	Mediator	35000	4
106	Chloe	Computer Programmer	33000	7

Again, note that the joining (WHERE) preceded the use of the analytical function RANK. The RANK and ORDER BY are done together — last.

The Order with GROUP BY Is Present

Now, suppose we used a GROUP BY in a query with no ordering or analytical function:

```
SELECT j.jobtitle, COUNT(*), MAX(orig_salary) maxsalary,
  MIN(orig_salary) minsalary
FROM employee e, job j
WHERE e.orig_salary < 43000
  AND e.empno = j.empno
GROUP BY j.jobtitle
```

Gives:

JOBTITLE	COUNT(*)	MAXSALARY	MINSALARY
Accountant	1	35000	35000
Chemist	1	35000	35000
Computer Programmer	1	33000	33000
Director Personnel	1	40000	40000
Mediator	3	40000	35000

Here we see the effect of the WHERE clause being applied before the GROUP BY.

Adding Ordering to the Query Containing the GROUP BY

This query can be reordered by the maximum original salary by adding an ORDER BY, which will keep the same number of rows but change the order of the display. Here is the statement:

```
SELECT j.jobtitle, COUNT(*), MAX(orig_salary) maxsalary,
  MIN(orig_salary) minsalary
FROM employee e, job j
WHERE e.orig_salary < 43000
  AND e.empno = j.empno
GROUP BY j.jobtitle
ORDER BY maxsalary
```

Which gives:

JOBTITLE	COUNT(*)	MAXSALARY	MINSALARY
Computer Programmer	1	33000	33000
Accountant	1	35000	35000
Chemist	1	35000	35000
Director Personnel	1	40000	40000
Mediator	3	40000	35000

The ORDER BY is applied last.

Adding an Analytical Function to the **GROUP BY** with **ORDER BY** Version

Notice that when the analytical function RANK is added to the statement, the RANK function is applied last, just before the ordering:

```
SELECT j.jobtitle, COUNT(*),
  MAX(orig_salary) maxsalary,
  MIN(orig_salary) minsalary,
  RANK() OVER(ORDER BY MAX(orig_salary)) rankorder
FROM employee e, job j
WHERE e.orig_salary < 43000
  AND e.empno = j.empno
GROUP BY j.jobtitle
ORDER BY rankorder
```

Gives:

JOBTITLE	COUNT(*)	MAXSALARY	MINSALARY	RANKORDER
Computer Programmer	1	33000	33000	1
Accountant	1	35000	35000	2
Chemist	1	35000	35000	2
Director Personnel	1	40000	40000	4
Mediator	3	40000	35000	4

The final ORDER BY is redundant to the ordering in the RANK function in this case. However, as we pointed out earlier, the use of the final ORDER BY is the preferred way to use the functions. The ranking and ordering is done last.

Changing the Final Ordering after Having Added an Analytical Function

The final ORDER BY can rearrange the order of the display, hence showing the place of the RANK function is between the GROUP BY and the ORDER BY:

```
SELECT j.jobtitle, COUNT(*), MAX(orig_salary) maxsalary,
  MIN(orig_salary) minsalary,
  RANK() OVER(ORDER BY MAX(orig_salary)) rankorder
FROM employee e, job j
WHERE e.orig_salary < 43000
  AND e.empno = j.empno
GROUP BY j.jobtitle
ORDER BY j.jobtitle desc
```

Gives:

JOBTITLE	COUNT(*)	MAXSALARY	MINSALARY	RANKORDER
Mediator	3	40000	35000	4
Director Personnel	1	40000	40000	4
Computer Programmer	1	33000	33000	1
Chemist	1	35000	35000	2
Accountant	1	35000	35000	2

Using HAVING with an Analytical Function

Finally, if a HAVING clause is added, it will have its effect just before the RANK. First, consider the previous statement with the analytical function commented out but with a HAVING clause added:

```
SELECT j.jobtitle, COUNT(*), MAX(orig_salary) maxsalary,
  MIN(orig_salary) minsalary
  -- RANK() OVER(ORDER BY MAX(orig_salary)) rankorder
FROM employee e, job j
WHERE e.orig_salary < 43000
  AND e.empno = j.empno
GROUP BY j.jobtitle
HAVING MAX(orig_salary) > 34000
ORDER BY j.jobtitle desc
```

Giving:

JOBTITLE	COUNT(*)	MAXSALARY	MINSALARY
Mediator	3	40000	35000
Director Personnel	1	40000	40000
Chemist	1	35000	35000
Accountant	1	35000	35000

Then, with the RANK in place we get this:

```
SELECT j.jobtitle, COUNT(*), MAX(orig_salary) maxsalary,
  MIN(orig_salary) minsalary,
  RANK() OVER(ORDER BY MAX(orig_salary)) rankorder
FROM employee e, job j
WHERE e.orig_salary < 43000
  AND e.empno = j.empno
GROUP BY j.jobtitle
HAVING MAX(orig_salary) > 34000
ORDER BY j.jobtitle desc
```

Giving:

JOBTITLE	COUNT(*)	MAXSALARY	MINSALARY	RANKORDER
Mediator	3	40000	35000	3
Director Personnel	1	40000	40000	3
Chemist	1	35000	35000	1
Accountant	1	35000	35000	1

The execution order is then: SELECT, FROM, WHERE, GROUP BY, HAVING, the analytical function, and then the final ORDER BY.

Where the Analytical Functions Can be Used in a SQL Statement

All of the examples we have seen thus far show the analytical function being used in the result set of the SQL statement. Since later versions of Oracle's SQL allow us to use subqueries in the result set as well as in the FROM and WHERE clauses, one might expect that analytical functions could be used in these clauses as well. This is not true.

The analytical functions are most usually used in the result sets as we have depicted. In some special cases, the functions may be used in an ORDER BY clause. However, the analytical functions are not allowed in WHERE or HAVING clauses.

If you need to use an analytical function in a WHERE clause, it can be handled using a virtual table like this:

```
SELECT *
FROM
  (SELECT empno, ename, orig_salary,
  DENSE_RANK() OVER(ORDER BY orig_salary) d_rank
```

```
    FROM employee) x
WHERE x.d_rank = 3
```

Giving:

EMPNO ENAME	ORIG_SALARY	DRANK
108 David	37000	3

This virtual table workaround can be used as many times as necessary to build a result. The performance of such a query is always a question; however, the logical progression of problem to solution often supercedes performance unless the query is just so slow that it will not return rows at all.

More Than One Analytical Function May Be Used in a Single Statement

The analytical functions are not restricted to just one function per SQL statement. One needs only be aware of the result that is produced to make sense of the answer if multiple analytical functions are used. Consider for example, this query:

```
SELECT empno, ename, orig_salary,
    RANK() OVER(ORDER BY orig_salary desc) toprank_orig,
       curr_salary,
    RANK() OVER(ORDER BY curr_salary desc) toprank_curr
FROM employee
ORDER BY ename
```

Which gives:

EMPNO	ENAME	ORIG_SALARY	TOPRANK_ORIG	CURR_SALARY	TOPRANK_CURR
106	Chloe	33000	7	44000	4
104	Christina	43000	2	55000	1
108	David	37000	4	39000	6
101	John	35000	5	39000	6
111	Katie	45000	1	49000	3
122	Lindsey	40000	3	52000	2
102	Stephanie	35000	5	44000	4

Note that Katie has the highest original salary and hence her rank is 1 on that attribute. For the current salary, Christina has the highest and hence holds the rank of 1 for that attribute.

As another example, you are not limited to the repeated use of the same analytical function. Further, the final ordering does not have to match the analytical function ordering. Consider this example:

```
SELECT empno, ename, orig_salary,
  ROW_NUMBER() OVER(ORDER BY orig_salary) rnum,
  RANK() OVER(ORDER BY curr_salary) rank,
  DENSE_RANK() OVER(ORDER BY orig_salary) drank
FROM employee
ORDER BY ename
```

Which gives:

EMPNO	ENAME	ORIG_SALARY	RNUM	RANK	DRANK
101	John	35000	2	1	2
106	Chloe	33000	1	3	1
104	Christina	43000	6	7	5
108	David	37000	4	1	3
111	Katie	45000	7	5	6
122	Lindsey	40000	5	6	4
102	Stephanie	35000	3	3	2

RNUM in this case is the ordering of salaries (low to high) with ties ignored had there not been other criteria. The RANK and DENSE_RANK functions return their expected results, but the final ordering is jumbled by the ORDER BY statement, which is applied last.

The Performance Implications of Using Analytical Functions

When an ORDER BY is used in a SQL statement, a sort is required. For example, the statement:

```
SELECT empno, ename
FROM employee
WHERE orig_salary > 38000
```

requires one pass through the Employee table. As each row is retrieved, it is examined; if the value of *orig_salary* meets the criteria set forth in the WHERE clause, the row is retrieved. If an ORDER BY is added to the statement, the result set has to be sorted and then returned, and hence ORDER BY requires a sort.

To examine the procedure by which Oracle processes queries, we can look at the EXPLAIN PLAN output (see the EXPLAIN PLAN sidebar).

The EXPLAIN PLAN Output

The EXPLAIN PLAN command may be used to find out how the Oracle Optimizer processes a statement. The Optimizer is a program that examines the SQL statement as presented by a user and then devises an execution plan to execute the statement. The execution plan can be seen by using either the EXPLAIN PLAN statement directly or by using the autotrace set option. In either case, one needs to ensure that the Plan Table has been created. The Plan Table must be created for each version of Oracle because the table varies with different versions. The Plan Table may be created with a utility called UTLXPLAN.SQL, which is in one of the Oracle directories.

If EXPLAIN PLAN is used directly, then the user must first create the Plan Table and then manage it. The sequence of managing the Plan Table goes like this:

1. Create the Plan Table.
2. Populate the Plan Table with a statement like:

```
EXPLAIN PLAN FOR [put your SQL statement here]
```

3. Query the Plan Table.
4. Truncate the Plan Table to set up for the next query to be analyzed.

To do some serious tuning of a query, the command ANALYZE TABLE x COMPUTER STATISTICS should be run for table x before the EXPLAIN PLAN command in order to allow the Optimizer to work as well as it can.

A simpler way to see the Optimizer plan is to set AUTOTRACE on. Unlike using EXPLAIN PLAN directly, setting AUTOTRACE on requires execution of the statement to see the EXPLAIN PLAN result. A better way to set AUTOTRACE on is like this:

```
SET AUTOTRACE TRACE EXP
```

because the command SET AUTOTRACE ON will produce a lot of statistics that will engender a study in themselves. (And unless you are already a DBA, you will spend a good deal of time figuring out what the statistics are trying to tell you about how internal memory is managed.)

One final point: You may have to visit your DBA to set AUTOTRACE on. If you get an error, you may have to ask for special permissions to use AUTOTRACE.

The sort operation may be seen in the execution plan display for the above SQL command.

1. Without the ordering:

```
SELECT empno, ename
FROM employee
WHERE orig_salary > 38000
```

Gives:

```
    EMPNO ENAME
---------- --------------------
      104 Christina
      111 Katie
      122 Lindsey


Execution Plan
----------------------------------------------------------
   0      SELECT STATEMENT Optimizer=CHOOSE
   1    0   TABLE ACCESS (FULL) OF 'EMPLOYEE'
```

No sorting was performed in the execution of the query. Note that these EXPLAIN PLAN outputs are read (generally speaking) from the bottom up and right indentation to left. In this case, the accessing of the table (TABLE ACCESS) precedes SELECT.

2. With an ordering clause added to the statement we get this:

```
SELECT empno, ename, orig_salary
FROM employee
WHERE orig_salary > 38000
ORDER BY orig_salary
```

Giving us:

```
   EMPNO ENAME                  ORIG_SALARY
---------- -------------------- -----------
     122 Lindsey                      40000
     104 Christina                    43000
     111 Katie                        45000


Execution Plan
----------------------------------------------------------------
   0      SELECT STATEMENT Optimizer=CHOOSE
   1    0    SORT (ORDER BY)
   2    1       TABLE ACCESS (FULL) OF 'EMPLOYEE'
```

In this case, EXPLAIN PLAN tells us that first the table was accessed (TABLE ACCESS) and then it was sorted (SORT) before returning the result set (SELECT).

What if an analytical function is included in the result set that sorts on the same order as the ORDER BY?

```
SELECT empno, ename, orig_salary,
   RANK() OVER(ORDER BY orig_salary)
FROM employee
WHERE orig_salary > 38000
ORDER BY orig_salary
```

Gives:

```
EMPNO ENAME                   ORIG_SALARY RANK()OVER(ORDERBYORIG_SALARY)
---------- ------------------ ----------- -----------------------------
  122 Lindsey                       40000                             1
  104 Christina                     43000                             2
  111 Katie                         45000                             3


Execution Plan
----------------------------------------------------------
   0      SELECT STATEMENT Optimizer=CHOOSE
   1   0   WINDOW (SORT)
   2   1    TABLE ACCESS (FULL) OF 'EMPLOYEE'
```

This EXPLAIN PLAN output tells us that there is still a sort, but it is not a "second" sort. Personifying the Optimizer, we can say that the Optimizer was "smart enough" to realize that another sort was not necessary. Only one sort takes place and hence the performance of the statement would be about the same as with a simple ORDER BY.

If the statement requests another ordering, another sort may result. For example:

```
SELECT empno, ename, orig_salary,
   RANK() OVER(ORDER BY orig_salary)
FROM employee
WHERE orig_salary > 38000
ORDER BY ename
```

Gives:

```
EMPNO ENAME                 ORIG_SALARY RANK()OVER(ORDERBYORIG_SALARY)
---------- ------------------- ----------- ------------------------------
   104 Christina               43000                              2
   111 Katie                   45000                              3
   122 Lindsey                 40000                              1


Execution Plan
-------------------------------------------------------------
   0       SELECT STATEMENT Optimizer=CHOOSE
   1    0    SORT (ORDER BY)
   2    1      WINDOW (SORT)
   3    2        TABLE ACCESS (FULL) OF 'EMPLOYEE'
```

The plan output in this case tells us that first the Employee table was accessed (TABLE ACCESS). Then the result was sorted by the analytical function (the WINDOW (SORT)). After that sort was completed, the result was sorted again due to the ORDER BY clause. Finally the result set was SELECTed and presented. Note that this example required two sorts to complete the result set.

If more analytical functions are added, yet more sorting may result (we say "may" here because the Optimizer may be able to shortcut some sorting). For example:

```
SELECT empno, ename, orig_salary, curr_salary,
   RANK() OVER(ORDER BY orig_salary) rank,
   DENSE_RANK() OVER(ORDER BY curr_salary) d_rank
FROM employee
WHERE orig_salary > 38000
ORDER BY ename
```

Gives:

```
   EMPNO ENAME            ORIG_SALARY CURR_SALARY        RANK      D_RANK
---------- ---------------- ----------- ----------- ---------- ----------
     104 Christina            43000       55000          2           3
     111 Katie                45000       49000          3           1
     122 Lindsey              40000       52000          1           2


Execution Plan
----------------------------------------------------------------
     0      SELECT STATEMENT Optimizer=CHOOSE
     1    0   SORT (ORDER BY)
     2    1    WINDOW (SORT)
     3    2      WINDOW (SORT)
     4    3        TABLE ACCESS (FULL) OF 'EMPLOYEE'
```

In this case, three sorts were performed to achieve the final result set: one for the RANK, one for the DENSE_RANK, and then one for the final ORDER BY.

Nulls and Analytical Functions

Nulls may be common in production databases. Nulls ordinarily mean that a value is unknown, and may present some query difficulties unless it is known how a query will perform with nulls present. It is strongly suggested that all queries be tested with nulls present even if a test data set needs to be created.

Suppose we create another table from the Employee table called Empwnulls that has this data in it:

```
SELECT * FROM empwnulls
```

Giving:

EMPNO	ENAME	HIREDATE	ORIG_SALARY	CURR_SALARY
101	John	02-DEC-97	35000	
102	Stephanie	22-SEP-98	35000	44000
104	Christina	08-MAR-98	43000	55000
108	David	08-JUL-01		
111	Katie	13-APR-00	45000	49000
106	Chloe	19-JAN-96	33000	44000
122	Lindsey	22-MAY-97	40000	52000

What effect will we see with the analytical functions we have discussed thus far? Here are some sample queries:

Without nulls:

```
SELECT empno, ename, curr_salary,
  ROW_NUMBER() OVER(ORDER BY curr_salary desc) salary
FROM employee /* Note this is from employee with no nulls
              in it */
ORDER BY curr_salary desc
```

Gives:

EMPNO	ENAME	CURR_SALARY	SALARY
104	Christina	55000	1
122	Lindsey	52000	2
111	Katie	49000	3
102	Stephanie	44000	4
106	Chloe	44000	5
101	John	39000	6
108	David	39000	7

With nulls:

```
SELECT empno, ename, curr_salary,
  ROW_NUMBER() OVER(ORDER BY curr_salary) salary
FROM empwnulls /* from "employee with nulls added"
                  (empwnulls) */
ORDER BY curr_salary
```

Gives:

EMPNO	ENAME	CURR_SALARY	SALARY
102	Stephanie	44000	1
106	Chloe	44000	2
111	Katie	49000	3
122	Lindsey	52000	4
104	Christina	55000	5
101	John		6
108	David		7

In descending order:

```
SELECT empno, ename, curr_salary,
  ROW_NUMBER() OVER(ORDER BY curr_salary desc) salary
FROM empwnulls /* from "employee with nulls added"
                  (empwnulls) */
ORDER BY curr_salary desc
```

Gives:

EMPNO	ENAME	CURR_SALARY	SALARY
101	John		1
108	David		2
104	Christina	55000	3
122	Lindsey	52000	4
111	Katie	49000	5
102	Stephanie	44000	6
106	Chloe	44000	7

When nulls are present, there is an option to place nulls first or last with the analytical function.

```
SELECT empno, ename, curr_salary,
   ROW_NUMBER() OVER(ORDER BY curr_salary NULLS LAST)
        salary
FROM empwnulls /* from "employee with nulls added"
                    (empwnulls) */
ORDER BY curr_salary
SQL> /
```

Gives:

EMPNO	ENAME	CURR_SALARY	SALARY
102	Stephanie	44000	1
106	Chloe	44000	2
111	Katie	49000	3
122	Lindsey	52000	4
104	Christina	55000	5
101	John		6
108	David		7

```
SELECT empno, ename, curr_salary,
   ROW_NUMBER() OVER(ORDER BY curr_salary NULLS FIRST)
        salary
FROM empwnulls /* from "employee with nulls added"
                    (empwnulls) */
ORDER BY curr_salary
SQL> /
```

Gives:

EMPNO	ENAME	CURR_SALARY	SALARY
102	Stephanie	44000	3
106	Chloe	44000	4
111	Katie	49000	5
122	Lindsey	52000	6
104	Christina	55000	7
101	John		1
108	David		2

The default is NULLS FIRST. To see nulls last in the sort order, the modifier NULLS LAST is used like this:

```
SELECT empno, ename, curr_salary,
  ROW_NUMBER() OVER(ORDER BY curr_salary desc NULLS LAST)
      salary
FROM empwnulls /* from "employee with nulls added"
                (empwnulls) */
ORDER BY curr_salary desc NULLS LAST
```

Giving:

EMPNO	ENAME	CURR_SALARY	SALARY
104	Christina	55000	1
122	Lindsey	52000	2
111	Katie	49000	3
102	Stephanie	44000	4
106	Chloe	44000	5
101	John		6
108	David		7

The modifier NULLS LAST or NULLS FIRST (which is the default) may be added to any ordering analytic clause. In the case of NULLS LAST, the ROW_NUMBER is reorganized to place the nulls at the end (sorted high). If NULLS LAST is left out of the final ORDER BY, the effect will be lost.

In the case of ranking, the result is:

```
SELECT empno, ename, curr_salary,
  RANK()
  OVER(ORDER BY curr_salary desc) salary
FROM empwnulls
ORDER BY curr_salary desc
```

Giving:

EMPNO	ENAME	CURR_SALARY	SALARY
101	John		1
108	David		1
104	Christina	55000	3
122	Lindsey	52000	4
111	Katie	49000	5
102	Stephanie	44000	6
106	Chloe	44000	6

Here, the ranking of the "top salary" is first because the rank of the null value defaults to NULLS FIRST. If the statement were rewritten with NULLS LAST, we'd get this result:

```
SELECT empno, ename, curr_salary,
  RANK()
  OVER(ORDER BY curr_salary desc NULLS LAST) salary
FROM empwnulls
ORDER BY curr_salary desc NULLS LAST
```

Gives:

EMPNO	ENAME	CURR_SALARY	SALARY
104	Christina	55000	1
122	Lindsey	52000	2
111	Katie	49000	3
102	Stephanie	44000	4
106	Chloe	44000	4
101	John		6
108	David		6

Note that in both cases, the null values are given a ranking and one may control where that ranking occurs. Of course, nulls may be excluded with a WHERE clause and the problem ignored, if it makes sense in a result set:

```
SELECT empno, ename, curr_salary,
  RANK()
  OVER(ORDER BY curr_salary desc NULLS LAST) salary
FROM empwnulls
WHERE curr_salary is not null
ORDER BY curr_salary desc NULLS LAST
```

Gives:

EMPNO	ENAME	CURR_SALARY	SALARY
104	Christina	55000	1
122	Lindsey	52000	2
111	Katie	49000	3
102	Stephanie	44000	4
106	Chloe	44000	4

Nulls could also be handled with a default value using the NVL function in the analytical function like this:

```
SELECT empno, ename, NVL(curr_salary,44444),
  RANK()
  OVER(ORDER BY NVL(curr_salary,44444) desc NULLS LAST)
      salary
FROM empwnulls
ORDER BY curr_salary desc NULLS LAST
```

Giving:

EMPNO	ENAME	NVL(CURR_SALARY,44444)	SALARY
104	Christina	55000	1
122	Lindsey	52000	2
111	Katie	49000	3
102	Stephanie	44000	6
106	Chloe	44000	6
101	John	44444	4
108	David	44444	4

You may notice a strange result in that the result was ordered with NULLS LAST, but the null values are given the default from the NVL. If the statement were redone without NULLS LAST, the values of the NVL'd nulls occur first:

```
SELECT empno, ename, NVL(curr_salary,44444),
  RANK()
  OVER(ORDER BY NVL(curr_salary,44444) desc) salary
FROM empwnulls
ORDER BY curr_salary desc
```

Giving:

```
    EMPNO ENAME          NVL(CURR_SALARY,44444)     SALARY
---------- -------------- ---------------------- ----------
      101 John                           44444          4
      108 David                          44444          4
      104 Christina                      55000          1
      122 Lindsey                        52000          2
      111 Katie                          49000          3
      102 Stephanie                      44000          6
      106 Chloe                          44000          6
```

But if the column alias for the analytical function is used in the final ORDER BY, the result is more like what is expected:

```
SELECT empno, ename, NVL(curr_salary,44444),
  RANK()
  OVER(ORDER BY NVL(curr_salary,44444) desc) salary
FROM empwnulls
ORDER BY salary
```

Giving:

```
    EMPNO ENAME          NVL(CURR_SALARY,44444)     SALARY
---------- -------------- ---------------------- ----------
      104 Christina                      55000          1
      122 Lindsey                        52000          2
      111 Katie                          49000          3
      101 John                           44444          4
      108 David                          44444          4
      102 Stephanie                      44000          6
      106 Chloe                          44000          6
```

When dealing with combinations of functions like this, it is always a good idea to run a test set of data to see how the function performs. This is especially true when nulls may be present. *Always test queries with data that contains null values.*

The DENSE_RANK function works in a similar way to RANK.

Partitioning with PARTITION_BY

Partitioning in an analytical function allows us to separate groupings of data and then perform a function from within that group. For example, let's consider our region attribute:

```
SELECT empno, ename, region
FROM employee
ORDER BY region, empno
```

Giving:

```
EMPNO ENAME                 REGION
---------- -------------------- ------
     108 David                E
     111 Katie                E
     122 Lindsey              E
     101 John                 W
     102 Stephanie            W
     104 Christina            W
     106 Chloe                W
```

Suppose now we'd like to partition the data to look at salaries within each region. To do this we use a partition analytical clause in the analytical function like this:

```
SELECT empno, ename, region, curr_salary,
   RANK() OVER(PARTITION BY region ORDER BY curr_salary desc)
      rank
FROM employee
ORDER BY region
```

Giving:

EMPNO	ENAME	REGION	CURR_SALARY	RANK
122	Lindsey	E	52000	1
111	Katie	E	49000	2
108	David	E	39000	3
104	Christina	W	55000	1
102	Stephanie	W	44000	2
106	Chloe	W	44000	2
101	John	W	39000	4

Note how the rankings occur within the region values ordered by descending salary. In the analytic clause, the PARTITION BY phrase must precede the ORDER BY phrase or else a syntax error will be generated.

A Problem that Uses ROW_NUMBER for a Solution

We will now take up a more interesting practical problem. Let's suppose that we have gathered data where people take a series of three tests, one after the other. The result of each test is stored with the result for each test on one line. Each entry contains the date and time for each test. Suppose further that the three tests must be taken in order. We'd like to write a query that checks the table to find out if any of the tests were taken out of order. Like all the examples in this book, we'll use a small sample table, but as you study it, please realize that the table we might be checking could contain millions of rows.

Let's use the values Test1, Test2, and Test3 for the names of the tests themselves. For each test there will be a test score. Suppose that a good, ordered set of data would look like this in a table called Subject:

```
SELECT name, test, score,
  TO_CHAR(dtime,'dd-Mon-yyyy hh24:mi') dtime
FROM subject
ORDER BY name, test
```

Which results in:

```
NAME       TEST    SCORE DTIME
---------- ------ ------ -----------------
Brenda     Test1     798 21-Dec-2006 08:19
Brenda     Test2     890 21-Dec-2006 09:49
Brenda     Test3     760 21-Dec-2006 10:55
Richard    Test1     888 21-Dec-2006 07:51
Richard    Test2     777 21-Dec-2006 09:21
Richard    Test3     678 21-Dec-2006 10:46
```

By inspecting the data, we can see that both Richard and Brenda took the tests in order — Test1, then Test2, then Test3. Remember that this is likely only a very small sample of the data that might be millions of rows long; hence, a visual inspection of the data would be practically impossible on a complete data set.

This type of data would not necessarily be ordered in a relational database; after loading, a "SELECT * FROM subject" might look more like this:

```
SELECT *
FROM subject
```

Giving:

```
NAME        TEST    SCORE DTIME
----------  ------  ------ ---------
Brenda      Test3     760 21-DEC-06
Brenda      Test2     890 21-DEC-06
Richard     Test2     777 21-DEC-06
Richard     Test3     678 21-DEC-06
Richard     Test1     888 21-DEC-06
Brenda      Test1     798 21-DEC-06
```

Remember that relational databases store data as sets of rows. The implication of "sets of rows" is that there is never an implied ordering of the rows and that there are no duplicate rows. In other words, when a relational database loads rows, it might internally place the rows anywhere in any order. Oracle does allow duplicate rows, but defining an appropriate primary key would prevent this. We will not pursue this issue at this time, but the point is that some data is loaded into a table and you cannot presume to know the internal order in a relational database.

The original ordered listing above was obtained with a SQL statement that had an ORDER BY in it like this:

```
SELECT name, test, score,
  TO_CHAR(dtime,'dd-Mon-yyyy hh24:mi') dtime
FROM subject
ORDER BY name, test
```

What we'd like to implement is a statement that would show all of the cases where the person did *not* have the proper test order sequence. In other words, we'd like to have a query that asked, for every group of tests for a person, "Is the first test Test1, the second test Test2, and the third test Test3?"

An output format of the data with partitioning and row numbering could look like this:

NAME	TEST	SCORE	Date/time	Test#
Brenda	Test1	798	21-Dec-2006 08:19	1
Brenda	Test2	890	21-Dec-2006 09:49	2
Brenda	Test3	760	21-Dec-2006 10:55	3
Richard	Test1	888	21-Dec-2006 07:51	1
Richard	Test2	777	21-Dec-2006 09:21	2
Richard	Test3	678	21-Dec-2006 10:46	3

Keep in mind that the data in the database is unordered. To cordon off the data by name in this fashion is called a *partition*. The analytic clause must contain not only a phrase to order the data by test, but also a way to partition the data by name. The Test# column data is generated by the ROW_NUMBER analytical function. Here is the query that produces the above result:

```
SELECT name, test, score,
  TO_CHAR(dtime, 'dd-Mon-yyyy hh24:mi') "Date/time",
  ROW_NUMBER() OVER(PARTITION BY name ORDER BY test) "Test#"
FROM subject
```

Now testing the result set is a matter of using it as a virtual table and first recreating the output like this:

```
SELECT x.name, x.test, x.score, x.dt, x.tnum
FROM
  (SELECT i.name, i.test, i.score,
    TO_CHAR(dtime, 'dd-Mon-yyyy hh24:mi') dt,
    ROW_NUMBER() OVER(PARTITION BY name ORDER BY dtime) tnum
  FROM subject i) x
WHERE (x.test like '%1' and x.tnum = 1)
OR (x.test like '%2' and x.tnum = 2)
OR (x.test like '%3' and x.tnum = 3)
```

Of course, this query returns the "good" rows and, with the above data, would return the same thing if no WHERE clause were present. To make it return any "bad" rows would involve a slight modification and some "bad" data. For example, if these rows were added to the Subject table:

```
NAME        TEST    SCORE DTIME
----------  ------  ------ -----------------
Jake        Test2      555 22-Dec-2002 12:15
Jake        Test1      735 22-Dec-2002 14:33
```

Then the WHERE clause query could be changed to the logical negative as follows to display the "bad" rows:

```
SELECT x.name, x.test, x.score, x.dt, x.tnum
FROM
  (SELECT i.name, i.test, i.score,
    TO_CHAR(dtime, 'dd-Mon-yyyy hh24:mi') dt,
    ROW_NUMBER() OVER(PARTITION BY name ORDER BY dtime) tnum
  FROM subject i) x
WHERE NOT((x.test like '%1' and x.tnum = 1)
OR (x.test like '%2' and x.tnum = 2)
OR (x.test like '%3' and x.tnum = 3))
```

The above query would result in this display, indicating tests taken out of order by Jake:

```
NAME        TEST    SCORE DT                      TNUM
----------  ------  ------ ------------------- ----------
Jake        Test2      555 22-Dec-2006 12:15           1
Jake        Test1      735 22-Dec-2006 14:33           2
```

NTILE

An analytical function closely related to the ranking
and row-counting functions is NTILE. NTILE groups
data by sort order into a variable number of percentile
groupings. The NTILE function roughly works by
dividing the number of rows retrieved into the chosen
number of segments. Then, the percentile is displayed
as the segment that the rows fall into. For example, if
you wanted to know which salaries where in the top
25%, the next 25%, the next 25%, and the bottom 25%,
then the NTILE(4) function is used for that ordering
(100%/4 = 25%). The algorithm for the function distrib-
utes the values "evenly." The analytical function
NTILE(4) for current salary in Employee would be:

```
SELECT empno, ename, curr_salary,
  NTILE(4) OVER(ORDER BY curr_salary desc) nt
FROM  employee
```

which results in:

EMPNO	ENAME	CURR_SALARY	NT
104	Christina	55000	1
122	Lindsey	52000	1
111	Katie	49000	2
102	Stephanie	44000	2
106	Chloe	44000	3
101	John	39000	3
108	David	39000	4

The range of salaries is broken up into (max – min)/4
for NTILE(4) and the rows are assigned after ranking.
Therefore, what you would expect would be:

```
55000 - 39000 = 16000.
16000/4 = 4000
```

```
55000 to 51000 is in the top 25%,
51000 to 47000 is in the 2nd 25%
47000 to 43000 is in the 3rd 25%
and 43000 to 39000 is in the bottom 25%.
```

As you can see from the result set of the above query, the NTILE function works from row order after a ranking takes place. In this example, we find the salary 44000 actually occurring in two different percentile groupings where theoretically we'd expect both Stephanie and Chloe to be in the same NTILE group. In NTILE, the edges of groups sometimes depend on other attributes (as in this case, the attribute employee number (EMPNO)). The following query and result reverses the grouping of Chloe and Stephanie:

```
SELECT empno, ename, curr_salary,
  NTILE(4) OVER(ORDER BY curr_salary desc, empno desc) nt
FROM employee
```

Gives:

EMPNO	ENAME	CURR_SALARY	NT
104	Christina	55000	1
122	Lindsey	52000	1
111	Katie	49000	2
106	Chloe	44000	2
102	Stephanie	44000	3
108	David	39000	3
101	John	39000	4

To get a clearer picture of the NTILE function, we can use it with several domains like this:

```
SELECT ename, curr_salary sal,
  ntile(2) OVER(ORDER BY curr_salary desc) n2,
  ntile(3) OVER(ORDER BY curr_salary desc) n3,
  ntile(4) OVER(ORDER BY curr_salary desc) n4,
  ntile(5) OVER(ORDER BY curr_salary desc) n5,
  ntile(6) OVER(ORDER BY curr_salary desc) n6,
  ntile(8) OVER(ORDER BY curr_salary desc) n8
FROM employee
```

Which gives:

ENAME	SAL	N2	N3	N4	N5	N6	N8
Christina	55000	1	1	1	1	1	1
Lindsey	52000	1	1	1	1	1	2
Katie	49000	1	1	2	2	2	3
Stephanie	44000	1	2	2	2	3	4
Chloe	44000	2	2	3	3	4	5
John	39000	2	3	3	4	5	6
David	39000	2	3	4	5	6	7

The use of NTILE with a small amount of data like we have done here is poor statistics, but a reasonable database demonstration. To truly deal with NTILE in a statistical sense, we'd have to use a lot more data.

What about nulls with the NTILE function? Here is an example using the same query on our Employee table with nulls (Empwnulls):

```
SELECT ename, curr_salary sal,
  ntile(2) OVER(ORDER BY curr_salary desc) n2,
  ntile(3) OVER(ORDER BY curr_salary desc) n3,
  ntile(4) OVER(ORDER BY curr_salary desc) n4,
  ntile(5) OVER(ORDER BY curr_salary desc) n5,
  ntile(6) OVER(ORDER BY curr_salary desc) n6,
  ntile(8) OVER(ORDER BY curr_salary desc) n8
FROM empwnulls
```

Gives:

ENAME	SAL	N2	N3	N4	N5	N6	N8
John		1	1	1	1	1	1
David		1	1	1	1	1	2
Christina	55000	1	1	2	2	2	3
Lindsey	52000	1	2	2	2	3	4
Katie	49000	2	2	3	3	4	5
Stephanie	44000	2	3	3	4	5	6
Chloe	44000	2	3	4	5	6	7

And with NULLS LAST:

```
SELECT ename, curr_salary sal,
   ntile(2) OVER(ORDER BY curr_salary desc NULLS LAST) n2,
   ntile(3) OVER(ORDER BY curr_salary desc NULLS LAST) n3,
   ntile(4) OVER(ORDER BY curr_salary desc NULLS LAST) n4,
   ntile(5) OVER(ORDER BY curr_salary desc NULLS LAST) n5,
   ntile(6) OVER(ORDER BY curr_salary desc NULLS LAST) n6,
   ntile(8) OVER(ORDER BY curr_salary desc NULLS LAST) n8
FROM empwnulls
```

Gives:

ENAME	SAL	N2	N3	N4	N5	N6	N8
Christina	55000	1	1	1	1	1	1
Lindsey	52000	1	1	1	1	1	2
Katie	49000	1	1	2	2	2	3
Stephanie	44000	1	2	2	2	3	4
Chloe	44000	2	2	3	3	4	5
John		2	3	3	4	5	6
David		2	3	4	5	6	7

The nulls are treated like a value for the NTILE and placed either at the beginning (NULLS FIRST, the default) or the end (NULLS LAST). The percentile algorithm places null values just before or just after the high and low values for the purposes of placing the row into a given percentile. As before, nulls can also be handled by either using NVL or excluding nulls from the result set using an appropriate WHERE clause.

RANK, PERCENT_RANK, and CUME_DIST

The final examples we present in the ranking function category are the PERCENT_RANK and CUME_DIST functions. For these functions we will use a table with more values — a table called Cities, with city names and temperatures (which might be in effect on some winter day):

ROWNUM	CNAME	TEMP
1	Mobile	70
2	Binghamton	20
3	Grass Valley	55
4	Gulf Breeze	77
5	Meridian	65
6	Baton Rouge	58
7	Reston	47
8	Bartlesville	35
9	Orlando	79
10	Carrboro	58
11	Alexandria	47
12	Starkville	58
13	Moundsville	63
14	Brewton	72
15	Davenport	77
16	New Milford	24
17	Hallstead	27
18	Provo	44
19	Tombstone	33
20	Idaho Falls	47

The syntax for the PERCENT_RANK and CUME_DIST functions are similar to those we've seen before:

```
PERCENT_RANK() OVER ([PARTITION clause] ORDER clause)
```

and

```
CUME_DIST() OVER ([PARTITION clause] ORDER clause)
```

The PARTITION clause is optional. To simplify the math, we will not use it in our example.

First, we'll look at an example of the use of these functions, and then discuss the calculations involved.

```
SELECT cname, temp,
  RANK() OVER(ORDER BY temp) RANK,
  PERCENT_RANK() OVER(ORDER BY temp) PR,
  CUME_DIST() OVER(ORDER BY temp) CD
FROM cities
ORDER BY temp
```

Gives:

CNAME	TEMP	RANK	PR	CD
Binghamton	20	1	.000	.050
New Milford	24	2	.053	.100
Hallstead	27	3	.105	.150
Tombstone	33	4	.158	.200
Bartlesville	35	5	.211	.250
Provo	44	6	.263	.300
Reston	47	7	.316	.450
Alexandria	47	7	.316	.450
Idaho Falls	47	7	.316	.450
Grass Valley	55	10	.474	.500
Baton Rouge	58	11	.526	.650
Starkville	58	11	.526	.650
Carrboro	58	11	.526	.650
Moundsville	63	14	.684	.700
Meridian	65	15	.737	.750
Mobile	70	16	.789	.800

Brewton	72		17	.842	.850
Gulf Breeze	77		18	.895	.950
Davenport	77		18	.895	.950
Orlando	79		20	1.000	1.000

PERCENT_RANK will compute the cumulative fraction of the ranking that exists for a particular ranking value. This calculation and the one for CUME_DIST are like the values one would see in a histogram. PERCENT_RANK is set to compute so that the first row is zero, and the other values in this column are computed based on the formula:

```
Percent_rank (PR) = (Rank-1)/(Number of rows-1)
```

By the row, the PERCENT_RANK calculation is:

	Rank	Rank-1	Calculation	Percent	Rank
Binghamton	20	1	0	(0/19)	0.000
New Milford	24	2	1	(1/19)	0.053
Hallstead	27	3	2	(2/19)	0.105
Provo	44	6	5	(5/19)	0.263
Reston	47	7	6	(6/19)	0.316
Alexandria	47	7	6	(6/19)	0.316
Idaho Falls	47	7	6	(6/19)	0.316
Grass Valley	55	10	9	(9/19)	0.474
Gulf Breeze	77	18	17	(17/19)	0.895
Davenport	77	18	17	(17/19)	0.895
Orlando	79	20	19	(19/19)	1.000

The CUME_RANK function calculates the cumulative distribution in a group of values. In our example, we have only one group, so the formula works like this:

```
Cumulative Distribution =
  the highest rank for that row (cr)/number of rows (nr)
```

The value of nr here is 20 (20 rows).
By the row, the CUME_RANK calculation is:

CNAME	TEMP	RANK	rownum	cr	calculation	CD
Binghamton	20	1	1	1	(1/20)	.050
New Milford	24	2	2	2	(2/20)	.100
Provo	44	6	6	6	(6/20)	.300
Reston	47	7	7	9	(9/20)	.450
Alexandria	47	7	8	9	(9/20)	.450
Idaho Falls	47	7	9	9	(9/20)	.450
Grass Valley	55	10	10	10	(10/20)	.500
Baton Rouge	58	11	11	13	(13/20)	.650
Starkville	58	11	12	13	(13/20)	.650
Carrboro	58	11	13	13	(13/20)	.650
Brewton	72	17	17	17	(17/20)	.850
Gulf Breeze	77	18	19	19	(19/20)	.950
Davenport	77	18	19	19	(19/20)	.950
Orlando	79	20	20	20	(20/20)	1.000

The cr value of 9 for row 7 occurs because the rank of 7 was given to all rows up to the ninth row, and hence rows 7, 8, and 9 get the same value of 9 for cr, the numerator in the function calculation.

The PERCENT_RANK and CUME_RANK functions are very specialized and far less common than RANK or ROW_NUMBER. Also, in our examples we have depicted only one grouping — one partition. A PARTITION BY clause may be added to the analytic clause of the function, and sub-grouping and sub-PERCENT_RANKs and CUME_DISTs may also be reported.

For example, using our Employee table with
PERCENT_RANK and CUME_DIST:

```
SELECT empno, ename, region,
  RANK() OVER(PARTITION BY region ORDER BY curr_salary)
    RANK,
  PERCENT_RANK() OVER(PARTITION BY region ORDER BY
    curr_salary) PR,
  CUME_DIST() OVER(PARTITION BY region ORDER BY curr_salary)
    CD
FROM employee
```

Gives:

EMPNO	ENAME	REGION	RANK	PR	CD
108	David	E	1	0	.333333333
111	Katie	E	2	.5	.666666667
122	Lindsey	E	3	1	1
101	John	W	1	0	.25
102	Stephanie	W	2	.333333333	.75
106	Chloe	W	2	.333333333	.75
104	Christina	W	4	1	1

In this result, first note the partitioning by region: The
result set acts like two different sets of data based on
the partition. Within each region, we see the calculation
of PERCENT_RANK and CUME_DIST as per the
previous algorithms.

References

SQL for Analysis in Data Warehouses, Oracle Corporation, Redwood Shores, CA, Oracle9i Data Warehousing Guide, Release 2 (9.2), Part Number A96520-01.

For an excellent discussion of how Oracle 10*g* has improved querying, see "DSS Performance in Oracle Database 10*g*," an Oracle white paper, September 2003. This article shows how the Optimizer has been improved in 10*g*.

Chapter 4

Aggregate Functions Used as Analytical Functions (Analytical Functions II)

The Use of Aggregate Functions in SQL

Many of the common aggregate functions can be used as analytical functions: SUM, AVG, COUNT, STDDEV, VARIANCE, MAX, and MIN. The aggregate functions used as analytical functions offer the advantage of partitioning and ordering as well. As an example, say you want to display each person's employee number, name, original salary, and the average salary of all employees. This cannot be done with a query like the following because you cannot mix aggregates and row-level results.

```
SELECT empno, ename, orig_salary,
  AVG(orig_salary)
FROM employee
ORDER BY ename
```

Gives:

```
SELECT empno, ename, orig_salary,
       *
ERROR at line 1:
ORA-00937: not a single-group group function
```

But we can use a Cartesian product/virtual table like this:

```
SELECT e.empno, e.ename, e.orig_salary,
  x.aos "Avg. salary"
FROM employee e,
  (SELECT AVG(orig_salary) aos FROM employee) x
ORDER BY ename
```

Which gives:

```
EMPNO ENAME      ORIG_SALARY Avg. salary
------ ---------- ----------- -----------
   101 John            35000  38285.7143
   106 Chloe           33000  38285.7143
   104 Christina       43000  38285.7143
   108 David           37000  38285.7143
   111 Kate            45000  38285.7143
   122 Lindsey         40000  38285.7143
   102 Stephanie       35000  38285.7143
```

This type of query is borderline cumbersome and may be done far more easily using AVG in an analytical function:

```
SELECT empno, ename, orig_salary,
  AVG(orig_salary) OVER() "Avg. salary"
FROM employee
ORDER BY ename
```

Giving:

```
EMPNO ENAME        ORIG_SALARY Avg. salary
------ ----------- ----------- -----------
   101 John              35000 38285.7143
   106 Chloe             33000 38285.7143
   104 Christina         43000 38285.7143
   108 David             37000 38285.7143
   111 Kate              45000 38285.7143
   122 Lindsey           40000 38285.7143
   102 Stephanie         35000 38285.7143
```

This display looks off-balance due to the decimal points in the average salary. We can modify the displayed result using the analytical function nested inside an ordinary row-level function; a better version of the query with a ROUND function added would be:

```
SELECT empno, ename, orig_salary,
  ROUND(AVG(orig_salary) OVER()) "Avg. salary"
FROM employee
ORDER BY ename
```

Giving:

```
EMPNO ENAME        ORIG_SALARY Avg. salary
------ ----------- ----------- -----------
   101 John              35000       38286
   106 Chloe             33000       38286
   104 Christina         43000       38286
   108 David             37000       38286
   111 Kate              45000       38286
   122 Lindsey           40000       38286
   102 Stephanie         35000       38286
```

The aggregate/analytical function uses an argument to specify which column is aggregated/analyzed (*orig_salary*). It should also be noted that there is a null OVER clause. When the OVER clause is null as it is here, it is said to be a reporting function and applies to the entire dataset.

We can use partitioning in the OVER clause of the aggregate-analytical function like this:

```
SELECT empno, ename, orig_salary, region,
  ROUND(AVG(orig_salary) OVER(PARTITION BY region))
    "Avg. Salary"
FROM employee
ORDER BY region, ename
```

Giving:

EMPNO	ENAME	ORIG_SALARY	REGION	Avg. Salary
108	David	37000	E	40667
111	Kate	45000	E	40667
122	Lindsey	40000	E	40667
101	John	35000	W	36500
106	Chloe	33000	W	36500
104	Christina	43000	W	36500
102	Stephanie	35000	W	36500

In this version of the query, we now have the average by region reported along with the other ordinary row data for an individual.

The result of the row-level reporting may be used in arithmetic in the result set. Suppose we wanted to see the difference between a person's salary and the average for his or her region. This example shows that query:

```
SELECT empno, ename, region, curr_salary,
  orig_salary,
  ROUND(AVG(orig_salary) OVER(PARTITION BY region))
      "Avg-group",
  ROUND(orig_salary - AVG(orig_salary) OVER(PARTITION
      BY region)) "Diff."
FROM employee
ORDER BY region, ename
```

Giving:

EMPNO	ENAME	REGION	CURR_SALARY	ORIG_SALARY	Avg-group	Diff.
108	David	E	39000	37000	40667	-3667
111	Kate	E	49000	45000	40667	4333
122	Lindsey	E	52000	40000	40667	-667
101	John	W	39000	35000	36500	-1500
106	Chloe	W	44000	33000	36500	-3500
104	Christina	W	55000	43000	36500	6500
102	Stephanie	W	44000	35000	36500	-1500

RATIO-TO-REPORT

Returning to the example of using an aggregate in a calculation, here we want to know what fraction of the total salary budget goes to which individual. We can find this result with a script like this:

```
COLUMN portion FORMAT 99.9999
SELECT ename, curr_salary,
  curr_salary/SUM(curr_salary) OVER() Portion
FROM employee
ORDER BY curr_salary
```

Giving:

```
ENAME                    CURR_SALARY  PORTION
--------------------     -----------  --------
John                           39000    .1211
David                          39000    .1211
Stephanie                      44000    .1366
Chloe                          44000    .1366
Kate                           49000    .1522
Lindsey                        52000    .1615
Christina                      55000    .1708
```

Notice that the PORTION column adds up to 100%:

```
COLUMN total FORMAT 9.9999
SELECT sum(o.portion) Total
FROM
  (SELECT i.ename, i.curr_salary,
    i.curr_salary/SUM(i.curr_salary) OVER() Portion
  FROM employee i
ORDER BY i.curr_salary) o
```

Gives:

```
 TOTAL
-------
 1.0000
```

The above query showing the fraction of salary apportioned to each individual can be done in one step with an analytical function called RATIO_TO_REPORT, which is used like this:

```
COLUMN portion2 LIKE portion
SELECT ename, curr_salary,
  curr_salary/SUM(curr_salary) OVER() Portion,
  RATIO_TO_REPORT(curr_salary) OVER() Portion2
FROM employee
ORDER BY curr_salary
```

Giving:

ENAME	CURR_SALARY	PORTION	PORTION2
John	39000	.1211	.1211
David	39000	.1211	.1211
Stephanie	44000	.1366	.1366
Chloe	44000	.1366	.1366
Kate	49000	.1522	.1522
Lindsey	52000	.1615	.1615
Christina	55000	.1708	.1708

The RATIO_TO_REPORT (and the SUM analytical function) can easily be partioned as well. For example:

```
SELECT ename, curr_salary, region,
   curr_salary/SUM(curr_salary) OVER(PARTITION BY Region)
      Portion,
   RATIO_TO_REPORT(curr_salary) OVER(PARTITION BY Region)
      Portion2
FROM employee
ORDER BY region, curr_salary
```

Gives:

ENAME	CURR_SALARY	RE	PORTION	PORTION2
David	39000	E	.2786	.2786
Kate	49000	E	.3500	.3500
Lindsey	52000	E	.3714	.3714
John	39000	W	.2143	.2143
Stephanie	44000	W	.2418	.2418
Chloe	44000	W	.2418	.2418
Christina	55000	W	.3022	.3022

117

Notice that the portion amounts add to 1.000 in each region:

```
SELECT ename, curr_salary, region,
   curr_salary/SUM(curr_salary) OVER(PARTITION BY Region)
      Portion,
   RATIO_TO_REPORT(curr_salary) OVER(PARTITION BY Region)
      Portion2
FROM employee
UNION
SELECT null, TO_NUMBER(null), region, sum(P1), sum(p2)
FROM
   (SELECT ename, curr_salary, region,
      curr_salary/SUM(curr_salary) OVER(PARTITION BY Region) P1,
      RATIO_TO_REPORT(curr_salary) OVER(PARTITION BY Region) P2
   FROM employee)
GROUP BY region
ORDER BY 3,2
```

Gives:

ENAME	CURR_SALARY	RE	PORTION	PORTION2
David	39000	E	.2786	.2786
Kate	49000	E	.3500	.3500
Lindsey	52000	E	.3714	.3714
		E	1.0000	1.0000
John	39000	W	.2143	.2143
Chloe	44000	W	.2418	.2418
Stephanie	44000	W	.2418	.2418
Christina	55000	W	.3022	.3022
		W	1.0000	1.0000

In this query, the TO_NUMBER(null) is provided to make the data types compatible.

A similar report can be had without the UNION workaround with the following SQL*Plus formatting commands included in a script:

```
BREAK ON region
COMPUTE sum of portion ON region
SELECT ename, curr_salary, region,
  curr_salary/SUM(curr_salary) OVER(PARTITION BY Region)
      Portion,
  RATIO_TO_REPORT(curr_salary) OVER(PARTITION BY Region)
      Portion2
FROM employee
ORDER BY region, curr_salary;
CLEAR COMPUTES
CLEAR BREAKS
```

Giving:

ENAME	CURR_SALARY	REGION	PORTION	PORTION2
David	39000	E	.278571429	.278571429
Kate	49000		.35	.35
Lindsey	52000		.371428571	.371428571
		******		
		sum	1	
John	39000	W	.214285714	.214285714
Stephanie	44000		.241758242	.241758242
Chloe	44000		.241758242	.241758242
Christina	55000		.302197802	.302197802
		******		
		sum	1	

Windowing Subclauses with Physical Offsets in Aggregate Analytical Functions

A windowing subclause is a way of capturing several rows of a result set (i.e., a "window") and reporting the result in one "window row." An example of this technique would be in applications where one wants to smooth data by finding a moving average. Moving averages are most often calculated based on sorted data and on a physical offset of rows. Once we have established how the physical (row) offsets function, we will explore logical (range) offsets. To illustrate the moving average using physical offsets, suppose we have some observations that have these values:

Time	Value
0	12
1	10
2	14
3	9
4	7

Suppose further we know that the data is noisy; that is, it contains a random factor that is added or subtracted from what we might consider a "true" value. One way to smooth out the data and remove some of the random noise is to use a moving average on *ordered* data by taking an average using n physical rows above and below each row. A moving average will operate in a window so that if the moving average is based on, say, three numbers ($n = 3$), the windows and their reported window rows would be:

Window 1:

```
Original time  Original value  Windowed (smoothed) value
      0             12
      1             10            12  = [(12 + 10 + 14)/3]
      2             14
```

Window 2:

```
Original time  Original value  Windowed (smoothed) value
      1             10
      2             14            11  = [(10 + 14 + 9)/3]
      3              9
```

Window 3:

```
Original time  Original value  Windowed (smoothed) value
      2             14
      3              9            10  = [(14 + 9 + 7)/3]
      4              7
```

These calculations result in this display of the data:

```
Time  Value  Moving Average
0     12
1     10     12
2     14     11
3      9     10
4      7
```

In this calculation, the end points (time = 0 and time = 5) usually are not reported because there are no values beyond the end points with which to average the other values. Many people who use moving averages are satisfied with the loss of the end points (along with the noise); others do workarounds to keep the original set of readings with only the "inside" numbers smoothed.

In Oracle's analytical functions, the way the aggregate functions work is that the end points are reported, but they are based on averages that include nulls in rows preceding and past the data points. In Oracle, nulls in calculations involving aggregate functions are ignored. Consider, for example, this query:

```
SELECT ename, curr_salary
FROM empwnulls
UNION
SELECT 'The average .......', average
FROM
   (SELECT avg(curr_salary) average
    FROM empwnulls)
```

Which gives:

```
ENAME                    CURR_SALARY
--------------------- -----------
Chloe                       44000
Christina                   55000
David
John
Kate                        49000
Lindsey                     52000
Stephanie                   44000
The average .......         48800
```

Note that 48800 = (44000 + 55000 + 49000 + 52000 + 44000)/5, and that the rows containing nulls are simply ignored in the calculation.

Returning to our simple example and the moving averages we have computed thus far:

Time	Value	Moving Average
0	12	
1	10	12
2	14	11
3	9	10
4	7	

The end points would be calculated as follows:

Window 0:

```
Original time  Original value  Windowed (smoothed) value
      0              12         11 = [(12 + 10 + null)]/2
      1              10
```

Window 5:

```
Original time  Original value  Windowed (smoothed) value
      3               9
      4               7          8 = [(9 + 7 + null)]/2
```

Oracle's SQL would report the three-period averages as:

```
Time  Value  Moving Average
0     12     11
1     10     12
2     14     11
3      9     10
4      7      8
```

The window analytical function requires that data be explicitly ordered. The syntax of the windowing analytic average function is:

```
AVG(attribute1) OVER (ORDER BY attribute2)
    ROWS BETWEEN x PRECEDING
        AND y FOLLOWING
```

where *attribute1* and *attribute2* do not have to be the same attribute. *Attribute2* defines the window, and *attribute1* defines the value on which to operate. The designation of "ROWS" means we will use a physical offset. The x and y values are the row limits — the number of physical rows below and above the window. (Later, we will look at another way to do these problems using a logical offset, RANGE, instead of ROWS.)

The ORDER BY in the analytical clause is absolutely necessary, and only one attribute may be used for ordering in the function. Also, only numeric or date data types would make sense in calculations of aggregates. Here is the above example in SQL using physical offsets for the moving average on a table called Testma:

```
SELECT * FROM testma;
```

Which gives:

MTIME	MVALUE
0	12
1	10
2	14
3	9
4	7

```
SELECT mtime, mvalue,
  AVG(mvalue) OVER(ORDER BY mtime
    ROWS BETWEEN 1 PRECEDING AND 1 FOLLOWING) ma
FROM testma
ORDER BY mtime
```

Gives:

MTIME	MVALUE	MA
0	12	11
1	10	12
2	14	11
3	9	10
4	7	8

If the ordering subclause is changed, then the row-ordering is done first and then the moving average:

```
SELECT mtime, mvalue,
  AVG(mvalue) OVER(ORDER BY mvalue
    ROWS BETWEEN 1 PRECEDING AND 1 FOLLOWING) ma
FROM testma
ORDER BY mvalue
```

Gives:

MTIME	MVALUE	MA
4	7	8
3	9	8.66666667
1	10	10.3333333
0	12	12
2	14	13

Note that, for example, $[(9 + 10 + 12)/3] = 10.3333$.

One is not restricted to the use of the AVG function for windowing as per this example — which shows other functions also used for windowing. Take a look at this example (with some SQL*Plus formatting in the script):

```
COLUMN ma FORMAT 99.999
COLUMN sum LIKE ma
COLUMN "sum/3" LIKE ma
SELECT mtime, mvalue,
  AVG(mvalue) OVER(ORDER BY mtime
    ROWS BETWEEN 1 PRECEDING AND 1 FOLLOWING) ma,
  SUM(mvalue) OVER(ORDER BY mtime
    ROWS BETWEEN 1 PRECEDING AND 1 FOLLOWING) sum,
  (SUM(mvalue) OVER(ORDER BY mtime
    ROWS BETWEEN 1 PRECEDING AND 1 FOLLOWING))/3 "Sum/3"
FROM testma
ORDER BY mtime
```

Which gives:

MTIME	MVALUE	MA	SUM	Sum/3
0	12	11.000	22.000	7.333
1	10	12.000	36.000	12.000
2	14	11.000	33.000	11.000
3	9	10.000	30.000	10.000
4	7	8.000	16.000	5.333

In this case, the end rows give different values in the Sum/3 column because the denominator is 2 in the AVG case and 3 in all rows in the "forced" Sum/3 column. The SUM column is misleading in that it contains the sum of three numbers in the middle, but only two numbers on the end.

Also, we can use the COUNT aggregate analytical function to show how many rows are included in each window like this:

```
SELECT mtime, mvalue,
  COUNT(mvalue) OVER(ORDER BY mtime
  ROWS BETWEEN 1 PRECEDING AND 1 FOLLOWING) Howmanyrows
FROM testma
ORDER BY mtime
```

Giving:

MTIME	MVALUE	HOWMANYROWS
0	12	2
1	10	3
2	14	3
3	9	3
4	7	2

An Expanded Example of a Physical Window

We will need some additional data to look at more examples of windowing functions. Let us consider the following data of some fictitious stock whose symbol is FROG:

```
COLUMN price FORMAT 9999.99
SELECT *
FROM stock
WHERE symb like 'FR%'
ORDER BY symb desc, dte
```

Which gives:

```
SYMB  DTE         PRICE
----- ---------- --------
FROG  06-JAN-06   63.13
FROG  09-JAN-06   63.52
FROG  10-JAN-06   64.30
FROG  11-JAN-06   65.11
FROG  12-JAN-06   65.07
FROG  13-JAN-06   65.67
FROG  16-JAN-06   65.60
FROG  17-JAN-06   65.99
FROG  18-JAN-06   66.11
FROG  19-JAN-06   66.26
FROG  20-JAN-06   67.03
FROG  23-JAN-06   67.51
FROG  24-JAN-06   67.23
FROG  25-JAN-06   67.43
FROG  26-JAN-06   67.27
FROG  27-JAN-06   66.85
FROG  30-JAN-06   66.95
FROG  31-JAN-06   67.82
FROG  01-FEB-06   68.21
FROG  02-FEB-06   68.60
FROG  03-FEB-06   68.76
```

```
FROG  06-FEB-06    69.55
FROG  07-FEB-06    69.89
FROG  08-FEB-06    70.18
FROG  09-FEB-06    70.18

28 rows selected.
```

To see how the moving average window can expand, we can change the clause ROWS BETWEEN x PRECEDING AND y FOLLOWING to have different values for x and y. In fact, x and y do not have to be the same value at all. For example, suppose we let $x = 3$ and $y = 1$, which gives more weight to three days before the row-window date and less to the one day after. The query and result look like this:

```
COLUMN ma FORMAT 99.999
SELECT dte, price,
  AVG(price) OVER(ORDER BY dte
  ROWS BETWEEN 3 PRECEDING AND 1 FOLLOWING) ma
FROM stock
WHERE symb like 'FR%'
ORDER BY dte
```

Giving:

```
DTE        PRICE      MA
---------  --------  -------
03-JAN-06   62.45    62.835
04-JAN-06   63.22    62.827
05-JAN-06   62.81    62.903
06-JAN-06   63.13    63.325
09-JAN-06   63.52    63.650
10-JAN-06   64.30    64.015
11-JAN-06   65.11    64.226
12-JAN-06   65.07    64.734
13-JAN-06   65.67    65.150
16-JAN-06   65.60    65.488
17-JAN-06   65.99    65.688
18-JAN-06   66.11    65.926
```

```
19-JAN-06    66.26  66.198
20-JAN-06    67.03  66.580
23-JAN-06    67.51  66.828
24-JAN-06    67.23  67.092
25-JAN-06    67.43  67.294
26-JAN-06    67.27  67.258
27-JAN-06    66.85  67.146
30-JAN-06    66.95  67.264
31-JAN-06    67.82  67.420
01-FEB-06    68.21  67.686
02-FEB-06    68.60  68.068
03-FEB-06    68.76  68.588
06-FEB-06    69.55  69.002
07-FEB-06    69.89  69.396
08-FEB-06    70.18  69.712
09-FEB-06    70.18  69.950
```

Here is the calculation (remember we are using three rows preceding and one row following):

```
DTE          PRICE      MA  Calculation of MA
---------  ---------- -------  ------------------
03-JAN-06    62.45  62.835  (62.45 + 63.22)/2
04-JAN-06    63.22  62.827  (62.45 + 63.22 + 62.81)/3
05-JAN-06    62.81  62.903  (62.45 + 63.22 + 62.81 + 63.13)/4
06-JAN-06    63.13  63.026  (62.45 + 63.22 + 62.81 + 63.13 + 63.52)/5
09-JAN-06    63.52  63.396  (63.22 + 62.81 + 63.13 + 63.52 + 64.30)/5
...
```

The trailing end is done similarly:

```
02-FEB-06    68.60  68.068
03-FEB-06    68.76  68.588
06-FEB-06    69.55  69.002
07-FEB-06    69.89  69.396  (68.60 + 68.76 + 69.55 + 69.89 + 70.18)/5
08-FEB-06    70.18  69.712  (68.76 + 69.55 + 69.89 + 70.18 + 70.18)/5
09-FEB-06    70.18  69.950  (69.55 + 69.89 + 70.18 + 70.18)/4
```

We can clarify the demonstration a bit by displaying which rows are used in these moving average calculations with two other analytical functions: FIRST_ VALUE and LAST_VALUE. These two functions tell us which rows are used in the calculation of the window function for each row.

```
COLUMN first FORMAT 9999.99
COLUMN last LIKE first
SELECT dte, price,
  AVG(price) OVER(ORDER BY dte
  ROWS BETWEEN 3 PRECEDING AND 1 FOLLOWING) ma,
  FIRST_VALUE(price) OVER(ORDER BY dte
  ROWS BETWEEN 3 PRECEDING AND 1 FOLLOWING) first,
  LAST_VALUE(price) OVER(ORDER BY dte
  ROWS BETWEEN 3 PRECEDING AND 1 FOLLOWING) last
FROM stock
WHERE symb like 'F%'
ORDER BY dte
```

Giving:

DTE	PRICE	MA	FIRST	LAST
03-JAN-06	62.45	62.835	62.45	63.22
04-JAN-06	63.22	62.827	62.45	62.81
05-JAN-06	62.81	62.903	62.45	63.13
06-JAN-06	63.13	63.325	63.13	63.52
09-JAN-06	63.52	63.650	63.13	64.30
10-JAN-06	64.30	64.015	63.13	65.11
11-JAN-06	65.11	64.226	63.13	65.07
12-JAN-06	65.07	64.734	63.52	65.67
13-JAN-06	65.67	65.150	64.30	65.60
16-JAN-06	65.60	65.488	65.11	65.99
17-JAN-06	65.99	65.688	65.07	66.11
18-JAN-06	66.11	65.926	65.67	66.26
19-JAN-06	66.26	66.198	65.60	67.03
20-JAN-06	67.03	66.580	65.99	67.51
23-JAN-06	67.51	66.828	66.11	67.23
24-JAN-06	67.23	67.092	66.26	67.43

25-JAN-06	67.43	67.294	67.03	67.27
26-JAN-06	67.27	67.258	67.51	66.85
27-JAN-06	66.85	67.146	67.23	66.95
30-JAN-06	66.95	67.264	67.43	67.82
31-JAN-06	67.82	67.420	67.27	68.21
01-FEB-06	68.21	67.686	66.85	68.60
02-FEB-06	68.60	68.068	66.95	68.76
03-FEB-06	68.76	68.588	67.82	69.55
06-FEB-06	69.55	69.002	68.21	69.89
07-FEB-06	69.89	69.396	68.60	70.18
08-FEB-06	70.18	69.712	68.76	70.18
09-FEB-06	70.18	69.950	69.55	70.18

Displaying a Running Total Using SUM as an Analytical Function

As we noted earlier, the aggregate function SUM may be used as an analytical function (as may AVG, MAX, MIN, COUNT, STDDEV, and VARIANCE). The SUM function is most easily seen when using a cumulative total calculation. For example, suppose we have the following receipts for a cash register application for several weeks ordered by date and location (DTE, LOCATION):

```
SELECT * FROM store
ORDER BY dte, location
```

Giving:

LOCATION	DTE	RECEIPTS
MOBILE	07-JAN-06	724.6
PROVO	07-JAN-06	969.61
MOBILE	08-JAN-06	88.76
PROVO	08-JAN-06	662.45
MOBILE	09-JAN-06	705.47

PROVO	09-JAN-06	928.37
MOBILE	10-JAN-06	217.26
PROVO	10-JAN-06	664.9
MOBILE	11-JAN-06	16.13
PROVO	11-JAN-06	694.51
MOBILE	12-JAN-06	421.59
PROVO	12-JAN-06	413.12
MOBILE	13-JAN-06	403.95
PROVO	13-JAN-06	645.78
MOBILE	14-JAN-06	831.12
PROVO	14-JAN-06	678.41
MOBILE	15-JAN-06	783.57
PROVO	15-JAN-06	491.05
MOBILE	16-JAN-06	878.15
PROVO	16-JAN-06	635.75
MOBILE	17-JAN-06	968.89
PROVO	17-JAN-06	378.25
MOBILE	18-JAN-06	351
PROVO	18-JAN-06	882.51
MOBILE	19-JAN-06	975.73
PROVO	19-JAN-06	24.52
MOBILE	20-JAN-06	191
PROVO	20-JAN-06	542.2
MOBILE	21-JAN-06	462.92
PROVO	21-JAN-06	294.19
MOBILE	22-JAN-06	707.57
PROVO	22-JAN-06	729.92
MOBILE	23-JAN-06	919.61
PROVO	23-JAN-06	272.24
MOBILE	24-JAN-06	217.91
PROVO	24-JAN-06	554.12

Now, suppose we'd like to have a running total of the receipts regardless of the location. One way to obtain this display is to use SUM and a slightly different physical offset. Previously we used this analytical function:

```
SELECT ...,
  AVG(...) OVER(ORDER BY z
  ROWS BETWEEN x PRECEDING AND y FOLLOWING) row-alias
FROM table
ORDER BY z
```

We will change:

```
ROWS BETWEEN x PRECEDING
```

to:

```
ROWS UNBOUNDED PRECEDING
```

This means that we will start with the first row and use all rows up to the current row of the window.

We will change:

```
AND y FOLLOWING
```

to:

```
CURRENT ROW
```

With the store-receipt data set we will use this function:

```
COLUMN "Running total" FORMAT 99,999.99
SELECT dte "Date", location, receipts,
  SUM(receipts) OVER(ORDER BY dte
    ROWS BETWEEN UNBOUNDED PRECEDING
    AND CURRENT ROW) "Running total"
FROM store
WHERE dte < '10-Jan-2006'
ORDER BY dte, location
```

Giving:

```
Date       LOCATION    RECEIPTS Running total
---------  ----------  ---------- -------------
07-JAN-06 MOBILE          724.6        724.60
07-JAN-06 PROVO          969.61      1,694.21
08-JAN-06 MOBILE          88.76      1,782.97
08-JAN-06 PROVO          662.45      2,445.42
09-JAN-06 MOBILE         705.47      3,150.89
09-JAN-06 PROVO          928.37      4,079.26
```

UNBOUNDED FOLLOWING

The clause UNBOUNDED FOLLOWING is used for the end of the window. Such a command is used like this:

```
SELECT dte "Date", location, receipts,
  SUM(receipts) OVER(ORDER BY dte
    ROWS BETWEEN CURRENT ROW
    AND UNBOUNDED FOLLOWING) "Running total"
FROM store
WHERE dte < '10-Jan-2006'
ORDER BY dte, location
```

Which results in:

```
Date       LOCATION    RECEIPTS Running total
---------  ----------  ---------- -------------
07-JAN-06 MOBILE          724.6       4079.26
07-JAN-06 PROVO          969.61      3354.66
08-JAN-06 MOBILE          88.76      2385.05
08-JAN-06 PROVO          662.45      2296.29
09-JAN-06 MOBILE         705.47      1633.84
09-JAN-06 PROVO          928.37       928.37
```

The summing takes place starting from the bottom of the window and works its way up rather than down.

This type of presentation could work well if the dates were inverted or if the sorting field were a sequence that counted down instead of up.

Partitioning Aggregate Analytical Functions

As with the ranking/row-numbering functions, the aggregates may be partitioned. Continuing with the receipt data, we can illustrate the effect of partitioning with this script:

```
COLUMN receipts FORMAT 99,999.99
COLUMN "Running total" LIKE receipts
SELECT rownum,
   dte "Date", location, receipts,
   rt "Running Total"
FROM
   (SELECT dte, location, receipts,
     SUM(receipts) OVER(PARTITION BY location
     ORDER BY dte
     ROWS BETWEEN UNBOUNDED PRECEDING
     AND CURRENT ROW) rt
FROM store
WHERE dte < '10-Jan-2006')
ORDER BY location, dte
```

Which gives:

ROWNUM	Date	LOCATION	RECEIPTS	Running Total
1	07-JAN-06	MOBILE	724.60	724.60
2	08-JAN-06	MOBILE	88.76	813.36
3	09-JAN-06	MOBILE	705.47	1,518.83
4	07-JAN-06	PROVO	969.61	969.61
5	08-JAN-06	PROVO	662.45	1,632.06
6	09-JAN-06	PROVO	928.37	2,560.43

Here we see, for example, that for row 2, 813.36 = (724.60 + 88.76). We also see that for the first PROVO row in row 4, the start of the second partition, the summing begins again. With the PARTITION BY clause, it can be seen that the partitions are not breached by the SUM aggregate/analytical function. One must be quite careful in displaying the result because this very similar statement gives misleading output:

```
SELECT dte "Date", location, receipts,
  SUM(receipts) OVER(PARTITION BY location
    ORDER BY dte
    ROWS BETWEEN UNBOUNDED PRECEDING
    AND CURRENT ROW) "Running total"
FROM store
WHERE dte < '10-Jan-2006'
ORDER BY dte, location
```

Gives:

Date	LOCATION	RECEIPTS	Running total
07-JAN-06	MOBILE	724.60	724.60
07-JAN-06	PROVO	969.61	969.61
08-JAN-06	MOBILE	88.76	813.36
08-JAN-06	PROVO	662.45	1,632.06
09-JAN-06	MOBILE	705.47	1,518.83
09-JAN-06	PROVO	928.37	2,560.43

In this latter case, the numbers are correct (compare the numbers to the previous version ordered by location first), but the presentation does not reflect the partitioning because of the final ORDER BY clause.

Logical Windowing

So far we have moved our window based on the physical arrangement of the ordered attribute. Recall that the ordering (sorting) in the analytical function takes place before SUM (or AVG, MAX, STDDEV, etc.) is applied. Logical partitions allow us to move our window according to some logical criterion, i.e., a value calculated "on the fly." Consider this example, which uses dates and logical offset of seven days preceding:

```
SELECT dte "Date", location, receipts,
  SUM(receipts) OVER(PARTITION BY location
    ORDER BY dte
    RANGE BETWEEN INTERVAL '7' day PRECEDING
    AND CURRENT ROW) "Running total"
FROM store
WHERE dte < '18-Jan-2006'
ORDER BY location, dte
```

Which gives:

Date	LOCATION	RECEIPTS	Running total
07-JAN-06	MOBILE	724.60	724.60
08-JAN-06	MOBILE	88.76	813.36
09-JAN-06	MOBILE	705.47	1,518.83
10-JAN-06	MOBILE	217.26	1,736.09
11-JAN-06	MOBILE	16.13	1,752.22
12-JAN-06	MOBILE	421.59	2,173.81
13-JAN-06	MOBILE	403.95	2,577.76
14-JAN-06	MOBILE	831.12	3,408.88
15-JAN-06	MOBILE	783.57	3,467.85
16-JAN-06	MOBILE	878.15	4,257.24
17-JAN-06	MOBILE	968.89	4,520.66

Date	LOCATION	RECEIPTS	Running total
07-JAN-06	PROVO	969.61	969.61
08-JAN-06	PROVO	662.45	1,632.06
09-JAN-06	PROVO	928.37	2,560.43
10-JAN-06	PROVO	664.90	3,225.33
11-JAN-06	PROVO	694.51	3,919.84
12-JAN-06	PROVO	413.12	4,332.96
13-JAN-06	PROVO	645.78	4,978.74
14-JAN-06	PROVO	678.41	5,657.15
15-JAN-06	PROVO	491.05	5,178.59
16-JAN-06	PROVO	635.75	5,151.89
17-JAN-06	PROVO	378.25	4,601.77

In this example, it may be noted that, while it takes seven days for the summing to "get started," the sums are quite useful after that time. Prior to the seven-day period specified, the analytical function, as before, uses nulls in the usual Oracle way in its calculation of the sum (Oracle ignores nulls in aggregate calculations).

Now it could be argued that the summing in this example could have used physical offsets and accomplished the same result. If there were gaps in the dates, then the logical offset would be useful in that one need not partition the data ahead of time. Consider the following amended receipt data with some dates missing:

First, we create a table called Store1 like this:

```
CREATE TABLE store1
as SELECT * FROM store
```

Then type:

```
DELETE FROM store1
WHERE location LIKE 'MOB%'
AND receipts < 500
```

Then, consider this query:

```
SELECT dte "Date", location, receipts,
  SUM(receipts) OVER(PARTITION BY location
    ORDER BY dte
    RANGE BETWEEN INTERVAL '7' day PRECEDING
    AND CURRENT ROW) "Running total"
FROM store1
WHERE location like 'MOB%'
ORDER BY location, dte
```

Which gives this result:

Date	LOCATION	RECEIPTS	Running total
07-JAN-06	MOBILE	724.60	724.60
09-JAN-06	MOBILE	705.47	1,430.07
14-JAN-06	MOBILE	831.12	2,261.19
15-JAN-06	MOBILE	783.57	2,320.16
16-JAN-06	MOBILE	878.15	3,198.31
17-JAN-06	MOBILE	968.89	3,461.73
19-JAN-06	MOBILE	975.73	4,437.46
22-JAN-06	MOBILE	707.57	4,313.91
23-JAN-06	MOBILE	919.61	4,449.95

Upon careful examination of the data, it may be noted that for the date 15-JAN-06, the value of the running total is only for the seven days prior to that date (a logical offset) — 2320.16 = 783.57 + 831.12 + 705.47.

Another example of logical summing would be one where the Stock table was queried and we were looking for the maximum and minimum values of a stock over the last two days — we want to start over each week. Here is such a query:

```
SELECT dte "Date", price,
  MIN(price) OVER( ORDER BY dte
    RANGE BETWEEN INTERVAL '2' day PRECEDING
    AND CURRENT ROW) "Min. price",
  MAX(price) OVER( ORDER BY dte
```

```
        RANGE BETWEEN INTERVAL '2' day PRECEDING
        AND CURRENT ROW) "Max. price"
FROM stock
ORDER BY dte
```

Which gives:

```
Date        PRICE Min. price Max. price
--------- -------- ---------- ----------
03-JAN-06   62.45     62.45      62.45
04-JAN-06   63.22     62.45      63.22
05-JAN-06   62.81     62.81      62.81
06-JAN-06   63.13     62.81      63.13
09-JAN-06   63.52     62.81      63.52
10-JAN-06   64.30     63.13      64.30
11-JAN-06   65.11     63.52      65.11
12-JAN-06   65.07     65.07      65.07
13-JAN-06   65.67     65.07      65.67
16-JAN-06   65.60     65.07      65.67
17-JAN-06   65.99     65.60      65.99
18-JAN-06   66.11     65.60      66.11
19-JAN-06   66.26     66.26      66.26
20-JAN-06   67.03     66.26      67.03
23-JAN-06   67.51     66.26      67.51
24-JAN-06   67.23     67.03      67.51
25-JAN-06   67.43     67.43      67.43
26-JAN-06   67.27     67.27      67.43
27-JAN-06   66.85     66.85      67.43
30-JAN-06   66.95     66.85      67.27
31-JAN-06   67.82     66.85      67.82
01-FEB-06   68.21     68.21      68.21
02-FEB-06   68.60     68.21      68.60
03-FEB-06   68.76     68.21      68.76
06-FEB-06   69.55     68.60      69.55
07-FEB-06   69.89     68.76      69.89
08-FEB-06   70.18     70.18      70.18
09-FEB-06   70.18     70.18      70.18
```

Consider the first few rows of this result:

```
Date        PRICE Min. price Max. price
--------- -------- ---------- ----------
03-JAN-06   62.45      62.45      62.45
04-JAN-06   63.22      62.45      63.22
05-JAN-06   62.81      62.81      62.81
06-JAN-06   63.13      62.81      63.13
09-JAN-06   63.52      62.81      63.52
```

We note that the maximum/minimum prices start over on 05-JAN-06 because of the two-day window on prior dates. But the max/min prices for each row during the week beginning 05-JAN-06 are correct.

If a person wanted to know only the weekly values of highs and lows on, say, a Tuesday, then this result could be put into a virtual table and found. First, Tuesdays in the dates of this table may be seen with this query:

```
SELECT dte, NEXT_DAY(dte-1,'Tuesday')
FROM stock
WHERE dte = NEXT_DAY(dte-1,'Tuesday')
```

Giving:

```
DTE       NEXT_DAY(
--------- ---------
03-JAN-06 03-JAN-06
10-JAN-06 10-JAN-06
17-JAN-06 17-JAN-06
24-JAN-06 24-JAN-06
31-JAN-06 31-JAN-06
07-FEB-06 07-FEB-06
```

and hence, a seven-day MAX and MIN on Tuesdays may be found like this:

```
SELECT 'Tuesday, '||TO_CHAR(x.dte,'Month dd,yyyy') "Tuesdays",
  x.minp "Minimum Price", x.maxp "Maximum Price"
FROM
  (SELECT i.dte, i.price,
    MIN(i.price) OVER( ORDER BY i.dte
      RANGE BETWEEN INTERVAL '7' day PRECEDING
      AND CURRENT ROW) minp,
    MAX(i.price) OVER( ORDER BY i.dte
      RANGE BETWEEN INTERVAL '7' day PRECEDING
      AND CURRENT ROW) maxp
  FROM stock i
  ORDER BY i.dte) x
WHERE x.dte in
  (SELECT z.dte -- , NEXT_DAY(z.dte-1,'Tuesday')
    FROM stock z
    WHERE z.dte = NEXT_DAY(z.dte-1,'Tuesday'))
```

Giving:

Tuesdays		Minimum Price	Maximum Price
Tuesday, January	03,2006	62.45	62.45
Tuesday, January	10,2006	62.45	64.30
Tuesday, January	17,2006	64.30	65.99
Tuesday, January	24,2006	65.99	67.51
Tuesday, January	31,2006	66.85	67.51
Tuesday, February	07,2006	66.95	69.55

Of course, the query could be further restricted by eliminating the first Tuesday in the WHERE clause subquery.

Another way to get Tuesdays would be to use the TO_CHAR transform on the date like this:

```
SELECT 'Tuesday, '||TO_CHAR(x.dte,'Month dd,yyyy') "Tuesdays",
  x.minp "Minimum Price", x.maxp "Maximum Price"
FROM
  (SELECT i.dte, i.price,
    MIN(i.price) OVER( ORDER BY i.dte
      RANGE BETWEEN INTERVAL '7' day PRECEDING
      AND CURRENT ROW) minp,
    MAX(i.price) OVER( ORDER BY i.dte
      RANGE BETWEEN INTERVAL '7' day PRECEDING
      AND CURRENT ROW) maxp
  FROM stock i
  ORDER BY i.dte) x
WHERE to_char(x.dte,'d') = 5
```

This query gives the same answer as the previous one.

The Row Comparison Functions — LEAD and LAG

At times during an analysis of data by rows, it is useful to see a previous row value on the same row as the current value. For example, suppose we wanted to see the value of our receipts along with the previous and next day's values. Such a query (using defaults for now) would look like this:

```
SELECT ROW_NUMBER() OVER(ORDER BY dte) rn,
  location, dte, receipts,
  LAG(receipts) OVER(ORDER BY dte) Previous,
  LEAD(receipts) OVER(ORDER BY dte) Next
FROM store
WHERE dte < '12-JAN-06'
  AND location like 'MOB%'
ORDER BY dte
```

Which gives:

RN	LOCATION	DTE	RECEIPTS	PREVIOUS	NEXT
1	MOBILE	07-JAN-06	724.60		88.76
2	MOBILE	08-JAN-06	88.76	724.6	705.47
3	MOBILE	09-JAN-06	705.47	88.76	217.26
4	MOBILE	10-JAN-06	217.26	705.47	16.13
5	MOBILE	11-JAN-06	16.13	217.26	

In this query, we see that on any one row, the previous day and the next day's receipts are displayed. Of course, since there is no previous day for row 1 and no next day for row 5, those values are null.

The row comparison function can also be partitioned as with other aggregates:

```
SELECT ROW_NUMBER() OVER(PARTITION BY location ORDER BY dte)
    rn, location, dte, receipts,
  LAG(receipts) OVER(PARTITION BY location ORDER BY dte)
        Previous,
  LEAD(receipts) OVER(PARTITION BY location ORDER BY dte) Next
FROM store
WHERE dte < '12-JAN-06'
ORDER BY location, dte
```

Which gives:

RN	LOCATION	DTE	RECEIPTS	PREVIOUS	NEXT
1	MOBILE	07-JAN-06	724.60		88.76
2	MOBILE	08-JAN-06	88.76	724.6	705.47
3	MOBILE	09-JAN-06	705.47	88.76	217.26
4	MOBILE	10-JAN-06	217.26	705.47	16.13
5	MOBILE	11-JAN-06	16.13	217.26	
1	PROVO	07-JAN-06	969.61		662.45
2	PROVO	08-JAN-06	662.45	969.61	928.37
3	PROVO	09-JAN-06	928.37	662.45	664.9
4	PROVO	10-JAN-06	664.90	928.37	694.51
5	PROVO	11-JAN-06	694.51	664.9	

Here we see the partitions clearly and, as expected, the aggregate does not breach the partition.

With these row comparison functions, the ORDER BY ordering analytic clause is required. Note that to produce this same result in ordinary SQL would be messy, but doable with multiple self-joins. For example, the first version of this query could be done this way for the PREVIOUS part:

```
SELECT rownum,
    a.location, a.dte, a.receipts, b.receipts Previous
    -- LAG(receipts) OVER(PARTITION BY location ORDER BY dte)
    --     Previous
    -- LEAD(receipts) OVER(PARTITION BY location ORDER BY dte)
    --     Next
FROM store a, store b
WHERE a.dte < '12-JAN-06'
    AND a.location like 'MOB%'
    AND b.location(+) like 'MOB%'
    AND a.dte = b.dte(+) + 1
```

Giving:

ROWNUM	LOCATION	DTE	RECEIPTS	PREVIOUS
1	MOBILE	07-JAN-06	724.60	
2	MOBILE	08-JAN-06	88.76	724.6
3	MOBILE	09-JAN-06	705.47	88.76
4	MOBILE	10-JAN-06	217.26	705.47
5	MOBILE	11-JAN-06	16.13	217.26

LAG and LEAD Options

The LAG and LEAD functions have options that allow specified offsets and default values for the nulls that result in non-applicable rows. The full syntax of the LAG or LEAD function looks like this:

```
LAG [or LEAD] (attribute, offset, default value) OVER (ORDER
    BY clause)
```

Using an example similar to the above, we can illustrate the options:

```
SELECT ROW_NUMBER() OVER(ORDER BY dte) rn,
   location, dte, receipts,
   LAG(receipts,3,999) OVER(ORDER BY dte) Previous,
   LEAD(receipts,2,-1) OVER(ORDER BY dte) Next
FROM store
WHERE dte < '19-JAN-06'
AND location like 'MOB%'
```

Which gives:

RN	LOCATION	DTE	RECEIPTS	PREVIOUS	NEXT
1	MOBILE	07-JAN-06	724.60	999	705.47
2	MOBILE	08-JAN-06	88.76	999	217.26
3	MOBILE	09-JAN-06	705.47	999	16.13
4	MOBILE	10-JAN-06	217.26	724.6	421.59
5	MOBILE	11-JAN-06	16.13	88.76	403.95
6	MOBILE	12-JAN-06	421.59	705.47	831.12
7	MOBILE	13-JAN-06	403.95	217.26	783.57
8	MOBILE	14-JAN-06	831.12	16.13	878.15
9	MOBILE	15-JAN-06	783.57	421.59	968.89
10	MOBILE	16-JAN-06	878.15	403.95	351
11	MOBILE	17-JAN-06	968.89	831.12	-1
12	MOBILE	18-JAN-06	351.00	783.57	-1

Here it will be noted that rows 1, 2, 3, 11, and 12 contain the chosen default values of 999 and –1 for the missing data. On row 4 we see that beside the 217.26 receipt, we get the lagged row (PREVIOUS) (three back) of 724.6 from row 1, and the forward row (NEXT) (two forward) of 421.59 from row 6.

Chapter 5

The Use of Analytical Functions in Reporting (Analytical Functions III)

In this chapter we will show how to use the analytical functions in a slightly different context. To illustrate the analytical functions in this "different" way, we need to introduce two other ideas. First, we want to show how to use the keyword GROUPING. To show how to use GROUPING, we introduce two functions that were pioneered in the Oracle 8 series — ROLLUP and CUBE — together with the ROW_NUMBER() analytical function. These two additions to the GROUP BY clause provide a wealth of information and also form the basis of more interesting reports that can be generated within SQL. The enhanced reporting uses both the GROUPING and the analytical function additions.

We begin by looking a little closer at the use of GROUP BY.

GROUP BY

First we look at some preliminaries with respect to the GROUP BY clause. When an aggregate is used in a SQL statement, it refers to a set of rows. The sense of the GROUP BY is to accumulate the aggregate on row-set values. Of course if the aggregate is used by itself there is only table-level grouping, i.e., the group level in the statement "SELECT MAX(hiredate) FROM employee" has the highest group level — that of the table, Employee.

The following example illustrates grouping below the table level.

Let's revisit our Employee table:

```
SELECT *
FROM employee
```

Which gives:

EMPNO	ENAME	HIREDATE	ORIG_SALARY	CURR_SALARY	REGION
101	John	02-DEC-97	35000	39000	W
102	Stephanie	22-SEP-98	35000	44000	W
104	Christina	08-MAR-98	43000	55000	W
108	David	08-JUL-01	37000	39000	E
111	Kate	13-APR-00	45000	49000	E
106	Chloe	19-JAN-96	33000	44000	W
122	Lindsey	22-MAY-97	40000	52000	E

Take a look at this example of using an aggregate with the GROUP BY clause to count by region:

```
SELECT count(*), region
FROM employee
GROUP BY region
```

Which gives:

```
 COUNT(*) REGION
---------- ------
        3 E
        4 W
```

Any row-level variable (i.e., a column name) in the result set must be mentioned in the GROUP BY clause for the query to make sense. In this case, the row-level variable is region. If you tried to run the following query, which does not have region in a GROUP BY clause, you would get an error.

```
SELECT count(*), region
FROM employee
```

Would give:

```
SELECT count(*), region
                 *
ERROR at line 1:
ORA-00937: not a single-group group function
```

The error occurs because the query asks for an aggregate (count) and a row-level result (region) at the same time without specifying that grouping is to take place.

GROUP BY may be used on a column without the column name appearing in the result set like this:

```
SELECT count(*)
FROM employee
GROUP BY region
```

Which would give:

```
COUNT(*)
----------
         3
         4
```

This latter type query is useful in queries that ask questions like, "in what region do we have the most employees?":

```
SELECT count(*), region
FROM employee
GROUP BY region
HAVING count(*) =
(SELECT max(count(*))
FROM employee
GROUP BY region)
```

Gives:

```
COUNT(*) REGION
---------- ------
         4 W
```

Now, suppose we add another column, a yes/no for certification, to our Employee table, calling our new table Employee1. The table looks like this:

```
SELECT *
FROM employee1
```

Gives:

EMPNO	ENAME	HIREDATE	ORIG_SALARY	CURR_SALARY	REGION	CERTIFIED
101	John	02-DEC-97	35000	39000	W	Y
102	Stephanie	22-SEP-98	35000	44000	W	N
104	Christina	08-MAR-98	43000	55000	W	N
108	David	08-JUL-01	37000	39000	E	Y
111	Kate	13-APR-00	45000	49000	E	N
106	Chloe	19-JAN-96	33000	44000	W	N
122	Lindsey	22-MAY-97	40000	52000	E	Y

Now suppose we'd like to look at the certification counts in a group:

```
SELECT count(*), certified
FROM employee1
GROUP BY certified
```

This would give:

COUNT(*)	CERTIFIED
4	N
3	Y

As with the region attribute, we have a count of the rows with the different certified values.

If nulls are present in the table, then their values will be grouped separately. Suppose we modify the Employee1 table to this:

EMPNO	ENAME	HIREDATE	ORIG_SALARY	CURR_SALARY	REGION	CERTIFIED
101	John	02-DEC-97	35000	39000	W	Y
102	Stephanie	22-SEP-98	35000	44000	W	N
104	Christina	08-MAR-98	43000	55000	W	
108	David	08-JUL-01	37000	39000	E	Y
111	Kate	13-APR-00	45000	49000	E	N
106	Chloe	19-JAN-96	33000	44000	W	N
122	Lindsey	22-MAY-97	40000	52000	E	

The previous query:

```
SELECT count(*), certified
FROM employee1
GROUP BY certified
```

Now gives:

```
COUNT(*) CERTIFIED
---------- ---------
       3 N
       2 Y
       2
```

Note that the nulls are counted as values. The null may be made more explicit with a DECODE statement like this:

```
SELECT count(*), DECODE(certified,null,'Null',certified)
  Certified
FROM employee1
GROUP BY certified
```

Giving:

```
COUNT(*) CERTIFIED
---------- ---------
       3 N
       2 Y
       2 Null
```

The same result may be had using the more modern CASE statement:

```
SELECT count(*),
  CASE NVL(certified,'x')
    WHEN 'x' then 'Null'
    ELSE certified
  END Certified -- CASE
FROM employee1
GROUP BY certified
```

As a side issue, the statement:

```
SELECT count(*),
  CASE certified
    WHEN 'N' then 'No'
    WHEN 'Y' then 'Yes'
    WHEN null then 'Null'
  END Certified -- CASE
FROM employee1
GROUP BY certified
```

returns "Null" for null values. In the more modern CASE statement example, we illustrate a variation of CASE where we used a workaround using NVL on the attribute certified, making it equal to "x" when null and then testing for "x" in the CASE clause. As illustrated in the last example, the workaround is not really necessary with CASE.

Grouping at Multiple Levels

To return to the subject at hand, the use of GROUP BY, we can use grouping at more than one level. For example, using the current version of the Employee1 table:

EMPNO	ENAME	HIREDATE	ORIG_SALARY	CURR_SALARY	REGION	CERTIFIED
101	John	02-DEC-97	35000	39000	W	Y
102	Stephanie	22-SEP-98	35000	44000	W	N
104	Christina	08-MAR-98	43000	55000	W	
108	David	08-JUL-01	37000	39000	E	Y
111	Kate	13-APR-00	45000	49000	E	N
106	Chloe	19-JAN-96	33000	44000	W	N
122	Lindsey	22-MAY-97	40000	52000	E	

The query:

```
SELECT count(*), certified, region
FROM employee1
GROUP BY certified, region
```

Produces:

```
COUNT(*) CERTIFIED REGION
---------- ---------- ------
       1              E
       1              W
       1 N            E
       2 N            W
       1 Y            E
       1 Y            W
```

Notice that because we used the GROUP BY ordering of certified and region, the result is ordered in that way. If we reverse the ordering in the GROUP BY like this:

```
SELECT count(*), certified, region
FROM employee1
GROUP BY region, certified
```

We get this:

```
COUNT(*) CERTIFIED REGION
---------- ---------- ------
       1              E
       1 N            E
       1 Y            E
       1              W
       2 N            W
       1 Y            W
```

The latter case shows the region breakdown first, then the certified values within the region. It would probably be more appropriate to have the GROUP BY ordering mirror the result set ordering, but as we illustrated here, it is not mandatory.

ROLLUP

In ordinary SQL, we can produce a summary of the grouped aggregate by using set functions. For example, if we wanted to see not only the grouped number of employees by region as above but also the sum of the counts, we could write a query like this:

```
SELECT count(*), region
FROM employee
GROUP BY region
UNION
SELECT count(*), null
FROM employee
```

Giving:

```
COUNT(*) REGION
---------- ------
       3 E
       4 W
       7
```

For larger result sets and more complicated queries, this technique begins to suffer in both efficiency and complexity. The ROLLUP function was provided to conveniently give the sum on the aggregate; it is used as an add-on to the GROUP BY clause like this:

```
SELECT count(*), region
FROM employee
GROUP BY ROLLUP(region)
```

Giving:

```
COUNT(*) REGION
---------- ------
       3 E
       4 W
       7
```

The name "rollup" comes from data warehousing where the concept is that very large databases must be aggregated to allow more meaningful queries at higher levels of abstraction. The use of ROLLUP may be extended to more than one dimension.

For example, if we use a two-dimensional grouping, we can also use ROLLUP, producing the following results. First, we use a ROLLBACK to un-null the nulls we generated in Employee1, giving us this version of the Employee1 table:

```
SELECT *
FROM employee1
```

Giving:

EMPNO	ENAME	HIREDATE	ORIG_SALARY	CURR_SALARY	REGION	CERTIFIED
101	John	02-DEC-97	35000	39000	W	Y
102	Stephanie	22-SEP-98	35000	44000	W	N
104	Christina	08-MAR-98	43000	55000	W	N
108	David	08-JUL-01	37000	39000	E	Y
111	Kate	13-APR-00	45000	49000	E	N
106	Chloe	19-JAN-96	33000	44000	W	N
122	Lindsey	22-MAY-97	40000	52000	E	Y

Now, using GROUP BY, we get the following results (first without ROLLUP, then with ROLLUP).

Without ROLLUP:

```
SELECT count(*), certified, region
FROM employee1
GROUP BY certified, region
```

Gives:

```
COUNT(*) CERTIFIED REGION
-------- --------- ------
       1 N         E
       3 N         W
       2 Y         E
       1 Y         W
```

With ROLLUP (and ROW_NUMBER added for explanation below):

```
SELECT ROW_NUMBER() OVER(ORDER BY certified, region) rn,
  count(*), certified, region
FROM employee1
GROUP BY ROLLUP(certified, region)
```

Gives:

```
    RN   COUNT(*) CERTIFIED REGION
--------- -------- --------- ------
        1        1 N         E
        2        3 N         W
        3        4 N
        4        2 Y         E
        5        1 Y         W
        6        3 Y
        7        7
```

The result shows the ROLLUP applied to certified first in row 3, which shows that we have four values of N for certified. Similarly, we see in result row 6 that we have three Y rows, and in result row 7 that we have seven rows overall.

Had we used a reverse ordering of the grouped attributes, we would see this:

```
SELECT ROW_NUMBER() OVER(ORDER BY region, certified) rn,
   count(*), region, certified
FROM employee1
GROUP BY ROLLUP(region, certified)
```

Giving:

RN	COUNT(*)	REGION	CERTIFIED
1	1	E	N
2	2	E	Y
3	3	E	
4	3	W	N
5	1	W	Y
6	4	W	
7	7		

In this version we have the information rolled up by region rather than by certified. Also note that we reversed the ordering in the row-number function to keep the presentation orderly. Is there a way to get rollups for both columns? Yes, by use of the ROLLUP extension, CUBE.

CUBE

If we wanted to see the summary data on both the certified and region attributes, we would be asking for the data warehousing "cube." The warehousing cube concept implies reducing tables by rolling up different columns (dimensions). Oracle provides a CUBE predicate to generate this result directly. Here is the CUBE ordered by region first:

```
SELECT ROW_NUMBER() OVER(ORDER BY region, certified) rn,
  count(*), region, certified
FROM employee1
GROUP BY CUBE(region, certified)
```

Giving:

```
   RN   COUNT(*) REGION CERTIFIED
---------- ---------- ------ ---------
        1          1 E      N
        2          2 E      Y
        3          3 E
        4          3 W      N
        5          1 W      Y
        6          4 W
        7          4        N
        8          3        Y
        9          7
```

On inspection of the result we note that we have two more rows and that both "rollups" are represented. The REGION rollup is still there, just as it is in the previous example, and rows 3 and 6 show the summary data for REGION (3 for E, 4 for W). Also, row 9 shows the overall summary data (seven rows in all). But the additional two rows, rows 7 and 8, are displaying the summary data for CERTIFIED (4 for N and 3 for Y).

Had we used the "other" presentation order of "certified, region," we would get the same result, but we change the order of the row numbering as well to be consistent:

```
SELECT ROW_NUMBER() OVER(ORDER BY certified, region) rn,
  count(*), certified, region
FROM employee1
GROUP BY ROLLUP(certified, region)
```

Giving:

```
RN    COUNT(*) CERTIFIED REGION
----------  ----------  ----------  ------
    1         1 N          E
    2         3 N          W
    3         4 N
    4         2 Y          E
    5         1 Y          W
    6         3 Y
    7         7
```

All of the same information as the previous example is shown, but it is presented in a different way.

GROUPING with ROLLUP and CUBE

When using ROLLUP and CUBE and when there are more values of the grouped attributes, it is most convenient to be able to identify the null ROLLUP or CUBE rows in the result set. As we saw above, the rows with nulls represent the summary data. By identifying the nulls, we can use either DECODE or CASE to change what is displayed as a null.

Oracle's SQL provides a function that will flag these rows that contain nulls: GROUPING. For ROLLUP and CUBE, the GROUPING function returns zeros and ones to flag the rolled up or cubed row. Here is an example of the use of the function:

```
SELECT ROW_NUMBER() OVER(ORDER BY certified, region) rn,
   count(*), certified, region,
   GROUPING(certified),
   GROUPING (region)
FROM employee1
GROUP BY CUBE(certified, region)
```

Giving:

RN	COUNT(*)	CERTIFIED	REGION	GROUPING(CERTIFIED)	GROUPING(REGION)
1	1	N	E	0	0
2	3	N	W	0	0
3	4	N		0	1
4	2	Y	E	0	0
5	1	Y	W	0	0
6	3	Y		0	1
7	3		E	1	0
8	4		W	1	0
9	7			1	1

Note that the value of the GROUPING(x) function is either zero or one, and is equal to one on the result row where the summary count for the attribute occurs. In the case of region, we see the summary data in rows 3, 6, and 9. For certified, the summary occurs in rows 7, 8, and 9.

We can use this GROUPING(x) function in a DECODE or CASE to enhance the result like this:

```
SELECT ROW_NUMBER() OVER(ORDER BY certified, region) rn,
   count(*), certified, region,
   DECODE(GROUPING(certified),0,null,'Count by "CERTIFIED"')
       "Count Certified",
   DECODE(GROUPING (region), 0, null,'Count by "REGION"')
       "Count Region"
FROM employee1
GROUP BY CUBE(certified, region)
```

Giving:

RN	COUNT(*)	C	RE	Count Certified	Count Region
1	1	N	E		
2	3	N	W		
3	4	N			Count by "REGION"
4	2	Y	E		
5	1	Y	W		
6	3	Y			Count by "REGION"
7	3		E	Count by "CERTIFIED"	
8	4		W	Count by "CERTIFIED"	
9	7			Count by "CERTIFIED"	Count by "REGION"

The same result may be had using the CASE function.
We could also use the BREAK reporting tool to space the display conveniently:

```
SQL>BREAK ON certified skip 1
```

Gives:

RN	COUNT(*)	C	RE	Count Certified	Count Region
1	1	N	E		
2	3		W		
3	4				Count by "REGION"
4	2	Y	E		
5	1		W		
6	3				Count by "REGION"
7	3		E	Count by "CERTIFIED"	
8	4		W	Count by "CERTIFIED"	
9	7			Count by "CERTIFIED"	Count by "REGION"

Chapter 6

The MODEL or SPREADSHEET Predicate in Oracle's SQL

The MODEL statement allows us to do calculations on a column in a row based on other rows in a result set. The MODEL or SPREADSHEET clause is very much like treating the result set of a query as a multidimensional array. The keywords MODEL and SPREAD-SHEET are synonymous.

The Basic MODEL Clause

Suppose we start with a table called Sales:

```
SELECT * FROM sales
ORDER BY location, product
```

Which gives:

LOCATION	PRODUCT	AMOUNT
Mobile	Cotton	24000
Mobile	Lumber	2800
Mobile	Plastic	32000
Pensacola	Blueberries	9000
Pensacola	Cotton	16000
Pensacola	Lumber	3500

The table has two locations and four products: Blueberries, Cotton, Lumber, and Plastic.

A query that returns a result based on "other rows" could be one like this:

```
SELECT a.location, a.amount
FROM sales a
WHERE a.amount in
  (SELECT max(b.amount)
  FROM sales b
  GROUP BY
  b.location)
```

Giving:

LOCATION	AMOUNT
Pensacola	16000
Mobile	32000

The above SQL statement creates a virtual table of grouped maximum values and then generates the result set based on the virtual table. The MODEL or SPREADSHEET clause allows us to compute a row in the result set that can retrieve data on some other row(s) without explicitly defining a virtual table. We will return to the above example presently, but before seeing the "row interaction" version of the SPREAD-SHEET clause, we will look at some simple examples to get the feel of the syntax and power of the statement. First of all, the overall syntax for the MODEL or SPREADSHEET SQL statement is as follows:

```
<prior clauses of SELECT statement>
MODEL [main]
[reference models]
[PARTITION BY (<cols>)]
DIMENSION BY (<cols>)
MEASURES (<cols>)
[IGNORE NAV] | [KEEP NAV]
[RULES
[UPSERT | UPDATE]
[AUTOMATIC ORDER | SEQUENTIAL ORDER]
[ITERATE (n) [UNTIL <condition>] ]
( <cell_assignment> = <expression> ... )
```

First we will look at an example and then more carefully define the terms used in the statement. Consider this example based on the Sales table:

```
SELECT product, location, amount, new_amt
FROM sales
SPREADSHEET
PARTITION BY (product)
DIMENSION BY (location, amount)
MEASURES (amount new_amt) IGNORE NAV
RULES (new_amt['Pensacola',ANY]=
    new_amt['Pensacola',currentv(amount)]*2)
ORDER BY product, location
```

Which gives:

```
PRODUCT               LOCATION                 AMOUNT    NEW_AMT
--------------------  --------------------   ---------- ----------
Blueberries           Pensacola                  9000      18000
Cotton                Mobile                    24000      24000
Cotton                Pensacola                 16000      32000
Lumber                Mobile                     2800       2800
Lumber                Pensacola                  3500       7000
Plastic               Mobile                    32000      32000
```

In brief, the PARTITION BY clause partitions the Sales table by one of the attributes. The DIMENSION BY clause determines the variables that will be used to compute results within each partition. MEASURES furnishes the rules by which the measured column will be computed. MEASURES involves RULES that affect the computation.

The above SQL statement allows us to generate the result set "new_amt" column with the RULES clause in line 7:

```
(new_amt['Pensacola',ANY]= new_amt['Pensacola',
    currentv(amount)]*2)
```

The RULES clause has an equal sign in it and hence has a left-hand side (LHS) and a right-hand side (RHS).

```
LHS:  new_amt['Pensacola',ANY]
RHS:  new_amt['Pensacola',currentv(amount)]*2
```

The *new_amt* on the LHS before the brackets ['Pen ...] means that we will compute a value for *new_amt*. The *new_amt* on the RHS before the brackets means we will use *new_amt* values (amount values) to compute the new values for *new_amt* on the LHS.

MEASURES and RULES use the DIMEN-SIONed columns such that for rows where the location

= 'Pensacola' and for ANY amount (LHS), then compute *new_amt* values for 'Pensacola' as the current value (currentv) of amount multiplied by 2 (RHS). The columns where location < > 'Pensacola' are unaffected and *new_amt* is simply reported in the result set as the amount value.

There are four syntax rules for the entire statement.

Rule 1. The Result Set

You have four columns in this result set:

```
SELECT product, location, amount, new_amt
```

As with any result set, the column ordering is immaterial, but it will help us to order the columns in this example as we have done here. We put the PARTITION BY column first, then the DIMENSION BY column(s), then the MEASURES column(s).

Rule 2. PARTITION BY

You must PARTITION BY at least one of the columns unless there is only one value. Here, we chose to partition by product and there are four product values: Blueberries, Lumber, Cotton, and Plastic. The results of the query are easiest to visualize if PARTITION BY is first in the result set. The sense of the PARTITION BY is that (a) the final result set will be logically "blocked off" by the partitioned column, and (b) the RULES clause may pertain to only one partition at a time. Notice that the result set is returned sorted by product — the column by which we are partitioning.

Rule 3. DIMENSION BY

Where PARTITION BY defines the rows on which the output is blocked off, DIMENSION BY defines the columns on which the spreadsheet calculation will be performed. If there are n items in the result set, $(n–p–m)$ columns must be included in the DIMENSION BY clause, where p is the number of columns partitioned and m is the number of columns measured. There are four columns in this example, so $n = 4$. One column is used in PARTITION BY ($p = 1$) and one column will be used for the SPREADSHEET (or MODEL) calculation ($m = 1$), leaving ($n–1–1$) or two columns to DIMENSION BY:

```
DIMENSION BY (location, amount)
```

We conveniently put the DIMENSION BY columns second and third in this result set.

Rule 4. MEASURES

The "other" result set column yet unaccounted for in PARTITION or DIMENSION clauses is column(s) to measure. MEASURES defines the calculation on the "spreadsheet" column(s) per the RULES. The DIMENSION clause defines which columns in the partition will be affected by the RULES. In this part of the statement:

```
MEASURES (amount new_amt) IGNORE NAV
```

we are signifying that we will provide a RULES clause to define the calculation that will take place based on calculating *new_amt*. We are aliasing the column "amount" with "new_amt"; the *new_amt* will be in the result set.

The optional "IGNORE NAV" part of the statement signifies that we wish to transform null values by treating them as zeros for numerical calculations and as null strings for character types.

In the sense of a spreadsheet, the MEASURES clause identifies a "cell" that will be used in the RULES part of the clause that follows. The sense of a "cell" in spreadsheets is a location on the spreadsheet that is defined by calculations based on other "cells" on that spreadsheet. The RULES will identify cell indexes (column values) based on the DIMENSION clause for each PARTITION. The syntax of the RULES clause is a before (LHS) and after (RHS) calculation based on the values of the DIMENSION columns:

```
New_amt[dimension columns] = calculation
```

ANY is a wildcard designation. Hence, we could set the RULES clause to make *new_amt* a constant for all values of location and amount with this RULES clause:

```
SELECT product, location, amount, new_amt
FROM sales
SPREADSHEET
PARTITION BY (product)
DIMENSION BY (location, amount)
MEASURES (amount new_amt) IGNORE NAV
RULES (new_amt[ANY,ANY]= 13)
ORDER BY product, location
```

Gives:

PRODUCT	LOCATION	AMOUNT	NEW_AMT
Blueberries	Pensacola	9000	13
Cotton	Mobile	24000	13
Cotton	Pensacola	16000	13
Lumber	Mobile	2800	13
Lumber	Pensacola	3500	13
Plastic	Mobile	32000	13

We can restrict the MEASURES/RULES to cover only one of the dimensions:

```
SELECT product, location, amount, new_amt
FROM sales
SPREADSHEET
PARTITION BY (product)
DIMENSION BY (location, amount)
MEASURES (amount new_amt) IGNORE NAV
    (new_amt['Pensacola',ANY]= 13)
ORDER BY product, location
```

Gives:

PRODUCT	LOCATION	AMOUNT	NEW_AMT
Blueberries	Pensacola	9000	13
Cotton	Mobile	24000	24000
Cotton	Pensacola	16000	13
Lumber	Mobile	2800	2800
Lumber	Pensacola	3500	13
Plastic	Mobile	32000	32000

In the first case, we are saying we want the value 13 for ANY value of location and amount. In the second case, we are setting the value of *new_amt* to 13 for those rows that contain location = 'Pensacola'.

A more realistic example of using RULES might be to forecast sales for each city with an increase of 10% for Pensacola and 12% for Mobile. Here we will set RULES for each city value and calculate new amounts based on the old amount. The query would look like this:

```
SELECT product, location, amount, fsales  "Forecast Sales"
FROM sales
SPREADSHEET
PARTITION BY (product)
DIMENSION BY (location, amount)
MEASURES (amount fsales) IGNORE NAV
    (fsales['Pensacola',ANY]=
    fsales['Pensacola',cv(amount)]*1.1,
    fsales['Mobile',ANY] = fsales['Mobile',cv()]*1.12)
ORDER BY product, location
```

Giving:

PRODUCT	LOCATION	AMOUNT	Forecast Sales
Blueberries	Pensacola	9000	9900
Cotton	Mobile	24000	26880
Cotton	Pensacola	16000	17600
Lumber	Mobile	2800	3136
Lumber	Pensacola	3500	3850
Plastic	Mobile	32000	35840

The query shows some flexibility in the current value function, abbreviating it as "CV" and showing it with and without an argument as "amount" is assumed since that is the column by which the statement is dimensioned as the second column on the LHS.

The rule:

```
fsales['Mobile',ANY] = fsales['Mobile',cv()]*1.12
```

says that we will compute a value on the RHS based on the LHS. The LHS value pair (location, amount) per DIMENSION BY is defined as:

```
location = 'Mobile' and for each value of amount (ANY) where
location = 'Mobile' proceed as follows:
```

Compute the value of fsales by using the current value [cv()] found for ('Mobile',amount) and multiply that amount value by 1.12.

The Pensacola case is handled in a similar way except that the CV function was written differently to illustrate another way to write it.

RULES that Use Other Columns

Let us first look at a result set/column structure for Sales like this:

```
SELECT product, location, amount
FROM sales
ORDER BY product, location
```

Which gives:

PRODUCT	LOCATION	AMOUNT
Blueberries	Pensacola	9000
Cotton	Mobile	24000
Cotton	Pensacola	16000
Lumber	Mobile	2800
Lumber	Pensacola	3500
Plastic	Mobile	32000

Now, suppose we want to force the amount of the Mobile sales into the Pensacola rows. We will again PARTITION BY product, but this time we will DIMENSION BY location only. We will recompute the amount values by simply reassigning the values for Pensacola rows to the corresponding values in the Mobile rows:

```
SELECT product, location, amount
FROM sales
SPREADSHEET
PARTITION BY (product)
DIMENSION BY (location)
MEASURES (amount) IGNORE NAV
    (amount['Pensacola']= amount['Mobile'])
ORDER BY product, location
```

Giving:

PRODUCT	LOCATION	AMOUNT
Blueberries	Pensacola	0
Cotton	Mobile	24000
Cotton	Pensacola	24000
Lumber	Mobile	2800
Lumber	Pensacola	2800
Plastic	Mobile	32000
Plastic	Pensacola	32000

The RULES here state that for each value of location = 'Pensacola' we report "amount" as equal to the value for "amount" in 'Mobile' *for that partition.* As we see, there is no value for the amount of Blueberries in Mobile, so the Pensacola amount gets set to zero per the IGNORE NAV option.

In previous examples we aliased the "amount" value because we reported both the "amount" and the new value for amount (*new_amt*); however, we used both "location" and "amount" in the DIMENSION BY. Here, we didn't DIMENSION "amount," but it is a good idea to alias what will be recomputed to avoid confusion:

```
SELECT product, location, new_amt
FROM sales
SPREADSHEET
PARTITION BY (product)
BY (location)
MEASURES (amount new_amt) IGNORE NAV
    (new_amt['Pensacola']= new_amt['Mobile'])
ORDER BY product, location
```

Gives:

PRODUCT	LOCATION	NEW_AMT
Blueberries	Pensacola	0
Cotton	Mobile	24000
Cotton	Pensacola	24000
Lumber	Mobile	2800
Lumber	Pensacola	2800
Plastic	Mobile	32000
Plastic	Pensacola	32000

Now suppose we'd like to display the greatest value for each partitioned product value in the Pensacola rows. We will set our RULES such that for each value of "amount" in 'Pensacola' we will replace the value of "amount" (aliased by "most") with the greatest value for that product in that partition. Here is the original table:

```
SELECT product, location, amount
FROM sales
ORDER BY product, location
```

Giving:

PRODUCT	LOCATION	AMOUNT
Blueberries	Pensacola	9000
Cotton	Mobile	24000
Cotton	Pensacola	16000
Lumber	Mobile	2800
Lumber	Pensacola	3500
Plastic	Mobile	32000

And now the query to possibly replace Pensacola rows with new values:

```
SELECT product, location, most
FROM sales
SPREADSHEET
PARTITION BY (product)
DIMENSION BY (location)
MEASURES (amount most) IGNORE NAV
    (most['Pensacola']= greatest(most['Mobile'],
    most['Pensacola']))
ORDER BY product, location
```

Gives:

PRODUCT	LOCATION	MOST
Blueberries	Pensacola	9000
Cotton	Mobile	24000
Cotton	Pensacola	24000
Lumber	Mobile	2800
Lumber	Pensacola	3500
Plastic	Mobile	32000
Plastic	Pensacola	32000

Blueberries had no Mobile counterpart and hence the greatest value occurred in the Blueberries partition where the location = 'Pensacola' and "most" got set to 9000.

For Cotton, the Mobile value was greater than the Pensacola value, and hence the Mobile value for the Cotton partition was reported in the Pensacola row.

For Lumber, the Pensacola row was already greater and hence no change in value occurred.

For Plastic, there was no value for Pensacola, and hence a new row was created to show Pensacola with the Mobile value for that product.

RULES that Use Several Other Rows to Compute New Rows

In the examples for the RULES clauses we have presented, we have made calculations for value combinations within the same partition. Another example of inter-row calculations in our spreadsheet could be had if we added another column, Year, in a new table called Sales1:

```
SQL> SELECT * FROM sales1 ORDER BY location, product, year
```

Giving:

LOCATION	PRODUCT	AMOUNT	YEAR
Mobile	Cotton	21600	2005
Mobile	Cotton	24000	2006
Mobile	Lumber	2520	2005
Mobile	Lumber	2800	2006
Mobile	Plastic	28800	2005
Mobile	Plastic	32000	2006
Pensacola	Blueberries	7650	2005
Pensacola	Blueberries	9000	2006
Pensacola	Cotton	13600	2005
Pensacola	Cotton	16000	2006
Pensacola	Lumber	2975	2005
Pensacola	Lumber	3500	2006

Now suppose we want to forecast 2007 based on the values in 2005 and 2006. Note that there are no values for 2007 in the table so we will be generating a new row for 2007. To keep the calculation simple (albeit non-creative), we will add the values from 2005 and 2006 to get 2007. This result can be had with one MODEL statement:

```
SELECT product, location, year, s "Forecast 2007 Sales"
FROM sales1
SPREADSHEET
PARTITION BY (product)
DIMENSION BY (location, year)
MEASURES (amount s) IGNORE NAV
    (s['Pensacola',2007]= s['Pensacola',
    2006]+s['Pensacola',2005],
    s['Mobile',2007]= s['Mobile',2006]+s['Mobile',2005])
ORDER BY product, location, year
```

Giving:

PRODUCT	LOCATION	YEAR	Forecast 2007 Sales
Blueberries	Mobile	2007	0
Blueberries	Pensacola	2005	7650
Blueberries	Pensacola	2006	9000
Blueberries	Pensacola	2007	16650
Cotton	Mobile	2005	21600
Cotton	Mobile	2006	24000
Cotton	Mobile	2007	45600
Cotton	Pensacola	2005	13600
Cotton	Pensacola	2006	16000
Cotton	Pensacola	2007	29600
Lumber	Mobile	2005	2520
Lumber	Mobile	2006	2800
Lumber	Mobile	2007	5320
Lumber	Pensacola	2005	2975
Lumber	Pensacola	2006	3500
Lumber	Pensacola	2007	6475
Plastic	Mobile	2005	28800

Plastic	Mobile	2006	32000
Plastic	Mobile	2007	60800
Plastic	Pensacola	2007	0

We used a simple alias, s, for the result set for the MEASURES and RULES, but we used a column alias for the overall display. If we cordon off some rows of the result set and look at the RULES we can see where the 2007 rows come from. For example, consider these rows:

Cotton	Mobile	2005	21600
Cotton	Mobile	2006	24000
Cotton	Mobile	2007	45600

The rule covering these rows is:

```
s['Mobile',2007]= s['Mobile',2006]+s['Mobile',2005]
```

and clearly, the amount reported for 2007, 45600, is the sum of the amounts for 2005 and 2006 (45600 = 21600 + 24000).

For the result row:

| Blueberries | Mobile | 2007 | 0 |

There are no values for 2006 or 2005 and hence due to the IGNORE NAV option, we get zero for a 2007 forecast for Mobile. Similar logic applies to this row:

| Plastic | Pensacola | 2007 | 0 |

Of course, more complicated formulas could be used in the RULES. Of interest, a shortcut attempt at this calculation will not work:

```
SELECT product, location, year, s
FROM sales1
SPREADSHEET
PARTITION BY (product)
DIMENSION BY (location, year)
MEASURES (amount s) IGNORE NAV
    (s[ANY,2007]= s[ANY,2006]+s[ANY,2005])
ORDER BY product, location, year
SQL> /
```

Gives:

```
    (s[ANY,2007]= s[ANY,2006]+s[ANY,2005])
                      *

ERROR at line 7:
ORA-32622: illegal multi-cell reference
```

The SQL engine has to be able to generate only one value on the RHS for each LHS row and this statement would generate multiple values for any one value on the LHS.

We could show only the result row for 2007 by filtering the overall result set with a WHERE in our query (the wrap and re-present technique):

```
SELECT * FROM
  (SELECT product, location, year, "Forecast 2007"
  FROM sales1
  MODEL
  PARTITION BY (product)
  DIMENSION BY (location, year)
  MEASURES (amount s) IGNORE NAV
    (s['Pensacola',2007]= s['Pensacola',
    2006]+s['Pensacola',2005],
    s['Mobile',2007]= s['Mobile',2006]+s['Mobile',2005])
ORDER BY product, location, year)
WHERE year = 2007
```

Giving:

PRODUCT	LOCATION	YEAR	Forecast 2007
Blueberries	Mobile	2007	0
Blueberries	Pensacola	2007	16650
Cotton	Mobile	2007	45600
Cotton	Pensacola	2007	29600
Lumber	Mobile	2007	5320
Lumber	Pensacola	2007	6475
Plastic	Mobile	2007	60800
Plastic	Pensacola	2007	0

If the filtering were attempted in the clauses of the core SELECT statement, no rows would result because the data needed for RULES would have been excised before the calculation could be made:

```
SELECT product, location, year, s
FROM sales1
WHERE year = 2007
MODEL
PARTITION BY (product)
DIMENSION BY (location, year)
MEASURES (amount s) IGNORE NAV
  (s['Pensacola',2007]= s['Pensacola',2006]+s['Pensacola',
  2005],s['Mobile',2007]= s['Mobile',2006]+s['Mobile',2005])
ORDER BY product, location, year
```

Gives:

```
no rows selected
```

RETURN UPDATED ROWS

There is an easier way to show only the "new rows" than to use a nested query — the RETURN UPDATED ROWS option will return only the 2007 rows in our example:

```
SELECT product, location, year, s "2007"
FROM sales1
SPREADSHEET
RETURN UPDATED ROWS
PARTITION BY (product)
DIMENSION BY (location, year)
MEASURES (amount s) -- IGNORE NAV
  (s['Pensacola',2007]= s['Pensacola',
  2006]+s['Pensacola',2005],
  s['Mobile',2007]= s['Mobile',2006]+s['Mobile',2005])
ORDER BY product, location, year
```

Gives:

PRODUCT	LOCATION	YEAR	2007
Blueberries	Mobile	2007	
Blueberries	Pensacola	2007	16650
Cotton	Mobile	2007	45600
Cotton	Pensacola	2007	29600
Lumber	Mobile	2007	5320
Lumber	Pensacola	2007	6475
Plastic	Mobile	2007	60800
Plastic	Pensacola	2007	

Also note the commenting out of the IGNORE NAV clause and its effect of not setting nulls to zero.

Using Comparison Operators on the LHS

Comparison operators may be used on the LHS attributes provided that we carry the values to the RHS with the CV function. Consider only the Pensacola rows in the Sales1 table:

```
SELECT product, location, year, amount
FROM sales1
WHERE location like 'Pen%'
ORDER BY product, year
```

Giving:

PRODUCT	LOCATION	YEAR	AMOUNT
Blueberries	Pensacola	2005	7650
Blueberries	Pensacola	2006	9000
Cotton	Pensacola	2005	13600
Cotton	Pensacola	2006	16000
Lumber	Pensacola	2005	2975
Lumber	Pensacola	2006	3500

In this example, we will compute a new value for "amount" (aliased by s) for each value of "amount" for the Pensacola rows:

```
SELECT product, location, year, s
FROM sales1
WHERE location like 'Pen%'
MODEL
RETURN UPDATED ROWS
PARTITION BY (product)
DIMENSION BY (location, year)
MEASURES (amount s) -- IGNORE NAV
  (s['Pensacola',year > 2000]= s['Pensacola',cv()]*1.2)
ORDER BY product, location, year
```

Gives:

PRODUCT	LOCATION	YEAR	S
Blueberries	Pensacola	2005	9180
Blueberries	Pensacola	2006	10800
Cotton	Pensacola	2005	16320
Cotton	Pensacola	2006	19200
Lumber	Pensacola	2005	3570
Lumber	Pensacola	2006	4200

New row values are calculated for each row as *updates* for that row. However, you cannot use this technique for creating new cells because "year > 2000" refers to multiple rows and you cannot have multiple cells in the calculation on the RHS of the RULES when you do it this way. Again, note that we used RETURN UPDATED ROWS in this example.

One should not confuse the term "update" as used in this context with the SQL UPDATE command. No table rows are actually updated. The phrase "update" as it applies to MODEL statements means that a value in a result set row is recomputed.

The use of the element "year > 2000" is called a *symbolic reference*. A symbolic reference may refer to different rows and *updates* to those rows. If we wrote a rule like this:

```
SELECT product, location, year, s
FROM sales1
WHERE location like 'Pen%'
MODEL
RETURN UPDATED ROWS
PARTITION BY (product)
DIMENSION BY (location, year)
MEASURES (amount s) -- IGNORE NAV
  (s['Pensacola', 2007] = s['Pensacola',2006])
ORDER BY product, location, year
```

Giving:

PRODUCT	LOCATION	YEAR	S
Blueberries	Pensacola	2007	9000
Cotton	Pensacola	2007	16000
Lumber	Pensacola	2007	3500

Then, the elements of the RULES clause would be a *positional reference* — the RULES refer to specific positions in the virtual array and a new row for year 2007 was *inserted*. The 2007 rows did not exist before the calculation of the values for that year. The positional reference is shorthand for (s[location='Pensacola',...]).

Adding a Summation Row — Using the RHS to Generate New Rows Using Aggregate Data

In the previous examples, we generated new rows with positional references on the LHS. If our logic requires that we generate new rows and the new rows are derived from aggregate data, we have to use an aggregate function on the RHS to reduce the calculation to a single value. To make the illustration a little clearer, suppose we add another row for Lumber in Pensacola, resulting in this version of the Sales table:

```
SELECT product, location, amount
FROM sales
ORDER BY product, location, amount
```

Giving:

```
PRODUCT                 LOCATION                 AMOUNT
--------------------    --------------------    ----------
Blueberries             Pensacola                  9000
Cotton                  Mobile                    24000
Cotton                  Pensacola                 16000
Lumber                  Mobile                     2800
Lumber                  Pensacola                   555
Lumber                  Pensacola                  3500
Plastic                 Mobile                    32000
```

To generate a sum row for every PARTITION
dimensioned by location and amount we can use this
query:

```
SELECT product, location, amount, s "Sum"
FROM sales
SPREADSHEET
PARTITION BY (product)
DIMENSION BY (location, amount)
MEASURES (amount s) IGNORE NAV
  (s['Pensacola',-1]= sum(s)[cv(),ANY])
ORDER BY product, location
```

Giving:

```
PRODUCT         LOCATION      AMOUNT       Sum
-------------   ----------   ----------   ----------
Blueberries     Pensacola       9000        9000
Blueberries     Pensacola         -1        9000
Cotton          Mobile         24000       24000
Cotton          Pensacola      16000       16000
Cotton          Pensacola         -1       16000
Lumber          Mobile          2800        2800
Lumber          Pensacola        555         555
Lumber          Pensacola       3500        3500
Lumber          Pensacola         -1        4055
Plastic         Mobile         32000       32000
Plastic         Pensacola         -1
```

In this query we did not use RETURN UPDATED ROWS and we created a new row with an amount value of –1. The value for the "–1" row was computed per the RULES as the sum of all values for that location:

```
s['Pensacola',-1]= sum(s)[cv(),ANY]
```

Note that per the RULES, Mobile's rows do not generate a new row and do not figure in the calculation of a sum. The result set becomes clearer if we do indeed use RETURN UPDATED ROWS and remove the AMOUNT column from the result to eliminate the –1 value:

```
SELECT product, location, -- amount,
    s "Sum"
FROM sales
SPREADSHEET
RETURN UPDATED ROWS
PARTITION BY (product)
DIMENSION BY (location, amount)
MEASURES (amount s) IGNORE NAV
  (s['Pensacola',-1]= sum(s)[cv(),ANY])
ORDER BY product, location
```

Giving:

PRODUCT	LOCATION	Sum
Blueberries	Pensacola	9000
Cotton	Pensacola	16000
Lumber	Pensacola	4055
Plastic	Pensacola	

Summing within a Partition

We can enhance the result set another way by renaming the summed row. Further, we do not have to restrict ourselves to a particular location within the partition. We can invent a "location" for our partitioned summed row. In summing we will use the aggregate function SUM, and we will use wildcards for arguments because we want all rows for a partition:

```
SELECT product, location, amount, s "Sum"
FROM sales
SPREADSHEET
PARTITION BY (product)
DIMENSION BY (location, amount)
MEASURES (amount s) IGNORE NAV
  (s['*** Partition sum = ',-1]= sum(s)[ANY,ANY])
ORDER BY product, location desc
```

Gives:

PRODUCT	LOCATION	AMOUNT	Sum
Blueberries	Pensacola	9000	9000
Blueberries	*** Partition sum =	-1	9000
Cotton	Pensacola	16000	16000
Cotton	Mobile	24000	24000
Cotton	*** Partition sum =	-1	40000
Lumber	Pensacola	3500	3500
Lumber	Pensacola	555	555
Lumber	Mobile	2800	2800
Lumber	*** Partition sum =	-1	6855
Plastic	Mobile	32000	32000
Plastic	*** Partition sum =	-1	32000

We have chosen the familiar PARTITION BY and DIMENSION BY clauses. Again, note that the data is partitioned by product. The Sum row appears as the sum of all rows *for a given partition* and we renamed the location for the Sum row as "*** Partition sum = ."

The query would also work with null amount values for the dummy Sum rows:

```
SELECT product, location, amount, s
FROM sales
SPREADSHEET
PARTITION BY (product)
DIMENSION BY (location, amount)
MEASURES (amount s) IGNORE NAV
   (s['*** Partition sum = ',null]= sum(s)[ANY,ANY])
ORDER BY product, location desc
```

Giving:

PRODUCT	LOCATION	AMOUNT	S
Blueberries	Pensacola	9000	9000
Blueberries	*** Partition sum =		9000
Cotton	Pensacola	16000	16000
Cotton	Mobile	24000	24000
Cotton	*** Partition sum =		40000
Lumber	Pensacola	3500	3500
Lumber	Pensacola	555	555
Lumber	Mobile	2800	2800
Lumber	*** Partition sum =		6855
Plastic	Mobile	32000	32000
Plastic	*** Partition sum =		32000

As a cosmetic variation, we can use the RETURN UPDATED ROWS option and further rename the result row like this:

```
SELECT product, location "Sales", -- amount,
     s "Sum"
FROM sales
SPREADSHEET
RETURN UPDATED ROWS
PARTITION BY (product)
```

```
DIMENSION BY (location, amount)
MEASURES (amount s) IGNORE NAV
RULES
   (s['Total Sales ... ',-1]= sum(s)[ANY,ANY])
ORDER BY product, location desc
```

Giving:

PRODUCT	Sales	Sum
Blueberries	Total Sales ...	9000
Cotton	Total Sales ...	40000
Lumber	Total Sales ...	6855
Plastic	Total Sales ...	32000

Although the use of location in the DIMENSION BY part of the statement seems superfluous, it is necessary to have two values in the RULES part of the statement, so both location and amount are used.

Aggregation on the RHS with Conditions on the Aggregate

Suppose we chose to use a group function on the RHS. First, we define the version of sales data we are going to work with:

```
SELECT product, location, year, amount
FROM sales1
WHERE location like 'Pen%'
ORDER BY product, location, year
```

Giving:

PRODUCT	LOCATION	YEAR	AMOUNT
Blueberries	Pensacola	2005	7650
Blueberries	Pensacola	2006	9000
Cotton	Pensacola	2005	13600
Cotton	Pensacola	2006	16000
Lumber	Pensacola	2005	2975
Lumber	Pensacola	2006	3500

Then, we will use the MAX aggregate function and a BETWEEN condition on the RHS:

```
SELECT product, location, year, s "Year Max"
FROM sales1
WHERE location like 'Pen%'
MODEL
RETURN UPDATED ROWS
PARTITION BY (product)
DIMENSION BY (location, year)
MEASURES (amount s) -- IGNORE NAV
  (s['Pensacola', ANY] = max(s)['Pensacola',year between 2005
  and 2006])
ORDER BY product, location, year
```

Giving:

PRODUCT	LOCATION	YEAR	Year Max
Blueberries	Pensacola	2005	9000
Blueberries	Pensacola	2006	9000
Cotton	Pensacola	2005	16000
Cotton	Pensacola	2006	16000
Lumber	Pensacola	2005	3500
Lumber	Pensacola	2006	3500

We are not constrained to using wildcards on the RHS calculation of aggregates. In this case we controlled which rows would be included in the aggregate using the BETWEEN predicate.

Revisiting CV with Value Offsets — Using Multiple MEASURES Values

We have seen how to use the CV function inside an RHS expression. The CV function copies the value from the LHS and uses it in a calculation. We can also use logical offsets from the current value. For example, "cv()–1" would indicate the current value minus one. Suppose we wanted to calculate the increase in sales for each year, cv(). We will need the sales from the previous year to make the calculation, cv()–1. We will restrict the data for the example; look first at sales in Pensacola:

```
SELECT product, location, year, amount
FROM sales1
WHERE location like 'Pen%'
ORDER BY product, location, year
```

Giving:

PRODUCT	LOCATION	YEAR	AMOUNT
Blueberries	Pensacola	2005	7650
Blueberries	Pensacola	2006	9000
Cotton	Pensacola	2005	13600
Cotton	Pensacola	2006	16000
Lumber	Pensacola	2005	2975
Lumber	Pensacola	2006	3500

We will PARTITION BY product in this example and we will DIMENSION BY location and year. We will use two new MEASURES, growth and pct (percent growth). We will calculate with RULES and display the two new values. In the MEASURES clause, we will need the amount value, although it does not appear in the result set. As before, we will alias "amount" as s to simplify the RULES statements. Also, we need to add the new result set columns growth and pct, but in the MEASURES clause, they are preceded by a zero so they can be aliased. We will use the RETURN UPDATED ROWS option to limit the output. Here is the query:

```
SELECT product, location, year, growth, pct
FROM sales1
WHERE location like 'Pen%'
MODEL
RETURN UPDATED ROWS
PARTITION BY (product)
DIMENSION BY (location, year)
MEASURES (amount s, 0 growth, 0 pct) -- IGNORE NAV
  (growth['Pensacola', year > 2005] = (s[cv(),cv()] -
  s[cv(),cv()-1]),
  pct['Pensacola', year > 2005]
  = (s[cv(),cv()] - s[cv(),cv()-1])/s[cv(),cv()-1])
ORDER BY location, product
```

Giving:

PRODUCT	LOCATION	YEAR	GROWTH	PCT
Blueberries	Pensacola	2006	1350	.176470588
Cotton	Pensacola	2006	2400	.176470588
Lumber	Pensacola	2006	525	.176470588

Let us consider several things in this example. First, we are using "amount" in the calculation although we do not report amount directly. Note the syntax of this RULE:

```
growth['Pensacola', year > 2005] = (s[cv(),cv()] -
    s[cv(),cv()-1])
```

The RULE says to compute a value for growth and hence growth appears on the LHS preceding the brackets. The RULE uses location and year to define the rows in the table for which growth will be computed. Note that the calculation is based on amounts, aliased by s, which appears as the computing value on the RHS before the brackets.

Remember that in the original explanation for this RULE:

```
(new_amt['Pensacola', ANY]= new_amt['Pensacola',
    currentv(amount)]*2)
```

We said:

> The *new_amt* on the LHS before the brackets ['Pen ...] means that we will compute a value for *new_amt*. The *new_amt* on the RHS before the brackets means we will use *new_amt* values (amount values) to compute the new values for *new_amt* on the LHS.

In this example, we have created a new variable on the LHS (*growth*) and used the old variable (*s*) on the RHS. Syntactically and logically, we must mention both the new variable and the old one in the MEASURES clause. We are not bound to report in the result set the values we use in the MEASURES clause. On the other hand, to use the values in the RULES we have to have defined them in MEASURES. To make the new variable (growth, for example) numeric, we precede the "declaration" of growth with a zero in the MEASURES clause.

Another quirk of this RULE:

```
growth['Pensacola', year > 2005] = (s[cv(),cv()] -
    s[cv(),cv()-1])
```

is that we have used logical offsets in the calculation. Rather than ask for amounts (s) for calculation of a given growth for a given year, we offset the current value by –1 in the difference expression. What we are saying here is that for a particular year, we will use the values for that year and the previous year. So, for 2006 we compute the growth for Pensacola as the "cv(),cv()" minus the "cv(),cv()–1", which would be (using amount rather than its alias, s):

```
amount('Pensacola',2006) - amount('Pensacola',2005)
```

The other calculation, "pct," is a bit more complex, but follows the same syntactical logic as the "growth" calculation.

We used the alias for amount for a shorthand notation, but the query works just as well and perhaps reads more clearly if we do not use the alias for amount:

```
SELECT product, location, year, growth, pct
FROM sales1
WHERE location like 'Pen%'
MODEL
RETURN UPDATED ROWS
PARTITION BY (product)
DIMENSION BY (location, year)
MEASURES (amount, 0 growth, 0 pct) -- IGNORE NAV
  (growth['Pensacola', year > 2005] = (amount[cv(),cv()] -
  amount[cv(),cv()-1]),
  pct['Pensacola', year > 2005]
  = (amount[cv(),cv()] - amount[cv(),cv()-1])/
  amount[cv(),cv()-1])
ORDER BY location, product
```

Giving:

PRODUCT	LOCATION	YEAR	GROWTH	PCT
Blueberries	Pensacola	2006	1350	.176470588
Cotton	Pensacola	2006	2400	.176470588
Lumber	Pensacola	2006	525	.176470588

The use of the alias here is a trade-off between understandability and brevity.

As an aside, this result could have been had with a traditional (albeit arguably more complex) self-join:

```
SELECT a.product, a.location, b.year,
   b.amount amt2006, a.amount amt2005,
   b.amount - a.amount growth,
   (b.amount - a.amount)/a.amount pct
FROM sales1 a, sales1 b
WHERE a.year = b.year -1
AND a.location LIKE 'Pen%'
AND b.location LIKE 'Pen%'
AND a.product = b.product
ORDER BY product
```

Giving:

PRODUCT	LOCATION	YEAR	AMT2006	AMT2005	GROWTH	PCT
Blueberries	Pensacola	2006	9000	7650	1350	.176470588
Cotton	Pensacola	2006	16000	13600	2400	.176470588
Lumber	Pensacola	2006	3500	2975	525	.176470588

Having developed the example for one location, we can expand the MODEL statement to get the growth volume and percents for all locations using the ANY wildcard and commenting out the WHERE clause of the core query:

```
SELECT product, location, year, growth, pct
FROM sales1
--    WHERE location like 'Pen%'
MODEL
RETURN UPDATED ROWS
PARTITION BY (product)
DIMENSION BY (location, year)
MEASURES (amount s, 0 growth, 0 pct) -- IGNORE NAV
   (growth[ANY, year > 2005] = (s[cv(),cv()] - s[cv(),cv()-1]),
   pct[ANY, year > 2005] = (s[cv(),cv()] - s[cv(),
   cv()-1])/s[cv(),cv()-1])
ORDER BY location, product
```

Giving:

PRODUCT	LOCATION	YEAR	GROWTH	PCT
Cotton	Mobile	2006	2400	.111111111
Lumber	Mobile	2006	280	.111111111
Plastic	Mobile	2006	3200	.111111111
Blueberries	Pensacola	2006	1350	.176470588
Cotton	Pensacola	2006	2400	.176470588
Lumber	Pensacola	2006	525	.176470588

Perhaps there is a lesson in query development here in that it is easier to see results if the original data is filtered before we attempt to compute all values.

Ordering of the RHS

When a range of cells is in the result set, ordering may be necessary when computing the values of the cells. Consider this derivative table created from previous data and enhanced:

Ordered by year *ascending*:

LOCATION	PRODUCT	AMOUNT	YEAR
Mobile	Cotton	19872	2004
Mobile	Cotton	21600	2005
Mobile	Cotton	24000	2006

Ordered by year *descending*:

LOCATION	PRODUCT	AMOUNT	YEAR
Mobile	Cotton	24000	2006
Mobile	Cotton	21600	2005
Mobile	Cotton	19872	2004

The MODEL statement creates a virtual table from which it calculates results. If the MODEL statement updates the result that appears in the result set, the result calculation may depend on the order in which the data is retrieved. As we know, one can never depend on the order in which data is actually stored in a relational database. Consider the following examples where the RULES are made to give us the sum of the amounts for the previous two years, for either year first, based on different orderings:

```
SELECT product, t, s
FROM sales2
MODEL
RETURN UPDATED ROWS
--      PARTITION BY (location)
DIMENSION BY (product, year t)
MEASURES (amount s)
  (s['Cotton', t>=2005] ORDER BY t asc =
  sum(s)[cv(),t between cv(t)-2 and cv(t)-1])
ORDER BY product
```

Giving:

PRODUCT	T	S
Cotton	2006	39744
Cotton	2005	19872

Note that the PARTITION BY statement is commented out, as the table contains only one location and hence partitioning is not necessary. Next, we compute a new value for s based on the sum of other values of s where on the RHS we sum over years cv()–1 and cv()–2. Second, we have added an ordering clause to the LHS to prescribe how we want to compute our new values — ascending by year in this case.

For ('Cotton',2006), you expect the new value of s to be the sum of the values for 2005 and 2004 (19872 + 21600) = 41472. You expect that the sum for 2005 would be just 2004 because there is no 2003. But instead, we get an odd value for 2006. What is going on here? The problem here is that in the calculation, we need to order the "input" to the RULES. In the above case, we have ordered the year to be ascending on the LHS, so 2005 was calculated first. 2005 was correct as there was no 2003 and so the new value for 2005 was reported as the value for 2004:

```
s['Cotton', t>=2005] = sum(s)[cv(),t between cv(t)-2 and
    cv(t)-1]
```

Becomes:

```
s['Cotton', 2005] = sum(s)[cv(),t between 2003 and 2004]
s['Cotton', 2005] = s['Cotton', 2004] + s['Cotton', 2003]
s['Cotton', 2005] = 19872 + 0 = 19872
```

When calculating 2006, the statement becomes:

```
s['Cotton', 2006] = sum(s)[cv(),t between 2004 and 2005]
s['Cotton', 2006] = s['Cotton', 2005] + s['Cotton', 2004]
```

But 2005 has been recalculated due to our ordering. So, the calculation for 2006 becomes:

```
s['Cotton', 2005] = 19872 + 19872 = 39744
```

Now look what happens if the LHS years are in descending order:

```
SELECT product, t, s
FROM sales2
MODEL
RETURN UPDATED ROWS
--     PARTITION BY (location)
DIMENSION BY (product, year t)
```

```
MEASURES (amount s)
  (s['Cotton', t>=2005] ORDER BY t desc =
  sum(s)[cv(),t between cv(t)-2 and cv(t)-1])
ORDER BY product
```

Gives:

```
PRODUCT                        T          S
-------------------- ---------- ----------
Cotton                      2006      41472
Cotton                      2005      19872
```

We get the correct answers because 2006 is recalculated based on original values for 2005 and 2004. Then, 2005 is recalculated.

Because of the ordering problem, in some statements where ordering is necessary, we may get an error if no ordering is specified.

```
SELECT product, t, s
FROM sales2
MODEL
RETURN UPDATED ROWS
--     PARTITION BY (location)
DIMENSION BY (product, year t)
MEASURES (amount s)
  (s['Cotton', t>=2005] = -- ORDER BY t desc =
  sum(s)[cv(),t between cv(t)-2 and cv(t)-1])
ORDER BY product
SQL> /
```

Gives:

```
FROM sales2
        *
ERROR at line 2:
ORA-32637: Self cyclic rule in sequential order MODEL
```

When no ORDER BY clause is specified, you might think that the ordering specified by the DIMENSION should take precedence; however, it is far better to dictate the order of the calculation if it would make a difference, as it did in this case.

AUTOMATIC versus SEQUENTIAL ORDER

Again, consider a partition of the Sales2 table but this time, we will use even sales amounts to make mental calculations easier:

```
SELECT * FROM sales2
WHERE product = 'Lumber'
ORDER BY year
```

Gives:

LOCATION	PRODUCT	AMOUNT	YEAR
Mobile	Lumber	2000	2005
Mobile	Lumber	3000	2006

Then consider using a SPREADSHEET (MODEL) clause to forecast 2005 sales as 10% higher than the existing value and 2006 sales as 20% higher:

```
SELECT product, t, orig, x projected
FROM sales2
MODEL
RETURN UPDATED ROWS
DIMENSION BY (product, amount orig, year t)
MEASURES (amount x)
RULES
  (x['Lumber',ANY,2005] = x[cv(),cv(),cv()]*1.1,
   x['Lumber',ANY,2006] = x[cv(),cv(),cv()]*1.2)
ORDER BY t
```

Gives:

```
PRODUCT               T        ORIG  PROJECTED
------------ ---------- ---------- ----------
Lumber              2005      2000      2200
Lumber              2006      3000      3600
```

In this example, we are simply updating rows based on a formula (a set of RULES). The amount calculated for 2005 is based on 2005 values, and the same is true for 2006.

Another way to write this statement could look like this:

```
SELECT product, t, x orig, projected
FROM sales2
MODEL
RETURN UPDATED ROWS
DIMENSION BY (product, year t)
MEASURES (amount x, 0 projected)
RULES
  (projected['Lumber', 2005] = x[cv(), cv()]*1.1,
   projected['Lumber', 2006] = x[cv(), cv()]*1.2)
ORDER BY t
```

Giving:

```
PRODUCT               T        ORIG  PROJECTED
------------ ---------- ---------- ----------
Lumber              2005      2000      2200
Lumber              2006      3000      3600
```

In the second version we compute "projected" based on "amount" (aliased by x).

Now suppose we decide to compute the projected values such that 2005 is based on a 10% increase and we compute 2006 based on 20% more than the projected value in 2005. It makes a difference whether we compute the 2005 projected value before we compute 2006, since 2006 is based on the projected value of 2005.

We could tackle this problem using ordering on the LHS as before, but we will do this a different way by explicitly calculating rows.

Consider this statement:

```
SELECT product, t, x orig, projected
FROM sales2
MODEL
RETURN UPDATED ROWS
DIMENSION BY (product, year t)
MEASURES (amount x, 0 projected)
RULES
  (projected['Lumber', 2005] = x[cv(), cv()]*1.1,
   projected['Lumber', 2006] = projected[cv(), cv()-1]*1.2)
ORDER BY t
```

Giving:

PRODUCT	T	ORIG	PROJECTED
Lumber	2005	2000	2200
Lumber	2006	3000	2640

Here, the projected value for 2006 is 2640 which is 1.2 * 2200 (projected 2006 is 20% more than projected 2005).

But suppose the RULES were reversed:

```
SELECT product, t, x orig, projected
FROM sales2
MODEL
RETURN UPDATED ROWS
DIMENSION BY (product, year t)
MEASURES (amount x, 0 projected)
RULES
  (projected['Lumber', 2006] = projected[cv(), cv()-1]*1.2,
   projected['Lumber', 2005] = x[cv(), cv()]*1.1)
ORDER BY t
```

Giving:

PRODUCT	T	ORIG	PROJECTED
Lumber	2005	2000	2200
Lumber	2006	3000	0

Here, when we compute the 20% increase in 2006 based on the projected 2005 value, we get zero because "projected 2005" has not been computed yet! The RULES say to compute 2006, then compute 2005. A way around this is to tell SQL that you want to compute these values automatically; let the SQL engine determine which needs to be computed first. The phrase AUTOMATIC ORDER may be put in the RULES like this:

```
SELECT product, t, x orig, projected
FROM sales2
MODEL
RETURN UPDATED ROWS
DIMENSION BY (product, year t)
MEASURES (amount x, 0 projected)
RULES AUTOMATIC ORDER
  (projected['Lumber', 2006] = projected[cv(), cv()-1]*1.2,
  projected['Lumber', 2005] = x[cv(), cv()]*1.1)
ORDER BY t
```

Giving:

PRODUCT	T	ORIG	PROJECTED
Lumber	2005	2000	2200
Lumber	2006	3000	2640

If you actually wanted your RULES to be evaluated in the order in which they are written, then the appropriate phrase would be SEQUENTIAL ORDER:

```
SELECT product, t, x orig, projected
FROM sales2
MODEL
RETURN UPDATED ROWS
DIMENSION BY (product, year t)
MEASURES (amount x, 0 projected)
RULES SEQUENTIAL ORDER
  (projected['Lumber', 2006] = projected[cv(), cv()-1]*1.2,
  projected['Lumber', 2005] = x[cv(), cv()]*1.1)
ORDER BY t
```

Giving:

PRODUCT	T	ORIG	PROJECTED
Lumber	2005	2000	2200
Lumber	2006	3000	0

When writing RULES, particularly if the RULES are more complex than this example, you may phrase RULES to be executed either way. It is necessary to know which RULE ordering is to be applied when one calculation depends on another.

The FOR Clause, UPDATE, and UPSERT

Consider this version of the Sales table (Sales2). In this version we display the amount and the amount multiplied by 2:

```
SELECT product, amount, amount*2, year
FROM sales2
WHERE product = 'Cotton'
ORDER BY product, year
```

Giving:

PRODUCT	AMOUNT	AMOUNT*2	YEAR
Cotton	19872	39744	2004
Cotton	21600	43200	2005
Cotton	24000	48000	2006

In most of the examples we have offered, we used values on the RHS to calculate new, updated values on the LHS. For example:

```
SELECT product, s  "Amount x 2", t
FROM sales2
SPREADSHEET
RETURN UPDATED ROWS
PARTITION BY (location)
DIMENSION BY (product, year t)
MEASURES (amount s) IGNORE NAV
  (s['Cotton', t ]
  ORDER BY t
  = s[cv(), cv(t)]*2)
ORDER BY product, t
```

Gives:

PRODUCT	Amount x 2	T
Cotton	39744	2004
Cotton	43200	2005
Cotton	48000	2006

In this example, we simply ask for a recomputation of the amount for each year in the table with the LHS referencing Cotton and whichever year (alias t) comes up. The RHS calculation is based on the current values in that row — "s[cv(), cv(t)]*2." As before, the first cv() refers to Product as it is specified first in the DIMENSION BY clause. The second argument on both sides also references the ordering specified by

DIMENSION BY. Here, we say that the column s, aliased by Amount x 2, is *updated*. A new value is computed and put in the appropriate place in the result set, replacing the original values of s.

If we use a symbolic reference to the year we get the same result:

```
SELECT product, s, t
FROM sales2
SPREADSHEET
RETURN UPDATED ROWS
PARTITION BY (location)
DIMENSION BY (product, year t)
MEASURES (amount s) IGNORE NAV
  (s['Cotton', t between 2002 and 2007]
  ORDER BY t
  = s[cv(), cv(t)]*2)
ORDER BY product, t
```

Gives:

PRODUCT	S	T
Cotton	39744	2004
Cotton	43200	2005
Cotton	48000	2006

In this case, we have asked for the years between 2002 and 2007. For those years where no value in this range exists we get no result. We get updated cells for the places where the calculation is made.

Now, suppose we want to have values for the years 2002 through 2007 whether data exists for those years or not. We can force the LHS to create rows for those years with a FOR statement. When we force the LHS to create values, the value is carried over to the RHS with the CV function. The syntax of the FOR statement is:

```
FOR column-name IN (appropriate set)
```

or

```
FOR column-name IN (SELECT clause with a result set matching
    column type)
```

Suppose we use this FOR on the LHS:

```
SELECT product, s, t
FROM sales2
SPREADSHEET
RETURN UPDATED ROWS
PARTITION BY (location)
DIMENSION BY (product, year t)
MEASURES (amount s) IGNORE NAV
  (s['Cotton', FOR t IN (2003, 2004, 2005, 2006, 2007)]
  = s[cv(), cv(t)]*2)
ORDER BY product, t
```

This gives:

PRODUCT	S	T
Cotton	0	2003
Cotton	39744	2004
Cotton	43200	2005
Cotton	48000	2006
Cotton	0	2007

When using a FOR loop, control can be exercised as to whether or not one wants to see the rows for which the data does not apply by using the UPSERT or UPDATE option. UPSERT means "update or insert" and is the default.

```
SELECT product, s, t
FROM sales2
SPREADSHEET
RETURN UPDATED ROWS
```

```
PARTITION BY (location)
DIMENSION BY (product, year t)
MEASURES (amount s) IGNORE NAV
RULES UPSERT
  (s['Cotton', FOR t IN (2003, 2004, 2005, 2006, 2007)]
  = s[cv(), cv(t)]*2)
ORDER BY product, t
```

Giving:

PRODUCT	S	T
Cotton	0	2003
Cotton	39744	2004
Cotton	43200	2005
Cotton	48000	2006
Cotton	0	2007

```
SQL> ed
Wrote file afiedt.buf
```

If UPDATE is specified, then only updated rows are presented:

```
SELECT product, s, t
FROM sales2
SPREADSHEET
RETURN UPDATED ROWS
PARTITION BY (location)
DIMENSION BY (product, year t)
MEASURES (amount s) IGNORE NAV
RULES UPDATE
  (s['Cotton', FOR t IN (2003, 2004, 2005, 2006, 2007)]
  = s[cv(), cv(t)]*2)
ORDER BY product, t
```

Giving:

PRODUCT	S	T
Cotton	39744	2004
Cotton	43200	2005
Cotton	48000	2006

Iteration

The MODEL statement also allows us to use iteration to calculate values. Iteration calculations are often used for approximations. As a first example of syntax and function, consider this:

```
SELECT s, n, x FROM dual
MODEL
DIMENSION BY (1 x)
MEASURES (50 s, 0 n)
RULES ITERATE (3)
  (s[1] = s[1]/2,
  n[1] = n[1] + 1)
```

Gives:

S	N	X
6.25	3	1

The statement has three values in the result set: s, n, and x. The MODEL uses DIMENSION BY (1 x). The s as used in this statement requires a subscript. The construct (1 x) in the dimension clause uses 1 arbitrarily; the 1 is used for the "subscript" for s in the RULES. The MEASURES clause defines two aliases that we will display in the result set, s and n. Initial values for s and n are 50 and 0 respectively.

The RULES clause says we will ITERATE exactly three times. After the first iteration, the value of $s[1]$ becomes 50/2, or 25; after the second iteration, $s[1]$ becomes $25/2 = 12.5$; and on the third iteration, $s[1]$ becomes $12.5/2 = 6.25$. Had we chosen some other number for x, we'd get the same result for s and n, but we just have to be consistent in writing the rules so that the information in the brackets agrees with the initial value for x:

```
SELECT s, n, x FROM dual
MODEL
DIMENSION BY (37 x)
MEASURES (50 s, 0 n)
RULES ITERATE (3)
  (s[37] = s[37]/2,
  n[37] = n[37] + 1)
```

Gives:

S	N	X
6.25	3	37

We can include an UNTIL clause in our iteration to terminate the loop like this:

```
SELECT s, n, x FROM dual
MODEL
DIMENSION BY (1 x)
MEASURES (50 s, 0 n)
RULES ITERATE (20) UNTIL (s[1]<=1)
  (s[1] = s[1]/2,
  n[1] = n[1] + 1)
```

Gives:

S	N	X
.78125	6	1

In this case, we place a maximum value on iterations of 20. We decided to terminate the iteration when the value of s[1] is less than or equal to 1. The iteration proceeded like this:

```
Step    S               N
-------- ---------- --------
Start   50              0
  1     25              1
  2     12.5            2
  3     6.25            3
  4     3.125           4
  5     1.5625          5
  6     0.71825         6
```

We can also compare a value with its predecessor in the iteration calculation like this:

```
SELECT s, n, x FROM dual
MODEL
DIMENSION BY (1 x)
MEASURES (50 s, 0 n)
RULES ITERATE (80) UNTIL (previous(s[1])-s[1]<=0.25)
  (s[1] = s[1]/2,
  n[1] = n[1] + 1)
```

Giving:

```
        S           N          X
---------- ---------- ----------
 .1953125       8          1
```

This time we used a maximum value of 80 for iterations. We decided to terminate the iteration when the difference between the previous value of s[1] and the new value of s[1] is less than or equal to 0.25. The iteration proceeded like this:

```
Step     S                N
-------- ---------- --------
Start    50               0
1        25               1
2        12.5             2
3        6.25             3
4        3.125            4
5        1.5625           5
6        0.71825          6
7        0.3906           7
8        0.1953           8
```

Note that the iteration stopped when the difference between the previous value and new value was less than 0.25 (0.39 − 0.19 = 0.20).

A Square Root Iteration Example

We will now create an example where we guess a square root and then use the guess to approach the actual value. To use the ITERATE command like this, we first create a table with labels and values:

```
DESC square_root
```

Gives:

```
Name                                       Null?    Type
------------------------------------------ -------- ------------
LABELS                                              VARCHAR2(20)
X                                                   NUMBER(8,2)
```

We put values in the table where:

```
SELECT * FROM square_root
```

Gives:

```
LABELS                        X
-------------------- ----------
original               21.000
root                   10.000
```

Here, we are going to try to find the square root of *original* whose value is 21. We predefined the column formatting here to be 9999999.999, so we get three decimal digits of precision. The value for *root* is a guess (and not a very good one). For our first try at getting the root, we will use 1,000 iterations. We hope to approximate the value of the root by computing a new value in each iteration based on the old value plus a correction factor. We will choose a correction constant (0.005) to use in computing the correction factor so that the iteration will proceed like this:

```
Step     Guess           N
-------- ---------- --------
Start    10              0

New value  = 10 + (21 — (10*10)) * 0.005
           = 10 + (-79) * 0.005
           = 10 — 0.395
           = 9.605

New value  = 9.605 + (21 — (9.605*9.605)) * 0.005
           = 9.605 + (-71.25) * 0.005
           = 9.05 — 0.356
           = 9.248
```

etc.

The method relies on the fact that the correction factor approaches the original value and as it gets closer, the correction gets smaller. In this technique we have a choice of the correction constant. The size of the correction constant affects how fast one wants to approach convergence, which in turn affects accuracy as we will see. If a larger correction constant were used, convergence would be quicker, but perhaps not as accurate.

The SELECT statement to calculate the square root looks like this:

```
SELECT labels, x
FROM square_root
MODEL IGNORE NAV
DIMENSION BY (labels)
MEASURES (x)
RULES SEQUENTIAL ORDER
ITERATE (1000)
  (x['root'] = x['root'] + ((x['original'] -
  (x['root']*x['root']))*0.005),
  x['Number of iterations'] = ITERATION_NUMBER + 1)
```

Giving:

```
LABELS                     X
-------------------- ---------
original               21.000
root                    4.583
Number of iterations 1000.000
```

This query uses the MODEL syntax we have seen previously. We can skip the PARTITION BY because we have only one set of data. We DIMENSION BY the labels and compute values based on the "X" values in the Square_root table, hence MEASURES (x).

In line 7 we instruct the statement to execute 1,000 times to try to find the root. Let's dissect this statement a bit:

```
(x['root'] = x['root'] + ((x['original'] -
            (x['root']*x['root']))*0.005)
```

In this statement, we are saying that in each iteration, we will compute a new value for x['root']:

```
x['root'] =
```

by taking the old value and adding to it 0.005 times the difference between the old value squared and the original value:

```
x['root'] + ((x['original'] − (x['root']*x['root']))*0.005)
```

Unfortunately the "old value-new value" designation is only marked by the position of the values in the expression. Since our formula has a sign in it, values will be added and subtracted as we get closer to the value we seek. After 1,000 iterations, the value for root has changed from our original guess of 10 to 4.583, which is close to the square root of 21. If we add more digits to the column format, we can see that the number calculated is actually closer to the real value of the square root:

```
COLUMN x FORMAT 9999999.9999999
```

Gives:

```
LABELS                         X
-------------------- ----------------
original              21.0000000
root                   4.5825757
Number of iterations 1000.0000000
```

We can use an alias for "x" if we choose to:

```
SELECT labels, y
FROM square_root
MODEL IGNORE NAV
DIMENSION BY (labels)
MEASURES (x y)
```

```
RULES SEQUENTIAL ORDER
ITERATE (1000)
  (y['root'] = y['root'] + ((y['original'] –
  (y['root']*y['root']))*0.005),
  y['Number of iterations'] = ITERATION_NUMBER + 1)
```

Gives:

```
LABELS                       Y
-------------------- ----------
original                    21
root                 4.58257569
Number of iterations      1000
```

y is an alias for "x" and, because we have not defined a column format, it defaults to a number with more decimal places in it. The y alias is actually superfluous, and is only there because we used aliases in previous examples.

To make the calculation more efficient, we can add an UNTIL clause to the iteration like this:

```
SELECT labels, y
FROM square_root
MODEL IGNORE NAV
DIMENSION BY (labels)
MEASURES (x y)
RULES SEQUENTIAL ORDER
ITERATE (1000) UNTIL (ABS(
PREVIOUS(y['root']) - y['root']) < 0.0000000000001)
  (y['root'] = y['root'] + ((y['original'] –
  (y['root']*y['root']))*0.005),
  y['Number of iterations'] = ITERATION_NUMBER + 1)
```

Giving:

```
LABELS                        Y
-------------------- ----------
original                     21
root                 4.58257569
Number of iterations        600
```

Here we note that the iteration was "close enough" after only 600 iterations. It would be a good experiment to try other numbers for "original" and for the correction factor. The original data could be changed to show other values and their roots:

```
SQL>update square_root set x = 385 where labels = 'original'
```

Then,

```
SELECT labels, x
FROM square_root
MODEL IGNORE NAV
DIMENSION BY (labels)
MEASURES (x)
RULES SEQUENTIAL ORDER
ITERATE (1000) UNTIL (ABS(
PREVIOUS(x['root']) - x['root']) < 0.0000000000001)
   (x['root'] = x['root'] + ((x['original'] -
   (x['root']*x['root']))*0.005),
   x['Number of iterations'] = ITERATION_NUMBER + 1)
```

Gives:

```
LABELS                        X
-------------------- ----------------
original             385.0000000
root                  19.6214169
Number of iterations 143.0000000
```

Here is the same problem with a larger correction factor:

```
SELECT labels, x
FROM square_root
MODEL IGNORE NAV
DIMENSION BY (labels)
MEASURES (x)
RULES SEQUENTIAL ORDER
ITERATE (1000) UNTIL (ABS(
PREVIOUS(x['root']) - x['root']) < 0.0000000000001)
  (x['root'] = x['root'] + ((x['original'] -
  (x['root']*x['root']))*0.05),
  x['Number of iterations'] = ITERATION_NUMBER + 1)
```

Gives:

```
LABELS                        X
-------------------- ----------
original                    385
root                 19.6214169
Number of iterations        824
```

And an even larger factor:

```
SELECT labels, x
FROM square_root
MODEL IGNORE NAV
DIMENSION BY (labels)
MEASURES (x)
RULES SEQUENTIAL ORDER
ITERATE (1000) UNTIL (ABS(
PREVIOUS(x['root']) - x['root']) < 0.0000000000001)
  (x['root'] = x['root'] + ((x['original'] -
  (x['root']*x['root']))*0.1),
  x['Number of iterations'] = ITERATION_NUMBER + 1)
SQL> /
```

Gives:

```
(x['root'] = x['root'] + ((x['original'] -
(x['root']*x['root']))*0.1)
                                          *
ERROR at line 9:
ORA-01426: numeric overflow
```

References

Haydu, John, "The SQL MODEL Clause of Oracle
Database 10*g*," Oracle Corp., Redwood Shores, CA,
2003. (A PDF version of the white paper is available at: http://otn.oracle.com/products/bi/pdf/
10gr1_twp_bi_dw_sqlmodel.pdf.)

Witkowski, A., Bellamkonda, S., Bozkaya, T., Folkert,
N., Gupta, A., Sheng, L., Subramanian, S., "Busi-
ness Modeling Using SQL Spreadsheets," Oracle
Corp., Redwood Shores, CA (paper given at the
Proceedings of the 29th VLDB Conference, Berlin,
Germany, 2003).

Chapter 7

Regular Expressions: String Searching and Oracle 10g

For many years, Oracle has supported string functions well ("strings" in Oracle are also known as character or text literals). This chapter presumes familiarity with the "ordinary" string functions, particularly INSTR, LIKE, REPLACE, and SUBSTR. A "regular expression" (RE) is a character string (a pattern) that is used to match another string (a search string or target string); REs are incorporated into new functions in Oracle 10*g* that have these names: REGEXP_x, where x = INSTR, LIKE, REPLACE, SUBSTR (e.g., REGEXP_INSTR). The new functions may be used in both SQL and PL/SQL.

The four new and improved functions operate on character strings and return the same types as the older counterparts:

▼ REGEXP_INSTR returns a number signifying where a pattern begins.

▼ REGEXP_LIKE returns a Boolean to signify the existence of a pattern.

▼ REGEXP_SUBSTR returns part of a string.

▼ REGEXP_REPLACE returns a string with part of it replaced.

The source string argument is usually of type VARCHAR2, but may also be used with type CHAR, CLOB, NCHAR, NVARCHAR2, and NCLOB. The placement of the source string and pattern is almost the same as the original functions and, like the original functions, there are other arguments that may enhance the use of the function. We will define each of the functions in turn, but we will primarily illustrate the function with minimal arguments.

The regular expressions (REs) are POSIX compliant. POSIX stands for the Portable Operating System Interface standardization effort, which is overseen by various international standardization committees like ISO/IEC, IEEE, etc. REs are used in computer languages, e.g., Java, XML, UNIX scripting, and particularly Perl. For a programmer who uses REs in a programming language, their use within Oracle will be very similar.

The conjunction of string searching, REs, Oracle 10g, and POSIX is that in rewriting the "normal" string functions like INSTR, one may use standardized POSIX symbols in REGEXP_INSTR (and other REGEXP_x functions) to express how a string is to be searched for a pattern. The POSIX symbols are standardized, albeit cryptic.

Why use REs? Rischert puts this well: "Data validation, identification of duplicate word occurrences, detection of extraneous white spaces, or parsing of strings are just some of the many uses of regular expressions."[1] There are many cumbersome tasks in data cleaning and validation that will be improved by this new feature. We will illustrate each of the new functions through usage scenarios.

A Simple Table to Illustrate an RE

As a first example, suppose we have a table of addresses:

```
DESC addresses
```

Giving:

```
Name                                       Null?    Type
------------------------------------------ -------- --------------
ADDR                                                VARCHAR2(30)
```

```
SELECT * FROM addresses
```

Gives:

```
ADDR
------------------------------
123 4th St.
4 Maple Ct.
2167 Greenbrier Blvd.
33 Third St.
One First Drive
1664 1/2 Springhill Ave
2003 Geaux Illini Dr.
```

---

1   Alice Rischert, "Inside Oracle Database 10g: Writing Better SQL Using Regular Expressions."

REGEXP_INSTR

We will begin our exploration of REs using the REGEXP_INSTR function. As with INSTR, the function returns a number for the position of matched pattern. Unlike INSTR, REGEXP_INSTR cannot work from the end of the string backward. The arguments for REGEXP_INSTR are:

```
REGEXP_INSTR(String to search, Pattern, [Position,
    [Occurrence, [Return-option, [Parameters]]]])
```

String to search, S, refers to the string that will be searched for the pattern.

Pattern, P, is the sought string, which will be expressed as an RE.

These first two arguments are not optional.

Example:

```
SELECT REGEXP_INSTR('Mary has a cold','a') position FROM dual
```

Gives:

```
 POSITION
----------
        2
```

The letter "a" is found in the second position of the target string (source string) "Mary has a cold."

Position is the place in S to begin the search for P. The default is 1.

Example:

```
SELECT REGEXP_INSTR('Mary has a cold','a',3) position
    FROM dual
```

Gives:

```
POSITION
----------
         7
```

Since we started in the third position of the search string, the first "a" after that was in the seventh position of the string. As mentioned above, *Position* in REGEXP_INSTR cannot be negative — one cannot work from the right end of the string.

Occurrence refers to the first, second, third, etc., occurrence of the pattern in S. The default is 1 (first).

Example:

```
SELECT REGEXP_INSTR('Mary has a cold','a',1,2) position
    FROM dual
```

Gives:

```
POSITION
----------
         7
```

This query illustrates searching for the second "a" starting at position 1. The second "a" is found at position 7.

A word of warning about Oracle syntax is in order. One might attempt to use the default value for *Position* and then ask for the second occurrence of the pattern like this:

```
SELECT REGEXP_INSTR('Mary has a cold','a',,2) position
    FROM dual
```

This query will fail because parameters cannot be left out as above. If we want to use the fourth parameter, we have to include the third even if we enter the default value.

Return-option returns the position of the start or end of the matched string. The default is 0, which returns the starting position of the pattern in the target; a value of 1 returns the starting position of the next character following the pattern match.

Example 1: The default (0) beginning of the position where the pattern is found:

```
SELECT REGEXP_INSTR('Mary has a cold','a',1,2,0) position
    FROM dual
```

Gives:

```
 POSITION
----------
        7
```

Example 2: The *Return-option* is set to 1 to indicate the end of the found pattern:

```
SELECT REGEXP_INSTR('Mary has a cold','a',1,2,1) position
    FROM dual
```

Gives:

```
 POSITION
----------
        8
```

In actuality, any non-zero, positive number for the *Return-option* will work to retrieve the next character position, but it is better to stay with 1 and 0 to avoid confusion.

Parameters is a field that may be used to define how one wants the search to proceed:

▼ i — to ignore case
▼ c — to match case

▼ n — to make the metacharacter dot symbol match new lines as well as other characters (more on this later in the chapter)

▼ m — to make the metacharacters ^ and $ match beginning and end of a line in a multiline string (more, later)

The default is "i".

Example 1: Find the "s" and match case.

```
SELECT REGEXP_INSTR('Sam told a story','s',1,1,0,'c') position
    FROM dual
```

Gives:

```
POSITION
----------
        12
```

Example 2: Find the "s" and ignore case.

```
SELECT REGEXP_INSTR('Sam told a story','s',1,1,0,'i') position
    FROM dual
```

Gives:

```
POSITION
----------
         1
```

We will defer the other options until later in the chapter. We will illustrate most of the REs using only the minimal parameters because once we learn to use the RE, the other parameters can be used in the special situations where they are warranted.

A Simple RE Using REGEXP_INSTR

The simplest regular expression matches letters, letter for letter. For example,

```
SELECT addr, REGEXP_INSTR(addr,'One') where_it_is
FROM addresses
WHERE REGEXP_INSTR(addr,'One') > 0
```

Gives:

```
ADDR                            WHERE_IT_IS
------------------------------- -----------
One First Drive                           1
```

The character string "One" (a *pattern* of letters to search for) would also find a match should the address have contained something like this: '444 Oneway drive' or '7 Muldoon-One.'

Example:

```
SELECT REGEXP_INSTR('444 Oneway drive','One') where_it_is
    FROM dual
```

Gives:

```
WHERE_IT_IS
-----------
          5
```

Note that other capitalizations of the word "One" will not match unless we use more optional parameters (see the above discussion on *Parameters*):

```
SELECT addr, REGEXP_INSTR(addr,'one') where_it_is
FROM addresses
WHERE REGEXP_INSTR(addr,'one') > 0
```

Gives:

```
no rows selected
```

To handle matching more effectively, the POSIX syntax allows us to create a "match string pattern" (usually just called a "pattern") using special characters and the idea of left-to-right placement within the pattern. We will introduce these special characters and the placement idea with examples.

Before proceeding, reconsider the previous example. The overall match for the string "One" should be considered as the letter "O", which when matched should immediately be followed by an "n", which when matched should be followed by an "e". It is not so much the word "One" that is being matched as it is a letter-by-letter, left-to-right matching process.

Metacharacters

In earlier Oracle versions, the metacharacters "%" and "_" were used as wildcards in the LIKE condition in WHERE clauses. Metacharacters add features to matching patterns. For example,

```
... WHERE Name LIKE 'Sm%'
```

says to acknowledge a match (return a Boolean True) for the column Name when it begins with the letters "Sm" followed by anything. In RE-Oracle functions, there are three special characters that are used in matching patterns:

> ▼ "^" — a caret is called an "anchoring operator," and matches the beginning of a string. The caret is overloaded — it has multiple meanings in pattern match expressions depending on where it is

used. The caret may also mean "not," which is at best confusing.

▼ "$" — a dollar sign is another anchoring operator and matches only the end of a string.

▼ "." — the period matches anything and is called the "match any character" operator. Many would call this a "wildcard" match character.

Let us see how these special characters may be used in our REGEXP_INSTR example. We will illustrate our examples by putting the RE and the match expression in the result set; when possible, we recommend you do the same while testing these new functions. First, the period may be substituted for any letter and still maintain a match:

```
SELECT addr, REGEXP_INSTR(addr,'O.e') where_it_is
FROM addresses
WHERE REGEXP_INSTR(addr,'O.e') > 0
```

Gives:

```
ADDR                            WHERE_IT_IS
------------------------------- -----------
One First Drive                           1
```

The match expression is a capital "O", followed by any character ("."), followed by an "n". We may use the caret-anchor to insist the matching start at the beginning of the string like this:

```
SELECT addr, REGEXP_INSTR(addr,'^O.e') where_it_is
FROM addresses
WHERE REGEXP_INSTR(addr,'^O.e') > 0
```

Gives:

```
ADDR                            WHERE_IT_IS
------------------------------  -----------
One First Drive                           1
```

In the following example, the match fails because we are asking for a match for a capital "F" followed by any character, but we are caret-anchored at the beginning of the string "addr":

```
SELECT addr, REGEXP_INSTR(addr,'^F.') where_it_is
FROM addresses
WHERE REGEXP_INSTR(addr,'^F.') > 0
```

Gives:

```
no rows selected
```

However, if we remove the caret-anchor, we get a match:

```
SELECT addr, REGEXP_INSTR(addr,'F.') where_it_is
FROM addresses
WHERE REGEXP_INSTR(addr,'F.') > 0
```

Gives:

```
ADDR                            WHERE_IT_IS
------------------------------  -----------
One First Drive                           5
```

We can also specify any series of letters and find matches, just like INSTR:

```
SELECT addr, REGEXP_INSTR(addr,'ing') where_it_is
FROM addresses
WHERE REGEXP_INSTR(addr,'ing') > 0
```

Gives:

```
ADDR                             WHERE_IT_IS
------------------------------   -----------
1664 1/2 Springhill Ave                   13
```

Or we can add anchors or "wildcard" match characters as need be.

One must be careful when anchoring and using the "other" arguments. Consider this example:

```
SELECT REGEXP_INSTR('Hello','^.',2) FROM dual;
```

Gives:

```
REGEXP_INSTR('HELLO','^.',2)
----------------------------
                           0
```

Here, we have anchored the pattern using the caret. Then we have contradicted ourselves by asking the pattern to begin looking in the second position of the string. The contradiction results in a non-match because the search string cannot be anchored at the beginning and then searched from some other position.

To return to the other "extra" arguments we discussed earlier, we noted that the *Parameters* optional argument allowed for special use of the period metacharacter. Let's delve further into the use of those arguments.

Suppose we had a table called Test_clob with these contents:

```
DESC test_clob
```

Giving:

```
Name                                              Null?    Type
------------------------------------------------- -------- -------------
NUM                                                        NUMBER(3)
CH                                                         CLOB
```

SELECT * FROM test_clob

Gives:

```
     NUM CH
---------- -------------------------------------------------------------
       1 A simple line of text
       2 This line contains two lines of text;
         it includes a carriage return/line feed
```

Here are some examples of the use of the "n" and "m" parameters:

Looking at the text in Test_clob where the value of num = 2, we see that there is a new line after the semi-colon. Further, the characters after the "x" in text may be searched as a "t" followed by a semicolon, followed by an "invisible" new line character, followed by a space, then the letters "it":

```
SELECT REGEXP_INSTR(ch, 't;. it',REGEXP_INSTR(ch,'x'),1,0,'n')
    "where is 't' after 'x'?"
FROM test_clob
WHERE num = 2
```

Gives:

```
where is 't' after 'x'?
-----------------------
                     36
```

The query shows the use of nested functions (a REGEXP_INSTR within another REGEXP_INSTR). Further, we specified that we wanted some character after the semicolon. In order to specify that the "some character" could be a new line, we had to use the "n" optional parameter. Had we used some other optional parameter, such as "i," we would not have found the pattern:

```
SELECT REGEXP_INSTR(ch, 't;. it',REGEXP_INSTR(ch,'x'),1,0,'i')
    "where is 't' after 'x'?"
FROM test_clob
WHERE num = 2
```

Gives:

```
where is 't' after 'x'?
-----------------------
                      0
```

Using the default *Parameter* would yield the same result:

```
SELECT REGEXP_INSTR(ch, 't;. it',REGEXP_INSTR(ch,'x'))
...
```

Would give:

```
where is 't' after 'x'?
-----------------------
                      0
```

The use of the "m" *Parameter* may be illustrated with the same text in Test_clob. Suppose we want to know if any lines in the CLOB column contain a space in the first position (the second line starts with a space). We write our query and use the default *Parameter* argument:

```
SELECT REGEXP_INSTR(ch, '^ it')
    "Space starting a line?"
FROM test_clob
WHERE num = 2
```

Gives:

```
Space starting a line?
----------------------
                     0
```

This query failed to show the space starting the second line because we didn't use the "m" optional argument. The "m" argument for *Parameters* is specifically for matching the caret-anchor to the beginning of a multi-line string. Here is the corrected version of the query:

```
SELECT REGEXP_INSTR(ch, '^ it',1,1,0,'m')
    "Space starting a line?"
FROM test_clob
WHERE num = 2
```

Giving:

```
Space starting a line?
----------------------
                    39
```

Brackets

The next special character we'll introduce is the bracket notation for a POSIX character class. If we use brackets, [*whatever*], we are asking for a match of *whatever* set of characters is included inside the brackets in any order. Suppose we wanted to devise a query to find addresses where there is either an "i" or an "r." The query is:

```
SELECT addr, REGEXP_INSTR(addr, '[ir]') where_it_is
FROM addresses
```

Giving:

```
ADDR                         WHERE_IT_IS
---------------------------- -----------
123 4th St.                            0
4 Maple Ct.                            0
2167 Greenbrier Blvd.                  7
33 Third St.                           6
One First Drive                        6
1664 1/2 Springhill Ave               12
2003 Geaux Illini Dr.                 15
```

All REs occur between quotes. The RE evaluates the target from left to right until a match occurs. The RE can be set up to look for one thing or, more frequently, a pattern of things in a target string. In this case, we have set up the pattern to find either an "i" or an "r".

As another example, suppose we want to create a match for any vowel followed by an "r" or "p". The query would look like this:

```
SELECT addr, REGEXP_INSTR(addr,'[aeiou][rp]') where_it_is
FROM addresses
WHERE REGEXP_INSTR(addr,'[aeiou][rp]') > 0
```

Giving:

```
ADDR                         WHERE_IT_IS
---------------------------- -----------
4 Maple Ct.                            4
2167 Greenbrier Blvd.                 14
33 Third St.                           6
One First Drive                        6
```

The matched characters are:

```
4 Maple Ct.
2167 Greenbrier Blvd.
33 Third St.
One First Drive
```

Ranges (Minus Signs)

We may also create a range for a match using a minus
sign. In the following example, we will ask for the letters "a" through "j" followed by an "n":

```
SELECT addr, REGEXP_INSTR(addr,'[a-j]n') where_it_is
FROM addresses
WHERE REGEXP_INSTR(addr,'[a-j]n') > 0
```

Gives:

ADDR	WHERE_IT_IS
2167 Greenbrier Blvd.	9
1664 1/2 Springhill Ave	13
2003 Geaux Illini Dr.	15

The matched characters are:

```
2167 Greenbrier Blvd.
1664 1/2 Springhill Ave
2003 Geaux Illini Dr
```

REGEXP_LIKE

To illustrate another RE function and to continue with
illustrations of matching, we will now use the Boolean-
returning REGEXP_LIKE function. The complete
function definition is:

```
REGEXP_LIKE(String to search, Pattern, [Parameters]),
```

where *String to search*, *Pattern*, and *Parameters* are
the same as for REGEXP_INSTR. As with
REGEXP_INSTR, the *Parameters* argument is usually used only in special situations. To introduce

REGEXP_LIKE, let's begin with the older LIKE function. Consider the use of LIKE in this query:

```
SELECT addr
FROM addresses
WHERE addr LIKE('%g%')
    OR  addr LIKE ('%p%')
```

Giving:

```
ADDR
-------------------------------
4 Maple Ct.
1664 1/2 Springhill Ave
```

We are asking for the presence of a "g" or a "p". The "%" sign metacharacter matches zero, one, or more characters and here is used before and after the letter we seek. The LIKE predicate has an RE counterpart using bracket classes that is simpler. The REGEXP_LIKE would look like this:

```
SELECT addr
FROM addresses
WHERE REGEXP_LIKE(addr,'[gp]')
```

Giving:

```
ADDR
-------------------------------
4 Maple Ct.
1664 1/2 Springhill Ave
```

Here, we are asking for a match in "addr" for either a "g" or a "p". The order of occurrence of [gp] or [pg] is irrelevant.

Negating Carets

As previously mentioned, the caret (" ^ ") may be either an anchor or a negating marker. We may negate the string we are looking for by placing a negating caret at the beginning of the string like this:

```
SELECT addr
FROM addresses
WHERE REGEXP_LIKE(addr,'[^gp]')
```

Giving:

```
ADDR
-------------------------------
123 4th St.
4 Maple Ct.
2167 Greenbrier Blvd.
33 Third St.
One First Drive
1664 1/2 Springhill Ave
2003 Geaux Illini Dr.
```

It appears at first that the negating caret did not work. However, look at what was asked for and what was matched. We asked for a match anywhere in the string for anything other than a "g" or a "p" and we got it — all rows have something other than a "g" or a "p".

To further illustrate the negating caret here, suppose we add a nonsense address that contains only "g"s and "p"s:

```
SELECT * FROM addresses
```

Gives:

```
ADDR
-----------------------------
123 4th St.
4 Maple Ct.
2167 Greenbrier Blvd.
33 Third St.
One First Drive
1664 1/2 Springhill Ave
2003 Geaux Illini Dr.
gggpppggpgpgpgpgp
```

Now execute the RE query again:

```
SELECT * FROM addresses
WHERE REGEXP_LIKE(addr,'[gp]')
```

Gives:

```
ADDR
-----------------------------
4 Maple Ct.
1664 1/2 Springhill Ave
gggpppggpgpgpgpgp
```

and use the negating caret:

```
SELECT * FROM addresses
WHERE REGEXP_LIKE(addr,'[^gp]')
```

Gives:

```
ADDR
-----------------------------
123 4th St.
4 Maple Ct.
2167 Greenbrier Blvd.
33 Third St.
One First Drive
```

```
1664 1/2 Springhill Ave
2003 Geaux Illini Dr.
```

If we wanted a "non-('g' or 'p')" followed by something else like an "l" (a lowercase "L"), we could write the query like this:

```
SELECT addr
FROM addresses
WHERE REGEXP_LIKE(addr,'[^gp]l')
```

Giving:

```
ADDR
--------------------------
2167 Greenbrier Blvd.
1664 1/2 Springhill Ave
2003 Geaux Illini Dr.
```

Here, the match succeeds because we are looking for a letter that is not a "g" or "p", followed by the letter "l".
The matches are:

```
2167 Greenbrier Blvd.
1664 1/2 Springhill Ave
2003 Geaux Illini Dr.
```

Bracketed Special Classes

Special classes are provided that use a special matching paradigm. Suppose we want to find any row where there are digits or lack of digits. The bracketed expression [[:digit]] matches numbers. If we wanted to find all addresses that begin with a number we could do this:

```
SELECT addr
FROM addresses
WHERE REGEXP_INSTR(addr,'^[[:digit:]]') = 1
```

Giving:

```
ADDR
--------------------------------
32 O'Neal Drive
32 O'Hara Avenue
123 4th St.
4 Maple Ct.
2167 Greenbrier Blvd.
33 Third St.
1664 1/2 Springhill Ave
2003 Geaux Illini Dr.
```

Another example:

```
SELECT addr
FROM addresses
WHERE REGEXP_INSTR(addr,'[[:digit:]]') = 0
```

Giving:

```
ADDR
--------------------------------
One First Drive
```

In both queries, the matching expression contains
[:digit:], which is a "match any numeric digit" class.
The brackets around the ":digit:" part come with the
expression. To use [:digit:] for "match any numeric
digit" we have to enclose the class within brackets or
else we would be asking for the component parts.

[[:digit:]] says to match digits.

[:digit:] by itself says "match a colon or a 'd' or an
'i'," etc. Match any letter in the collection. The fact that
some characters are repeated is inconsequential.

So in the second example, when we used [[:digit:]]
inside of the REGEXP_INSTR function, we found the
row where digits were not in the target string. If we
wanted another expression that would match "addr"
where there were no digits at all anywhere in the

string we could have used the bracket notation, a range of numbers, and the NOT predicate.

```
SELECT addr
FROM addresses
WHERE NOT REGEXP_LIKE(addr,'[0-9]')
```

Gives:

```
ADDR
-------------------------------
One First Drive
```

It is a bit dangerous to try to use negation inside of the match expression because of any non-digit matches (letters, spaces, punctuation). It is far easier to find *all* of what you don't want and then "NOT it." Asking for any match for a "non-zero to nine" returns all rows because all rows have a non-digit:

```
SELECT addr
FROM addresses
WHERE REGEXP_LIKE(addr,'[^0-9]')
```

Gives:

```
ADDR
-----------------------------
123 4th St.
4 Maple Ct.
2167 Greenbrier Blvd.
33 Third St.
One First Drive
1664 1/2 Springhill Ave
2003 Geaux Illini Dr.
```

Similarly, matching for a non-digit gives all rows:

```
SELECT addr
FROM addresses
WHERE NOT REGEXP_LIKE(addr,'[[:digit]]')
```

Gives:

```
ADDR
-------------------------
123 4th St.
4 Maple Ct.
2167 Greenbrier Blvd.
33 Third St.
One First Drive
1664 1/2 Springhill Ave
2003 Geaux Illini Dr.
```

Other Bracketed Classes

Similar to the [:digit:] class, there are other classes:

- ▼ [:alnum:] matches all numbers and letters (alphanumerics).
- ▼ [:alpha:] matches characters only.
- ▼ [:lower:] matches lowercase characters.
- ▼ [:upper:] matches uppercase characters.
- ▼ [:space:] matches spaces.
- ▼ [:punct:] matches punctuation.
- ▼ [:print:] matches printable characters.
- ▼ [:cntrl:] matches control characters.

These classes may be used the same way the [:digit:] class was used. For example:

```
SELECT addr,
    REGEXP_INSTR(addr,'[[:lower:]]')
FROM addresses
WHERE REGEXP_INSTR(addr,'[[:lower:]]') > 0
```

Gives:

ADDR	REGEXP_INSTR(ADDR,'[[:LOWER:]]')
123 4th St.	6
4 Maple Ct.	4
2167 Greenbrier Blvd.	7
33 Third St.	5
One First Drive	2
1664 1/2 Springhill Ave	11
2003 Geaux Illini Dr.	7

Notice that in each case, the position of the first occurrence of a lowercase letter is returned.

The Alternation Operator

When specifying a pattern, it is often convenient to specify the string using logical "OR." The alternation operator is a single vertical bar: "|". Consider this example:

```
SELECT addr,
    REGEXP_INSTR(addr,'r[ds]|pl')
FROM addresses
WHERE REGEXP_INSTR(addr,'r[ds]|pl') > 0
```

Which gives:

ADDR	REGEXP_INSTR(ADDR,'R[DS]|PL')
4 Maple Ct.	5
33 Third St.	7
One First Drive	7

In this expression, we are asking for either an "r" followed by a "d" or an "s" OR the letter combination "p" followed by an "l".

Repetition Operators — aka "Quantifiers"

REs have operators that will repeat a particular pattern. For example, suppose we first search for vowels in any address.

Recall our current Addresses table:

```
SELECT * FROM addresses
```

Gives:

```
ADDR
-----------------------------
123 4th St.
4 Maple Ct.
2167 Greenbrier Blvd.
33 Third St.
One First Drive
1664 1/2 Springhill Ave
2003 Geaux Illini Dr.
```

Now, to select only addresses that contain vowels we can use this statement:

```
SELECT addr, REGEXP_INSTR(addr,'[aeiou]')
    where_pattern_starts
FROM addresses
WHERE REGEXP_INSTR(addr,'[aeiou]') > 0
```

Gives:

ADDR	WHERE_PATTERN_STARTS
4 Maple Ct.	4
2167 Greenbrier Blvd.	8
33 Third St.	6
One First Drive	3

```
1664 1/2 Springhill Ave                    13
2003 Geaux Illini Dr.                       7
```

Note that the address "123 4th St." is not in the result set because it contains no vowels.

Now, let's look for two consecutive vowels:

```
SELECT addr,
    REGEXP_INSTR(addr,'[aeiou][aeiou]')
    where_pattern_starts
FROM addresses
```

Gives:

```
ADDR                          WHERE_PATTERN_STARTS
----------------------------- ---------------------
2167 Greenbrier Blvd.                     8
2003 Geaux Illini Dr.                     7
```

We can simplify the writing of the latter RE with a repeat operator, which is put in curly brackets {}. Here is an example of repeating the vowel match a second time:

```
SELECT addr,
    REGEXP_INSTR(addr,'[aeiou]{2}') where_pattern_starts
FROM addresses
WHERE REGEXP_INSTR(addr,'[aeiou]{2}') > 0
```

Giving:

```
ADDR                          WHERE_PATTERN_STARTS
----------------------------- ---------------------
2167 Greenbrier Blvd.                     8
2003 Geaux Illini Dr.                     7
```

A quantifier $\{m\}$ matches exactly m repetitions of the preceding RE; e.g., {2} matches exactly two occurrences. Note that there is no match for one occurrence of a vowel because two were specified in this example.

The quantifier may be expressed as a two-part argument {*m,n*} where *m,n* specifies that the match should occur from *m* to *n* times.

Now, suppose we are more specific with our quantifier in that we want matches from two to three times:

```
SELECT addr,
    REGEXP_INSTR(addr,'[aeiou]{2,3}') where_pattern_starts
FROM addresses
WHERE REGEXP_INSTR(addr,'[aeiou]{2,3}') > 0
```

Gives:

```
ADDR                            WHERE_PATTERN_STARTS
------------------------------  --------------------
2167 Greenbrier Blvd.                              8
2003 Geaux Illini Dr.                              7
```

Had we specified from three to five consecutive vowels, we'd get this:

```
SELECT addr,
    REGEXP_INSTR(addr,'[aeiou]{2,3}') where_pattern_starts
FROM addresses
WHERE REGEXP_INSTR(addr,'[aeiou]{3,5}') > 0
```

Gives:

```
ADDR                            WHERE_PATTERN_STARTS
------------------------------  --------------------
2003 Geaux Illini Dr.                              7
```

Another version of the repetition operator would say, "at least *m* times" with {*m,*}:

```
SELECT addr,
    REGEXP_INSTR(addr,'[aeiou]{2,3}')
    where_pattern_starts
FROM addresses
WHERE REGEXP_INSTR(addr,'[aeiou]{3,}') > 0
SQL> /
```

Giving:

```
ADDR                            WHERE_PATTERN_STARTS
-----------------------------   --------------------
2003 Geaux Illini Dr.                              7
```

This match succeeds because there are three vowels in a row in the word "Geaux," and the query asks for at least three consecutive vowels.

More Advanced Quantifier Repeat Operator Metacharacters — *, %, and ?

Suppose we wanted to match a letter, e.g., "e", followed by any number of "e"s later in the expression. First of all, the RE "ee" would match two "e"s in a row, but not "e"s separated by other characters.

```
SELECT addr,
    REGEXP_INSTR(addr,'ee') where_pattern_starts
FROM addresses
WHERE REGEXP_INSTR(addr,'ee') > 0
```

Gives:

```
ADDR                            WHERE_PATTERN_STARTS
-----------------------------   --------------------
2167 Greenbrier Blvd.                              8
```

If we wanted to find a letter and then whatever until there was another of the same letter, we could start with a query like this for "e"s:

```
SELECT addr,
    REGEXP_INSTR(addr,'e.e') where_pattern_starts
FROM addresses
WHERE REGEXP_INSTR(addr,'e.e') > 0
```

Giving:

```
no rows selected
```

The problem here is that we asked for an "e" followed by anything, followed by another "e", and we don't have that configuration in our data. To match any number of things between the same letters we may use one of the repeat operators. The three operators are:

▼ + — which matches one or more repetitions of the preceding RE

▼ * — which matches zero or more repetitions of the preceding RE

▼ ? — which matches zero or one repetition of the preceding RE

Suppose we reconsider our data and ask for "i"s instead of "e"s ("i" followed by any one character, followed by another "i"). Had we asked for "i"s, we get a result because our data has two "i"s separated by some other letter.

```
SELECT addr,
    REGEXP_INSTR(addr,'i.i') where_pattern_starts
FROM addresses
WHERE REGEXP_INSTR(addr,'i.i') > 0
```

Gives:

ADDR	WHERE_PATTERN_STARTS
2003 Geaux Ill**ini** Dr.	15

To further illustrate how these repetition matches work, we will introduce another RE now available in Oracle 10*g*: REGEXP_SUBSTR.

REGEXP_SUBSTR

As with the ordinary SUBSTR, REGEXP_SUBSTR returns part of a string. The complete syntax of REGEXP_SUBSTR is:

```
REGEXP_SUBSTR(String to search, Pattern, [Position,
    [Occurrence, [Return-option, [Parameters]]]])
```

The arguments are the same as for INSTR. For example, consider this query:

```
SELECT REGEXP_SUBSTR('Yababa dababa do','a.a') FROM dual
```

Gives:

```
REG
---
aba
```

Here, we have set up a string ("Yababa dababa do") and returned part of it based on the RE "a.a".

We can repeat the metacharacter using the repeat operators. The pattern "a.a" looks for an "a" followed by anything followed by an "a". If we use a repeat operator after the period, then the pattern looks for a repeated "wildcard." Therefore, the pattern "a.*a" looks for an "a" followed by any character zero or more times (because it's a "*"), followed by another "a". We can see the effect of using our repeat quantifiers with these simple examples:

"*" (match zero or more repetitions):

```
SELECT REGEXP_SUBSTR('Yababa dababa do','a.*a') FROM dual
```

Gives:

```
REGEXP_SUBST
------------
ababa dababa
```

The query matches an "a" followed by anything repeated zero or more times followed by another "a". In this case, the matching occurs from the first "a" to the last.

"+" (match one or more repetitions):

```
SELECT REGEXP_SUBSTR('Yababa dababa do','a.+a') FROM dual
```

Gives:

```
REGEXP_SUBST
------------
ababa dababa
```

Similar to the first example, the use of "+" requires at least one intervening character between the first and last "a".

"?" (match exactly zero or one repetition):

```
SELECT REGEXP_SUBSTR('Yababa dababa do','a.?a') FROM dual
```

Gives:

```
REG
---
aba
```

In the case of "+" and "*" we have examples of *greedy matching* — matching as much of the string as possible to return the result. In the "*" case we are returning a substring based on zero or more characters between the "a"s. In the case of the greedy operator "*" as many characters as possible are matched; the match takes place from the first "a" to the last one.

The same logic is applied to the use of "+" — also greedy and matching from one to as many "a"s as the matching software/algorithm can find.

The "?" repetition metacharacter matches zero or one time and the match is satisfied after finding an "a" followed by something (".") (here a "b"), and then followed by another "a". The "?" repeating metacharacter is said to be non-greedy. When the match is satisfied, the matching process quits.

To see the difference between "*" and "+", consider the next four queries.

Here, we are asking to match an "a" and zero or more "b"s:

```
SELECT REGEXP_SUBSTR('a','ab*') FROM dual
```

Gives:

```
R
-
a
```

Since there are no more "b"s in the target string ("a"), the match succeeds and returns the letter "a".

If we had a series of "b"s immediately following the "a", we would get them all due to our greedy "*":

```
SELECT REGEXP_SUBSTR('abbbb','ab*') FROM dual
```

Gives:

```
REGEX
-----
abbbb
```

If we changed the "*" to "+" we would be insisting on matching at least one "b"; with only a single "a" in a target string we get no result:

```
SELECT REGEXP_SUBSTR('a','ab+') FROM dual
```

Giving:

```
R
-
```

But, if we have succeeding "b"s, we get the same greedy result as with "*":

```
SELECT REGEXP_SUBSTR('abbbb','ab+') FROM dual
```

Giving:

```
REGEX
-----
abbbb
```

In our table of addresses, if we want an "e" followed by any number of other characters and then another "e", we may use each of the repeat operators with these results:

```
SELECT addr,
    REGEXP_SUBSTR(addr,'e.+e'),
    REGEXP_INSTR(addr, 'e.+e') "@"
FROM addresses
```

Giving:

ADDR	REGEXP_SUBSTR(ADDR,'E.+E')	@
123 4th St.		0
4 Maple Ct.		0
2167 Greenbrier Blvd.	eenbrie	8
33 Third St.		0
One First Drive	e First Drive	3

```
1664 1/2 Springhill Ave                                     0
2003 Geaux Illini Dr.                                       0
```

Note the greedy "+" finding one or more things between "e"s; it "stretches" the letters between "e"s as far as possible. Note that the query returned "eenbrie" and not just "ee".

```
SELECT addr,
    REGEXP_SUBSTR(addr,'e.*e')
FROM addresses
```

Gives:

```
ADDR                            REGEXP_SUBSTR(ADDR,'E.*E')            @
------------------------------- ------------------------------- ----------
123 4th St.                                                            0
4 Maple Ct.                                                            0
2167 Greenbrier Blvd.           eenbrie                               8
33 Third St.                                                          0
One First Drive                 e First Drive                         3
1664 1/2 Springhill Ave                                               0
2003 Geaux Illini Dr.                                                 0
```

Again, our greedy "*" finds multiple characters between "e"s. But look what happens if we use the non-greedy "?":

```
SELECT addr,
    REGEXP_SUBSTR(addr,'e.?e')
FROM addresses
```

Gives:

```
ADDR                            REGEXP_SUBSTR(ADDR,'E.?E')
------------------------------- -------------------------------
123 4th St.
4 Maple Ct.
2167 Greenbrier Blvd.                 ee
33 Third St.
One First Drive
```

```
1664 1/2 Springhill Ave
2003 Geaux Illini Dr.
```

In the first two examples, we matched an "e" followed by other characters, then another "e". In the "?" case, we got only two non-null rows returned because "?" is non-greedy.

Empty Strings and the ? Repetition Character

The "?" metacharacter seeks to match zero or one repetition of a pattern. This characteristic works well as long as one expects some match to occur. Consider this example (from the "Introducing Oracle Regular Expressions" white paper):

```
SELECT REGEXP_INSTR('abc','d') FROM dual
```

Gives:

```
REGEXP_INSTR('ABC','D')
-----------------------
                      0
```

We get zero because the match failed. On the other hand, if we include the "?" repetition character, we get this seemingly odd result:

```
SELECT REGEXP_INSTR('abc','d?') FROM dual
```

Gives:

```
REGEXP_INSTR('ABC','D?')
-----------------------
                      1
```

The "?" says to match zero or one time. Since no "d" occurs in the string, then it is matching the empty string in the first position and hence responds accordingly. If we repeat the experiment with *Return-option* 1, we can see that the empty string was matched when using "?":

```
SELECT REGEXP_INSTR('abc','d',1,1,1) FROM dual
```

Gives:

```
REGEXP_INSTR('ABC','D',1,1,1)
-----------------------------
                            0
```

Here, there is no "d" in the string, and therefore the function returns zero, indicating "no 'd'" and there is no confusion. But, if we include the "?" in the argument-enhanced RE, we still get a 1 for the place of the match.

```
REGEXP_INSTR('ABC','D?',1,1,1)
-----------------------------
                            1
```

This latter result indicates that we got a match for the "d?" both before and after 1, indicating we matched the empty string.

REGEXT_REPLACE

We have one other RE function in Oracle 10*g* that is quite useful — REGEXP_REPLACE. There is an analog to the REPLACE function in previous versions of Oracle. An example of the REPLACE function looks like this:

```
SELECT REPLACE('This is a test','t','XYZ') FROM dual
```

Gives:

```
REPLACE('THISISATE
------------------
This is a XYZesXYZ
```

All occurrences of a lowercase "t" are replaced with the string "XYZ". Note that the capital "T" was not replaced as all of these string functions exhibit case sensitivity. Further note that the lengths of the match and replace fields are not required to be equal.

The REGEXP_REPLACE function may have these arguments:

```
REGEXP_INSTR(String to search, Pattern, [Position,
    [Occurrence, [Return-option, [Parameters]]]])
```

These arguments are the same as those for REGEXP_ INSTR. The power of regular expressions for our second argument allows us to edit strings more easily than with the ordinary REPLACE function. For example, if we wanted to replace everything from one lowercase "t" to the next with some field, it would be easily done with REs:

```
SELECT REGEXP_REPLACE('This is a test',
    't.+t','XYZ') FROM dual
```

Gives:

```
REGEXP_REPLAC
-------------
This is a XYZ
```

Grouping

There are times when we would like to treat a pattern as a group. For example, suppose we wanted to find all occurrences of the letter sequence "irs" or "ird". We could, of course, write our regular expression like this:

```
SELECT addr, REGEXP_SUBSTR(addr,'ird|irs')
FROM addresses
```

Giving:

```
ADDR                            REGEXP_SUBSTR(ADDR,'IRD|IRS')
------------------------------  ------------------------------
123 4th St.
4 Maple Ct.
2167 Greenbrier Blvd.
33 Third St.                    ird
One First Drive                 irs
1664 1/2 Springhill Ave
2003 Geaux Illini Dr.
```

Thus we would get a match for any row that contained either "ird" or "irs". Another way to express this request is to group the letters "ir" together by putting them in parentheses and then parenthesizing the suffix using alternation:

```
SELECT addr, REGEXP_SUBSTR(addr,'(ir)(d|s)')
FROM addresses
```

Giving:

```
ADDR                            REGEXP_SUBSTR(ADDR,'(IR)(D|S)'
------------------------------  ------------------------------
123 4th St.
4 Maple Ct.
2167 Greenbrier Blvd.
33 Third St.                    ird
```

```
One First Drive              irs
1664 1/2 Springhill Ave
2003 Geaux Illini Dr.
```

Note that we need to parenthesize both expressions. If we leave the parentheses off of the alternation, like this:

```
SELECT addr, REGEXP_SUBSTR(addr,'(ir)d|s')
FROM addresses
```

We get:

```
ADDR                               REGEXP_SUBSTR(ADDR,'(IR)D|S')
---------------------------------- -----------------------------
123 4th St.
4 Maple Ct.
2167 Greenbrier Blvd.
33 Third St.                       ird
One First Drive                    s
1664 1/2 Springhill Ave
2003 Geaux Illini Dr.
```

This latter example matches either "ird" or "s".

The Backslash (\)

The backslash (\) is another overloaded metacharacter. It is normally used in two contexts. First, it may be used as an "escape character" to literally use a metacharacter in an expression. Second, it may be used as a backreference. The escape character is used in context — it takes on different meanings depending on what follows. Let's first explore the backslash as the escape character.

The Backslash as an Escape Character

If what follows the backslash is a metacharacter, then the intent is to find the literal character. There are times where we would like to recognize a special character in an RE. For example, the dollar sign is a metacharacter that anchors an RE at the end of an expression. Suppose we'd like to change a dollar sign to a blank space. For an RE to recognize a dollar sign literally, we have to "escape it." Consider the following query:

```
SELECT REGEXP_REPLACE('$1,234.56','$',' ') FROM dual
```

Giving:

```
REGEXP_REP
----------
$1,234.56
```

This query "failed" because what was intended was a match for a "$" rather than the use of the "$" as an anchor. To match the "$" in an RE, we use the escape character like this:

```
SELECT REGEXP_REPLACE('$1,234.56','\$',' ') FROM dual
```

Giving:

```
REGEXP_RE
---------
 1,234.56
```

The escape character followed by $ means a literal dollar sign as opposed to a "$" anchor. Other metacharacters may be "escaped" similarly.

Alternative Quoting Mechanism in Oracle 10g

Anyone who has had to deal with quotes in character strings in prior versions of Oracle has had to resort to the "two quotes really means one quote" system. For example,

```
INSERT INTO addresses VALUES ('32 O''Neal Drive')
```

results in this row being added to the Addresses table:

```
ADDR
------------------
32 O'Neal Drive
```

In Oracle 10*g*, there is a new alternative quoting mechanism that uses a "q" as the leading character after the parentheses and allows specification of a "different" sequence to define quotes. For example, in the following we use the curly brackets to define the input string. Here is an example:

```
INSERT INTO addresses VALUES (q'{32 O'Hara Avenue}')
```

which results in the following addition to the Addresses table:

```
ADDR
------------------------------
32 O'Hara Avenue
```

The characters inside the curly brackets are handled literally.

Backreference

The backslash may also be followed by a number. This indicates the RE contains a "backreference," which stores the matched part of an expression in a buffer and then allows the user to write code based on it. As a first example, we can use the backreference in a manner similar to the repeat operator. Consider these two queries:

```
SELECT REGEXP_SUBSTR('Yababa dababa do','(ab)')
FROM dual
```

Giving:

```
RE
--
ab
```

This first query simply returns "ab" when the pattern is matched. If we use the backreference option, the query looks like this:

```
SELECT REGEXP_SUBSTR('Yababa dababa do','(ab)\1')
FROM dual
```

Giving:

```
REGE
----
abab
```

In this query, which gives the same result as:

```
SELECT REGEXP_SUBSTR('Yababa dababa do','(ab){2}') ...
```

the backward slash is used as a backreference when written as "\1". In the version with the repeat operator, {2}, we are explicitly looking for two "ab"s, one after the other. In the backreference version, "\1" says to match the same string as was matched by the *n*th subexpression. There is only one subexpression — the letter sequence "ab". It looks like we're saying "match 'ab' and then look for another occurrence of the same match," but that is not quite right. If there are fewer expressions than the number after the backslash, then the query fails because there are insufficient subexpressions to look for. Therefore, if we tried to find three "ab"s in a row with a query like this:

```
SELECT REGEXP_SUBSTR('Yababa dababa do','ab\2')
FROM dual
```

We'd get an error:

```
SELECT REGEXP_SUBSTR('Yababa dababa do','ab\2')
                                            *
ERROR at line 1:
ORA-12727: invalid back reference in regular expression
```

The error occurs because there are not two subexpressions to search for. If we really wanted to find three "ab"s, we can use the repeat operator. If we changed the repeat operator to {3} as in:

```
SELECT REGEXP_SUBSTR('Yababa dababa do','(ab){3}') ...
```

We would get a null result because there are not three "ab"s one after the other; however, we would not get an error.

For a better example of using backreference, let's suppose we wanted to convert a name in the form "first middle last" into the "last, middle first" format. Consider this command:

```
SELECT REGEXP_REPLACE('Hubert Horatio Hornblower',
    '(.*) (.*) (.*)',
    '\3, \2 \1')
FROM dual   "Reformatted Name"
```

Gives:

```
Reformatted Name
--------------------------
Hornblower, Horatio Hubert
```

The first RE in the REGEXP_REPLACE matches the three character strings separated by spaces: '(.*) (.*) (.*)'. Then, since the RE contains three patterns that are matched, they are referred to by \1, \2, and \3 as backreferences. We can then effect the replacement by choosing to use the backreferenced matches in a different order. "\3" is the last name. We then follow that by a comma and a space, followed by the middle name, "\2", and then the first name, "\1."

References

The Python Library Reference web page, http://docs.python.org/lib/re-syntax.html, is a good page for RE syntax.

Ault, M., Liu, D., Tumma, M., *Oracle Database 10g New Features*, Rampant Tech Press, 2003.

Alice Rischert, "Inside Oracle Database 10*g*: Writing Better SQL Using Regular Expressions," Oracle web page: http://www.oracle.com/technology/oramag/webcolumns/2003/techarticles/rischert_reg exp_pt1.html.

Although written for Perl programming, the web page http://www.felixgers.de/teaching/perl/regular_ expressions.html, is part of an online tutorial but contains a short explanation of REs.

"Introducing Oracle Regular Expressions," an Oracle White Paper, Oracle Corp., Redwood Shores, CA.

Example taken from an online newsletter from Quest Software, Alice Rischert, "Writing Better SQL Using Regular Expressions," available at http://www.quest-pipelines.com/newsletter-v5/0204_A.htm.

www.minmaxplsql.com/downloads/Oracle10g.ppt contains a PowerPoint presentation by Steven Feuerstein entitled, "New PL/SQL Toys in Oracle10*g*," that contains examples of alternative quoting mechanisms (slide 18).

Chapter 8

Collection and OO SQL in Oracle

Collection objects have been available in PL/SQL since Oracle 7. In the O7 version of Oracle, TABLEs (aka INDEX-BY TABLEs) were introduced in PL/SQL. The PL/SQL TABLE is much like the idea that programmers have of an array. In ordinary programming languages like C, Visual BASIC, etc., an array is a collection of memory spaces all of the same type and indexable by some subscript — usually numeric. In PL/SQL there are TABLEs that mimic the functionality of programming arrays; however, in PL/SQL TABLEs, there is flexibility and a connection to SQL with TYPEing with these array-like structures. The use of PL/SQL TYPEing to SQL began in Oracle 8 where SQL programmers could use defined TYPEs in DML expressions.

Oracle provides three types of "collection objects": VARRAYs, nested tables, and associative arrays. As the name implies, "collection objects" are organized collections of things.

Associative Arrays

The associative array is a PL/SQL construct that behaves like an array (although it is called a TABLE or INDEX-BY TABLE). The "associative" part of the object comes from the PL/SQL ability to use non-numeric subscripts. Let's look at a PL/SQL example.

First, suppose that there is a table defined in SQL like this:

```
DESC chemical
```

Which produces a table like this:

Name	Null?	Type
NAME		VARCHAR2(20)
SYMBOL		VARCHAR2(2)

And that:

```
SELECT *
FROM chemical
```

Produces:

NAME	SY
Iron	Fe
Oxygen	O
Beryllium	Be

Then, within a PL/SQL procedure we can create a TABLE that references the Chemical table. Note that in the following procedure, the table is indexed using a binary integer.

```
CREATE OR REPLACE PROCEDURE chem0
AS
CURSOR ccur is SELECT name, symbol FROM chemical;
TYPE chemtab IS TABLE OF chemical.name%type
INDEX BY BINARY INTEGER;
ch chemtab;
i integer := 0;
imax integer;
BEGIN
  FOR j IN ccur LOOP
    i := i + 1;
    ch(i) := j.name;
  END LOOP;
  imax := i;
  i := 0;
  dbms_output.put_line('number of values read: '||imax);
  FOR k IN 1..imax LOOP
    dbms_output.put_line('Chemical ... '||ch(k));
  END LOOP;
END chem0;
exec chem0
number of values read: 3
```

Gives:

```
Chemical ... Iron
Chemical ... Oxygen
Chemical ... Beryllium
```

The key definition in the procedure is this:

```
TYPE chemical_table IS TABLE OF chemical.name%TYPE
    INDEX BY BINARY_INTEGER;
Chems chemical_table;
```

The defined table would be the Chemical table in the database where this INDEX-BY TABLE defines the type to be the same as a column, "names," in the Chemical table. Here, in PL/SQL one could refer to Chems(3), for example, to access the third element of the TABLE once it was loaded. The value of the associative array is its ability to be indexed by non-numeric elements. For example, we could redefine our INDEX-BY TABLE like this:

```
TYPE chemical_table1 IS TABLE OF chemical.name%TYPE
    INDEX BY chemical.symbol%TYPE;
Chems1 chemical_table;
```

Now we can refer to Chems1('Fe') to access our INDEX-BY TABLE. Here is an example:

```
CREATE OR REPLACE PROCEDURE chem1
AS
CURSOR ccur IS SELECT name, symbol FROM chemical;
TYPE chemtab IS TABLE OF chemical.name%type
INDEX BY chemical.symbol%type;
ch chemtab;
i integer := 0;
imax integer;
BEGIN
  FOR j IN ccur LOOP
  /*  i := i + 1;  */
    ch(j.symbol) := j.name;
  END LOOP;
  /* imax := i;
  i := 0;
  dbms_output.put_line('number of values read: '||imax); */
  dbms_output.put_line('Chemical ... '||ch('Fe'));
END chem1;
exec chem1
```

Gives:

```
Chemical ... Iron
```

Associative arrays are not used in SQL, but the other collection types may be used.

As a caveat, collection objects may allow for more efficient SQL (performance wise) in that a join of tables may be avoided; the cost of avoiding the join is non-3NF data, which promotes redundancy. The VARRAY is probably the most used collection object, but we will also look at nested tables. First, we will explore how TYPEs are defined and used in SQL. We will look at object definition based on composite attributes, then VARRAYs, then nested tables.

The OBJECT TYPE — Column Objects

A "column object" is an entity that can be used as a column in an Oracle table. Column objects usually consist of columns defined with predefined types. For example:

```
CREATE TABLE test (one NUMBER(3,0), two VARCHAR2(20))
```

In this table, Test, there are two columns defined with predefined types: column one, defined as a number with three digits and no decimal parts, and column two, defined as a character string of up to 20 characters.

To create a new column type, we define the type first as an object, and then use the defined type in a CREATE TABLE statement. The general syntax for creating a new column type is:

```
Create a column object type (a composite type)
```

For example, to create a column type called address_ obj that consists of street, city, state, and zip, we would type:

```
CREATE OR REPLACE TYPE address_obj as OBJECT
street VARCHAR2(20),
city VARCHAR2(20),
state CHAR(2),
zip CHAR(5))
```

273

It is important to note here that we have created (defined) a "type" as an "object." Our defined "type" is really a "class" in the object-oriented sense. In older programming languages, types are defined and then variables are declared as of a particular defined (or predefined) type. In object-oriented programming, we say that classes are defined and then objects are instantiated for a class. There is more to the sense of an object's class than there is to a variable's type, but in the object-oriented world, the use of the word object is variable — sometimes it really means instantiated "object" and (like here) it refers to the creation of class.

CREATE a TABLE with the Column Type in It

Now that we have created a column object type (a class), we can use the column object in a table creation:

```
CREATE TABLE emp (empno NUMBER(3),
name VARCHAR2(20),
address ADDRESS_OBJ)
```

Here, we have created a table with a class in it — address_obj. We still have not actually created an object, but rather used our class definition to create a table that contains the class.

INSERT Values into a Table with the Column Type in It

When you insert values into a table that contains a column object (a composite type), the format for the insert looks like this:

```
INSERT INTO emp VALUES (101, 'Adam',
ADDRESS_OBJ('1 A St.','Mobile','AL','36608'))
```

Here, the line that contains "ADDRESS_OBJ('1 A ..." uses "ADDRESS_OBJ" as a "constructor." In object-oriented (OO) programming, objects are usually allocated dynamic storage; hence, to use an object one needs to invoke a constructor to instantiate an object of a class (otherwise the object would not exist). In the OO version of Oracle, the use of a constructor to invoke the "OO feature" is also required although the sense of dynamic memory allocation is somewhat disassociated. Here we are instantiating an object in a table using the default constructor (the name of the class).

Display the New Table (SELECT * and SELECT by Column Name)

The use of SELECT * to show all the fields in a table may be used to display the result of some inserted rows. Following is an example of a query that shows the new table after some columns and rows have been inserted in it:

```
SELECT *
FROM emp
```

Which gives:

```
   EMPNO NAME
--------- --------------------
ADDRESS(STREET, CITY, STATE, ZIP)
-------------------------------------------------------------
     101 Adam
ADDRESS_OBJ('1 A St.', 'Mobile', 'AL', '36608')

     102 Baker
ADDRESS_OBJ('2 B St.', 'Pensacola', 'FL', '32504')

     103 Charles
ADDRESS_OBJ('3 C St.', 'Bradenton', 'FL', '34209')
```

Addressing specific columns works as well. Specific columns including the composite are addressed by their name in the result set:

```
SELECT empno, name, address -- you can use discrete attribute
  -- names
FROM emp
```

Gives:

```
   EMPNO NAME
--------- --------------------
ADDRESS(STREET, CITY, STATE,  IP)
-------------------------------------------------------------
     101 Adam
ADDRESS_OBJ('1 A St.', 'Mobile', 'AL', '36608')

     102 Baker
ADDRESS_OBJ('2 B St.', 'Pensacola', 'FL', '32504')

     103 Charles
ADDRESS_OBJ('3 C St.', 'Bradenton', 'FL', '34209')
```

COLUMN Formatting in SELECT

Since the above output looks sloppy, some column formatting is in order:

```
SQL> COLUMN name FORMAT a9
SQL> COLUMN empno FORMAT 999999
SQL> COLUMN address FORMAT a50
SQL> /
```

Now the above query would give:

```
EMPNO NAME      ADDRESS(STREET, CITY, STATE, ZIP)
------- --------- --------------------------------------------------
  101 Adam      ADDRESS_OBJ('1 A St.', 'Mobile', 'AL', '36608')
  102 Baker     ADDRESS_OBJ('2 B St.', 'Pensacola', 'FL', '32504')
  103 Charles   ADDRESS_OBJ('3 C St.', 'Bradenton', 'FL', '34209')
```

Note that here we formatted the entire address field and not the individual attributes of the column objects.

SELECTing Only One Column in the Composite

Fields within the column object may be addressed individually. A query that recalls names and cities in our example might look like this:

```
SELECT name, e.address.city
FROM emp e
```

Giving:

```
NAME      ADDRESS.CITY
--------- --------------------
Adam      Mobile
Baker     Pensacola
Charles   Bradenton
```

You must use a table alias and the qualifier "ADDRESS" with the alias. If the alias is not used, the query will fail with a syntax error.

SELECT with a WHERE Clause

In a WHERE clause, alias and qualifier are also used:

```
SELECT name, e.address.city
FROM emp e
WHERE e.address.state = 'FL'
```

Gives:

```
NAME       ADDRESS.CITY
---------  --------------------
Baker      Pensacola
Charles    Bradenton
```

Using UPDATE with TYPEed Columns

To use UPDATE, the alias must also be used:

```
UPDATE emp SET address.zip = '34210'
  WHERE address.city like 'Brad%'
```

Gives:

```
UPDATE emp set address.zip = '34210'
  WHERE address.city like 'Brad%'
             *
ERROR at line 1:
ORA-00904: invalid column name
```

Now type,

```
UPDATE emp e
SET e.address.zip = '34210'
WHERE e.address.city LIKE 'Brad%'
```

And,

```
SELECT *
FROM emp
```

Gives:

```
EMPNO NAME       ADDRESS(STREET, CITY, STATE, ZIP)
------- --------- ----------------------------------------------------
    101 Adam      ADDRESS_OBJ('1 A St.', 'Mobile', 'AL', '36608')
    102 Baker     ADDRESS_OBJ('2 B St.', 'Pensacola', 'FL', '32504')
    103 Charles   ADDRESS_OBJ('3 C St.', 'Bradenton', 'FL', '34210')
```

Create Row Objects — REF TYPE

What are "row objects"? They are tables containing rows of objects of a defined class that will be referenced using addresses to point to another table.

Why would you want to use "row objects"? The reason is that a table containing row objects is easier to maintain than objects that are embedded into another table. We can create a table of rows of a defined type and then reference the rows in this object table using the REF predicate. The following example illustrates this.

Create a table that contains only the address objects:

```
CREATE TABLE address_table OF ADDRESS_OBJ
```

Note that the syntax of this CREATE TABLE is different from an ordinary CREATE TABLE command in that the keyword OF plus the object type is used.

So far, the newly created table of column objects is empty:

```
SELECT *
FROM address_table
```

Gives:

```
no rows selected
```

Now:

```
DESC address_table
```

Gives:

Name	Null?	Type
STREET		VARCHAR2(20)
CITY		VARCHAR2(20)
STATE		CHAR(2)
ZIP		CHAR(5)

The fact that Address_table contains an object type is hidden; the table and its structure look like an ordinary table when SELECTing and DESCribing.

Loading the "row object" Table

How do we load the Address_table with row objects? One way is to use the existing ADDRESS_OBJ values in some other table (e.g., Emp) like this:

```
INSERT INTO Address_table
SELECT e.address
FROM emp e
```

Actually, the table alias is not necessary in this command, but to be consistent, it is better to use the table alias when it seems that it is required in some statements and not required in others.

Now:

```
SELECT *
FROM address_table
```

Gives:

STREET	CITY	ST	ZIP
1 A St.	Mobile	AL	36608
2 B St.	Pensacola	FL	32504
3 C St.	Bradenton	FL	34210

And Address_table (although it was created using a defined type) functions just like an ordinary table. For example:

```
SELECT city
FROM address_table
```

Gives:

```
CITY
--------------------
Mobile
Pensacola
Bradenton
```

A second way to add data to Address_table is to insert just as one would ordinarily do with a common SQL table:

```
INSERT INTO address_table VALUES ('4 D St.', 'Gulf
  Breeze','FL','32563')
```

Thus:

```
SELECT *
FROM address_table
```

Would give:

```
STREET                CITY                   ST ZIP
--------------------  --------------------   -- -----
1 A St.               Mobile                 AL 33608
2 B St.               Pensacola              FL 32504
3 C St.               Bradenton              FL 34209
4 D St.               Gulf Breeze            FL 32563
```

UPDATE Data in a Table of Row Objects

Updating data in the Address_table table of row objects is also straightforward:

```
UPDATE address_table
SET zip = 32514
WHERE zip = 32504

UPDATE address_table
SET street = '11 A Dr'
WHERE city LIKE 'Mob%'
```

Now:

```
SELECT *
FROM address_table
```

Would give:

STREET	CITY	ST	ZIP
11 A Dr	Mobile	AL	33608
2 B St.	Pensacola	FL	32514
3 C St.	Bradenton	FL	34209
4 D St.	Gulf Breeze	FL	32563

In these examples note that no special syntax is required for inserts or updates.

CREATE a Table that References Our Row Objects

Now, suppose we create a table that references our table of row objects. The syntax is a little different from other ordinary CREATE TABLE commands:

```
CREATE TABLE client (name VARCHAR2(20),
  address REF address_obj scope is address_table)
```

Now, if you type:

```
DESC client
```

You get:

Name	Null?	Type
NAME		VARCHAR2(20)
ADDRESS		REF OF ADDRESS_OBJ

In the CREATE TABLE command, we defined the column address as referencing address_obj, which is contained in an object table, Address_table.

INSERT Values into a Table that Contains Row Objects (TCRO)

How do we get values into this table that contains row objects? One way to begin is to insert into the client table and null the address_obj:

```
INSERT INTO client VALUES ('Jones',null)
```

Now,

```
SELECT *
FROM client
```

Will give:

```
NAME
--------------------
ADDRESS
-------------------------------
Jones
```

UPDATE a Table that Contains Row Objects (TCRO)

Then, having created a row with nulls for address, you can update the client table by referencing the Address_table of row objects using a REF function like this:

```
UPDATE client SET address =
(SELECT REF(aa)
FROM address_table aa
WHERE aa.city LIKE 'Mob%')
WHERE name = 'Jones'
```

In this query, we find an appropriate row in the Address_table by constraining the subquery to some row (here we used aa.city LIKE 'Mob%'). Then, we constrained the UPDATE to the Client table by using a filter (WHERE name = 'Jones') in the outer query.

The inner query must return only one row/value. If the subquery were written so that more than one row were returned, an error would result:

```
UPDATE client set address =
(SELECT REF(aa)
FROM address_table aa
WHERE aa.zip like '3%')
WHERE name = 'Jones'
SQL> /
```

Will give the following error:

```
(SELECT REF(aa)
   *
ERROR at line 2:
ORA-01427: single-row subquery returns more than one row
```

SELECT from the TCRO — Seeing Row Addresses

Now that the Client table has been updated, it may be viewed. If the statement "SELECT * FROM client" is used, only the address of the reference to the Address_ table will be in the result set.

```
SELECT *
FROM client
```

Will give:

```
NAME
--------------------
ADDRESS
---------------------------------------------------------------------
Jones
00002202089036C05DB23C4FDE9B82C00E36D92D0F864BF1821AF245BF97D37D2AC67D
A996
```

DEREF (Dereference) the Row Addresses

If the desired output is the data itself and not the address of the data, we must dereference the reference using the DEREF function:

```
SELECT name, DEREF(address)
FROM client
```

Gives:

```
NAME
--------------------
DEREF(ADDRESS)(STREET, CITY, STATE, ZIP)
------------------------------------------------------------
Jones
ADDRESS_OBJ('1 A St.', 'Mobile', 'AL', '36608')
```

One-step INSERTs into a TCRO

There is another way to insert data into the table. We can use a reference to Address_table in the insert without going through the INSERT-null-UPDATE sequence we introduced in the last section:

```
INSERT INTO client
SELECT 'Walsh', REF(aa)
FROM address_table aa
WHERE zip = '32563'
```

Now,

```
SELECT name, DEREF(address)
FROM client
```

Gives:

```
NAME
--------------------
DEREF(ADDRESS)(STREET, CITY, STATE, ZIP)
------------------------------------------------------------
Jones
ADDRESS_OBJ('11 A Dr', 'Mobile', 'AL', '33608')

Smith
ADDRESS_OBJ('3 C St.', 'Bradenton', 'FL', '34209')
```

```
Kelly
ADDRESS_OBJ('2 B St.', 'Pensacola', 'FL', '32514')

Walsh
ADDRESS_OBJ('4 D St.', 'Gulf Breeze', 'FL', '32563')
```

SELECTing Individual Columns in TCROs

Getting at individual parts of the referenced Address_table is easier than looking at the whole "DEREFed" field. Recall the description of the Client table:

```
DESC client
```

Giving:

```
Name                          Null?    Type
--------------------------- -------- --------------------
NAME                                   VARCHAR2(20)
ADDRESS                                REF OF ADDRESS_OBJ
```

The following query shows that the dereferencing may be done automatically:

```
SELECT c.name, c.address.city
FROM client c
```

Giving:

```
NAME                  ADDRESS.CITY
-------------------- --------------------
Jones                 Mobile
Smith                 Bradenton
Kelly                 Pensacola
Walsh                 Gulf Breeze
```

Note that in the above query, the alias, c, was used for the Client table. A table alias has to be used here. As shown by the following query, you will get an error message if a table alias is not used:

```
SELECT name, address.city
FROM client
```

Gives the following error message:

```
SELECT name, address.city FROM client
              *
ERROR at line 1:
ORA-00904: "ADDRESS"."CITY": invalid identifier
```

Deleting Referenced Rows

What happens if you delete a referenced row in Address_table?

First, let's look at the Address_table once again:

```
SELECT *
FROM address_table
```

Which gives:

STREET	CITY	ST	ZIP
11 A Dr	Mobile	AL	33608
2 B St.	Pensacola	FL	32514
3 C St.	Bradenton	FL	34209
4 D St.	Gulf Breeze	FL	32563

Now delete a row from Address_table:

```
DELETE FROM address_table
WHERE zip = '32563'
```

And now, SELECT from the Client table that contains a reference to the Address_table:

```
SELECT *
FROM client
```

Gives:

```
NAME
--------------------
ADDRESS
-------------------------------------------------------------------------
-----
Jones
0000220208949865D61CEA458686C25DFE27E28A2B1F4DF548022F434BAE5846A01A4C74BB

Smith
0000220208C3F689D219D24EA2A39D418A593968B71F4DF548022F434BAE5846A01A4C74BB

Kelly
00002202080B1E9F84B6EA44C981573524372C49991F4DF548022F434BAE5846A01A4C74BB

Walsh
000022020882FD946C58C940F2B7ECD94C688FD04C1F4DF548022F434BAE5846A01A4C74BB
```

Although the entry in Address_table was deleted, the reference to the deleted row still exists in the Client table. But looking at the dereferenced address shows that the referenced row is deleted:

```
SELECT name, DEREF(address)
FROM client
```

Gives:

```
NAME
--------------------
DEREF(ADDRESS)(STREET, CITY, STATE, ZIP)
------------------------------------------------------------
Jones
ADDRESS_OBJ('11 A Dr', 'Mobile', 'AL', '33608')

Smith
ADDRESS_OBJ('3 C St.', 'Bradenton', 'FL', '34209')

Kelly
ADDRESS_OBJ('2 B St.', 'Pensacola', 'FL', '32514')

Walsh
```

We can, of course, delete the row in the Client table:

```
DELETE FROM client
WHERE name LIKE 'Wa%'
```

The Row Object Table and the VALUE Function

Looking again at a version of the table that contains row objects (TCRO):

```
SELECT *
FROM address_table
```

Gives:

```
STREET                  CITY                  ST ZIP
--------------------    --------------------  -- -----
11 A Dr                 Mobile                AL 36608
22 B Dr                 Pensacola             FL 32504
33 C Dr                 Bradenton             FL 34210
```

There is another way to look at the Address_table (which contains row objects) using the VALUE function:

```
SELECT VALUE(aa)
FROM address_table aa
```

Which gives:

```
VALUE(AA)(STREET, CITY, STATE, ZIP)
---------------------------------------------------------------
ADDRESS_OBJ('11 A Dr', 'Mobile', 'AL', '36608')
ADDRESS_OBJ('22 B Dr', 'Pensacola', 'FL', '32504')
ADDRESS_OBJ('33 C Dr', 'Bradenton', 'FL', '34210')
```

The VALUE function is used to show the values of column objects, keeping all the attributes of the object together.

Creating User-defined Functions for Column Objects

In objected-oriented programming one expects not only to be able to create objects with attributes per the class definition, but also to be able to create functions to handle the attributes. Not only will the class exhibit properties (it will have attributes), but it will also have defined actions (methods) associated with the attributes.

While Oracle provides some aforementioned functions as built-ins (VALUE, REF, DEREF) for object classes, it may be convenient to define functions for a class for some applications. Following is an example of a type creation (a class definition), a table containing the type, and the use of a defined function for the class.

First a type is created as a class containing attributes and a function:

```
CREATE OR REPLACE TYPE aobj AS object (
  state CHAR(2), amt NUMBER(5),
MEMBER FUNCTION mult (times in number) RETURN number,
PRAGMA RESTRICT_REFERENCES(mult, WNDS))
```

Here, we have defined two columns (attributes) — *state* and *amt* (amount) — as well as a MEMBER FUNCTION for our class. The PRAGMA statement is standard Oracle practice and says that the function will not update the database when it is used. The function mult will return the *amt* multiplied by the value of *times*. When creating a TYPE with a MEMBER FUNCTION, the line:

```
MEMBER FUNCTION mult (times in number) RETURN number
```

is called a "function prototype." The word "in" in the parameter list of the function prototype means that the value of times will be input to the function.

The complete definition of the TYPE, like the definition of packages, is called a "specification" or, more appropriately, an "object specification" (a class definition). To complete the definition of the function we have to supply a "type body," much like the package body of a CREATE PACKAGE exercise. Here is the body of the TYPE, aobj, for our example:

```
CREATE OR REPLACE TYPE BODY aobj AS
MEMBER FUNCTION mult (times in number) RETURN number
IS
BEGIN
RETURN times * self.amt;  /* SEE BELOW */
END; /* end of begin */
END; /* end of create body */
```

The TYPE BODY must contain the MEMBER
FUNCTION line exactly as it appears in the specification. If the function needs to be changed, then the
whole sequence of "create-the-type," then "create-the-
type-body" has to be repeated. For packages, the term
"synchronized" is used to describe type-body, type-
specification matching.

Now, suppose we create a table that has an attribute with our newly defined TYPE (that contains a
function) in it:

```
CREATE TABLE aobjtable (arow aobj)
```

Which gives:

```
Table created.
```

Now,

```
DESC aobjtable
```

Gives:

```
Name                            Null?    Type
------------------------------- -------- ---------------------
AROW                                     AOBJ
```

Here, as before, we create a column object, but this
time arow has composite parts and a function as well.

The MEMBER FUNCTION in the TYPE BODY
looks about like any ordinary PL/SQL function except
that the return statement contains the word "self." Self
is necessary because to use an object, the object must
first be instantiated with the default constructor, aobj.
The definition of the "type as object" does not really
create an object *per se*, but rather creates a class that
is used to instantiate objects. To ask Oracle to multiply
some number times a value of *amt* in an object requires
that you first tell Oracle which object you are

referencing. To show how this comes together in a table containing objects, we first created a table (above) that uses our defined class, aobj. We may then insert some values into our table like this (note the use of the constructor aobj):

```
INSERT INTO aobjtable VALUES (aobj('FL',25))
INSERT INTO aobjtable VALUES (aobj('AL',35))
INSERT INTO aobjtable VALUES (aobj('OH',15))
```

To check what we have done, we can use the wildcard SELECT * (SELECT all) like this:

```
SELECT *
FROM aobjtable
```

Which gives:

```
AROW(STATE, AMT)
-----------------------------------------------------------
AOBJ('FL', 25)
AOBJ('AL', 35)
AOBJ('OH', 15)
```

When we reference particular object parts, we must use a table alias and the name of the object as before:

```
SELECT x.arow.state, x.arow.amt
FROM aobjtable x
```

Which gives:

```
AR   AROW.AMT
--   ----------
FL         25
AL         35
OH         15
```

And, to use the function we created, we must also use the table alias in our SELECT as well as the qualifier, arow:

```
SELECT x.arow.state, x.arow.amt, x.arow.mult(2)
FROM aobjtable x
```

This gives:

```
AR    AROW.AMT X.AROW.MULT(2)
--    ---------- ---------------
FL        25              50
AL        35              70
OH        15              30
```

The use of the word "self" in the function definition is now clearer in that when a row is fetched, we must reference the value of *amt* for that row (the row itself). Look at the following:

```
CREATE OR REPLACE TYPE BODY aobj AS
MEMBER FUNCTION mult (times in number) RETURN NUMBER
IS
  BEGIN
    RETURN times * self.amt;
  END; /* end of begin */
END; /* end of create body */
```

Methods have available a special tuple variable SELF, which refers to the "current" tuple. If SELF is used in the definition of the method, then the context must be such that a particular tuple is referred to.[1]

So we must get a row (a tuple) and use the value in that row to make a calculation, and the self refers to the value of the object (as created by the constructor, arow) for that row.

Why the PRAGMA?

---

[1] From the article "Object-Relational Features of Oracle" by J. Ullman.

Note the PRAGMA that says the length method will not modify the database (WNDS = write no database state). This clause is necessary if we are to use length in queries.

In the article, "length" was the name of their function example and "mult" is the name of ours.

VARRAYs

In the last section we saw how to create objects and tables of objects with composite attributes and with and without functions. We will now turn our attention to tables that contain other types of non-atomic columns. In this section, we will create an example that uses a repeating group. The term "repeating group" is from the 1970s when one referred to non-atomic values for some column in what was then called a "not quite flat file." A repeating group, aka an array of values, has a series of values all of the same type. In Oracle this repeating group is called a VARRAY (a variable array).

We will use some built-in methods for the VARRAY construction during this process and then demonstrate how to "write your own" methods for VARRAYs.

Suppose we had some data on a local club (social club, science club, whatever), and suppose that the data looks like this:

```
Club(Name, Address, City, Phone, (Members))
```

where (Members) is a repeating group.

Here is some data in a file/record format:

Club

Name	Address	City	Phone	Members
AL	111 First St.	Mobile	222-2222	Brenda, Richard
FL	222 Second St.	Orlando	333-3333	Gen, John, Steph, JJ

Technically, you cannot call this a table because the term "table" in relational databases refers to a two-dimensional arrangement of atomic data. Since "Members" contains a repeating group it is not atomic.

In relational databases we convert the data in the table to two or more two-dimensional tables — we normalize it. To normalize the above file, we decompose it into two tables — one containing the atomic parts of Club, and the other containing the repeating group with a reference to the key of Club. The normalized version of this small database would look like this:

Club_details

Name	Address	City	Phone
AL	111 First St.	Mobile	222-2222
FL	222 Second St.	Orlando	333-3333

Club_members

Name	Member
AL	Brenda
AL	Richard
FL	Gen
FL	John
FL	Steph
FL	JJ

We assume that Name in the table Club_details is unique and defines a primary key for that table. This assumption demands that further additions to the Club_details table will entail unique Names. The primary key of Club_members is the concatenation of the two columns, Name + Member. Further, the column

Name in Club_members is a foreign key referencing
the primary key, Name, in Club_details.

The focus on this section is not on the traditional
relational database representation, but rather on how
one might create the un-normalized version of the data.

CREATE TYPE for VARRAYs

As with ordinary programming language arrays (like in
C or Visual BASIC), with VARRAYs we can create a
collection of variables all of the same type. The basic
Oracle syntax for the CREATE TYPE statement for a
VARRAY type definition would be:

```
CREATE OR REPLACE TYPE name-of-type IS VARRAY(nn) of type
```

Where *name-of-type* is a valid attribute name, *nn* is the
number of elements (maximum) in the array, and *type*
is the data type of the elements of the array.

An example could look like this:

```
SQL> CREATE OR REPLACE TYPE mem_type IS VARRAY(10) of
  VARCHAR2(15);
  2  /
```

Giving:

```
Type created.
```

(Note the semicolon and slash are used in the
SQL*Plus syntax.)

In ordinary programming we have the ability to
define types that are later used in the declaration of
variables. A *data type* defines the kinds of operations
and the range of values that declared variables of that
type may use and take on. For example, if we defined a
variable to be of type NUMBER(3,0), we expect to be

able to perform the operations of addition, multiplication, etc., and we would define our range of variables to be –999 to 999. In the "mem_type" definition, we are defining our type to be a VARRAY with 10 elements, where each element is a varying character string of up to 15 characters.

CREATE TABLE with a VARRAY

Now that we have created a type, we can use our type in a table declaration similar to the way we used defined column types:

```
CREATE TABLE club (Name VARCHAR2(10),
Address VARCHAR2(20),
City VARCHAR2(20),
Phone VARCHAR2(8),
Members mem_type)
```

Now,

```
DESC club
```

Gives:

Name	Null?	Type
NAME		VARCHAR2(10)
ADDRESS		VARCHAR2(20)
CITY		VARCHAR2(20)
PHONE		VARCHAR2(8)
MEMBERS		MEM_TYPE

Loading a Table with a VARRAY in It — INSERT VALUEs with Constants

A VARRAY is actually more than just a defined type. Oracle's VARRAYs behave like classes in object-oriented programming. Classes are instantiated into objects using constructors. In Oracle's VARRAYs, the constructor defaults to being named the name of the declared type and may be used in an INSERT statement like this:

```
INSERT INTO club VALUES ('AL','111 First St.','Mobile',
'222-2222', mem_type('Brenda','Richard'))
INSERT INTO club VALUES ('FL','222 Second St.','Orlando',
'333-3333', mem_type('Gen','John','Steph','JJ'))
```

The "mem_type('*name*','*name2*',..)" is the constructor part of the statement.

We can then use a rather ordinary statement to access the entire content of Club like this:

```
SELECT *
FROM club
```

Giving:

```
NAME       ADDRESS                CITY              PHONE
--------   --------------------   ---------------   --------
MEMBERS
-----------------------------------------------------------
AL         111 First St.          Mobile            222-2222
MEM_TYPE('Brenda', 'Richard')

FL         222 Second St.         Orlando           333-3333
MEM_TYPE('Gen', 'John', 'Steph', 'JJ')
```

Notice that in the output, the values of the constructed mem_type appear qualified by the name of the type.

Also, we can use column names in the result set like this:

```
SELECT name, city, members
FROM club
```

Giving:

```
NAME        CITY
----------  --------------------
MEMBERS
-----------------------------------------------------
AL          Mobile
MEM_TYPE('Brenda', 'Richard')

FL          Orlando
MEM_TYPE('Gen', 'John', 'Steph', 'JJ')
```

Manipulating the VARRAY

Now the question naturally arises as to how to get at individual elements of the VARRAY. Although all good programmers want to access members of the VARRAY with statements like the below one (e.g., "SELECT c.members(3) FROM club c," to extract the third member from the VARRAY), the direct approach does not work, as shown here:

```
SELECT name, c.members(3)
FROM club c
SQL> /
```

Gives:

```
SELECT name, c.members(3) FROM club c
                 *
ERROR at line 1:
ORA-00904: "C"."MEMBERS": invalid identifier
```

So, how do we get at individual members of the VARRAY members?

You can access VARRAY elements in several ways: by using the TABLE function, by using a VARRAY self-join, by using the THE function, or by using PL/SQL. We will explain each of these ways in the next few sections.

The TABLE Function

The TABLE function can be used to indirectly access data in the VARRAY by using an IN predicate:

```
SELECT name "Clubname"
FROM club
WHERE 'Gen' IN
(SELECT *
    FROM TABLE(club.members))
```

This gives:

```
Clubname
----------
FL
```

To try to help this query by using a table alias inconsistently will cause an error, as shown by:

```
SELECT c.name "Clubname"
FROM club c
WHERE 'Gen' IN
(SELECT *
    FROM TABLE(club.members))
SQL> /
```

This gives:

```
WHERE 'Gen' IN (SELECT * FROM TABLE(club.members))
                                         *
ERROR at line 3:
ORA-00904: "CLUB"."MEMBERS": invalid identifier
```

If aliases are used, they must be used consistently, as shown below:

```
SELECT c.name "Clubname"
FROM club c
WHERE 'Gen' IN
(SELECT *
    FROM TABLE(c.members))
```

Giving:

```
Clubname
----------
FL
```

The subquery in the IN clause generates a virtual table from which values are obtained. The subquery by itself will not generate results:

```
SELECT *
FROM TABLE(club.members)
```

Gives an error message:

```
SELECT * FROM TABLE(club.members)
                        *
ERROR at line 1:
ORA-00904: "CLUB"."MEMBERS": invalid identifier
```

The VARRAY Self-join

A statement can be created that joins the values of the virtual table (created with the TABLE function) to the rest of the values in the table like this:

```
SELECT c.name, c.address, p.column_value
FROM club c, TABLE(c.members) p
```

Giving:

NAME	ADDRESS	COLUMN_VALUE
AL	111 First St.	Brenda
AL	111 First St.	Richard
FL	222 Second St.	Gen
FL	222 Second St.	John
FL	222 Second St.	Steph
FL	222 Second St.	JJ

Column_value is a built-in function/pseudo-variable that is held over from the DBMS_SQL package, which allowed programmers some shortcuts in PL/SQL. The self-join may be used in more complicated SQL as well as the example we just offered:

```
SELECT c.name, p.column_value, COUNT(p.column_value)
FROM club c, TABLE(c.members) p
-- WHERE c.name = 'AL'
GROUP by c.name, p.column_value
```

Giving:

```
NAME         COLUMN_VALUE      COUNT(P.COLUMN_VALUE)
----------   ---------------   ---------------------
AL           Brenda                              1
AL           Richard                             1
FL           JJ                                  1
FL           Gen                                 1
FL           John                                1
FL           Steph                               1
```

The THE and VALUE Functions

We can access all of the elements of the VARRAY simply by:

```
SELECT members
FROM club
WHERE name = 'FL'
```

Giving:

```
MEMBERS
------------------------------------------------------------
MEM_TYPE('Gen', 'John', 'Steph', 'JJ')
```

Extracting individual members of a VARRAY may be accomplished using two other functions — THE and VALUE:

```
SELECT VALUE(x) FROM
THE(SELECT c.members FROM club c
WHERE c.name = 'FL') x
WHERE VALUE(x) is not null
```

Giving:

```
VALUE(X)
----------------
Gen
John
Steph
JJ
```

The THE function generates a virtual table, which is displayed using the VALUE function for the elements. Using the COLUMN_VALUE function instead of the VALUE function will also work:

```
SELECT COLUMN_VALUE val FROM
THE(SELECT c.members FROM club c
WHERE c.name = 'FL') x
WHERE COLUMN_VALUE IS NOT NULL
```

Giving:

```
VAL
----------------
Gen
John
Steph
JJ
```

One way to make the "members" behave like an array is first to include the row number in the result set like this:

```
SELECT n, val
FROM
(SELECT rownum n, COLUMN_VALUE val FROM
THE(SELECT c.members FROM club c
WHERE c.name = 'FL') x
WHERE COLUMN_VALUE IS NOT NULL)
```

Which gives:

```
N VAL
---------- ----------------
       1 Gen
       2 John
       3 Steph
       4 JJ
```

Then, the individual array element can be extracted with a WHERE filter:

```
SELECT n, val
FROM
(SELECT rownum n, COLUMN_VALUE val FROM
THE(SELECT c.members FROM club c
WHERE c.name = 'FL') x
WHERE COLUMN_VALUE IS NOT NULL)
WHERE n - 3
```

Giving:

```
 N VAL
---------- ----------------
       3 Steph
```

The CAST Function

The THE function is one way to get individual members from the VARRAY.

The CAST function is used to convert collection types to ordinary, common types in Oracle. CAST may be used in a SELECT to explicitly define that a collection type is being converted:

```
SELECT COLUMN_VALUE FROM
THE(SELECT CAST(c.members as mem_type)
FROM club c
WHERE c.name = 'FL')
```

Which gives:

```
COLUMN_VALUE
----------------
Gen
John
Steph
JJ
```

The CAST function converts an object type (such as a VARRAY) into a common type that can be queried. As we saw in the discussion of the THE function in the previous section, Oracle 10*g* automatically converts the VARRAY without the CAST.

The CAST function may also be used with the MULTISET function to perform DML operations on VARRAYs. MULTISET is the "reverse" of CAST in that MULTISET converts a nonobject set of data to an object set. Suppose we create a new table of names:

```
CREATE TABLE newnames (n varchar2(20))
```

Which gives:

```
Table created.
```

Now:

```
INSERT INTO newnames VALUES ('Beryl')
INSERT INTO newnames VALUES ('Fred')
```

And:

```
SELECT *
FROM newnames
```

Gives:

```
N
--------------------
Beryl
Fred
```

Now suppose we use our new table of names (Newnames) to insert values into our old Club table using the INSERT and UPDATE technique:

```
DESC club
```

Gives:

Name	Null?	Type
NAME		VARCHAR2(10)
ADDRESS		VARCHAR2(20)
CITY		VARCHAR2(20)
PHONE		VARCHAR2(8)
MEMBERS		MEM_TYPE

Now:

```
INSERT INTO club VALUES ('VA',null,null,null,null)
```

We can now use CAST and MULTISET together to add data via an UPDATE to our Club table that contains a VARRAY:

```
UPDATE club SET members =
CAST(MULTISET(SELECT n FROM newnames) as mem_type)
WHERE name = 'VA'
```

Here, we are reverse-casting the collection of names (*n*) from the table Newnames using MULTISET, and then we're CASTing these names into our Club table as the expected type.

Also, we can insert values into our Club table by casting a MULTISET version of Newnames directly:

```
INSERT INTO club VALUES('MD',null, null,null,
CAST(MULTISET(SELECT * FROM newnames) as mem_type))
```

Using PL/SQL to Create Functions to Access Elements

Functions may be created in PL/SQL to manipulate VARRAYs. The functions may be placed in the object definition or they may be external (created outside of the object). Here is an example of an external function that allows us to extract individual elements from a VARRAY:

```
CREATE OR REPLACE FUNCTION vs
(vlist club.members%type, sub integer)
RETURN VARCHAR2
IS
BEGIN
  IF sub <= vlist.last THEN
    RETURN vlist(sub);
  END IF;
    RETURN NULL;
END vs;
```

The function uses a built-in function, LAST, to determine whether the subscript, sub, is less than the last subscript for "members."

```
SELECT vs(members,2)
FROM club
```

Gives:

```
VS(MEMBERS,2)
-------------------------------------------------------
Richard
John
```

This approach is quite interesting because we are doing in PL/SQL what we were not allowed to do in SQL — access an individual member of an array. Here is a permutation of the above query:

```
SELECT DECODE(vs(members,3),null,'No members',vs(members,3))
FROM club
WHERE name IN ('FL', 'MD')
```

Giving:

```
DECODE(VS(MEMBERS,3),NULL,'NOMEMBERS',VS(MEMBERS,3))
--------------------------------------------------------------
No members
Steph
```

This function works well as long as there are some members in the collection. As we shall see, we have to ensure that members exist before applying this function. As we have already noted, some built-in functions exist for use with collections; however, not all functions apply to VARRAYs. The function names are: EXISTS, COUNT, LIMIT, FIRST and LAST, PRIOR and NEXT, EXTEND, TRIM, and DELETE.

DELETE does not apply to VARRAYs because all VARRAYs must be dense and removing individual elements is not allowed.

EXISTS and LAST

Suppose we add a row with no members to the Club table:

```
INSERT INTO club values ('NY','55 Fifth Ave.','NYC',
  '999-9999',null)
```

Now:

```
SELECT *
FROM club
```

Will give:

```
NAME        ADDRESS              CITY             PHONE
----------  --------------------  ----------------  --------
MEMBERS
------------------------------------------------------------
NY          55 Fifth Ave.         NYC              999-9999

VA
MEM_TYPE('Beryl', 'Fred')

MD
MEM_TYPE('Beryl', 'Fred')

AL          111 First St.         Mobile           222-2222
MEM_TYPE('Brenda', 'Richard')

FL          222 Second St.        Orlando          333-3333
MEM_TYPE('Gen', 'John', 'Steph', 'JJ')
```

If we use our function from above with this enhanced data and with no WHERE filter, the query fails:

```
SELECT vs(members,3) FROM club
```

Gives an error message:

```
SELECT vs(members,3) FROM club
       *
ERROR at line 1:
ORA-06531: Reference to uninitialized collection
ORA-06512: at "RICHARD.VS", line 6
```

The reason that the query fails is because we now have a row with no member data in it (the NY club).

We can use the EXISTS built-in function to correct this problem. EXISTS returns a Boolean that acknowledges the presence (T) or absence (F) of a member of a VARRAY.

```
CREATE OR REPLACE FUNCTION vs
(vlist club.members%type, sub integer)
RETURN VARCHAR2
IS
BEGIN
  IF vlist.exists(1) THEN
    IF sub <= vlist.last THEN
      RETURN vlist(sub);
    ELSE
      RETURN 'Less than '||sub||' members';
    END IF;
  ELSE
    RETURN 'No members';
  END IF;
END vs;
```

The EXISTS function requires an argument to tell which element of the VARRAY is referred to. In the above function we are saying in the coded if-statement that if there is no first element, then return "No members." If a first member of the array is present, then the array is not null and we can look for whichever member is sought (per the value of sub). If the value of sub is less than the value of the last subscript, then the return of "'Less than '||sub||' members'" is effected.

```
SELECT c.name, vs(members,3) member_name
FROM club c
```

Gives:

NAME	MEMBER_NAME
NY	No members
VA	Less than 3 members
MD	Less than 3 members
AL	Less than 3 members
FL	Steph

We can also create a procedure to handle access to the VARRAY. Following is a procedure that uses EXISTS and LAST in a fashion similar to the function. We will access Club, taking into account the null values in one of the members (i.e., members in this case is uninitialized):

```
CREATE OR REPLACE PROCEDURES vs3
(sub integer)
IS
CURSOR vcur IS
  SELECT name, members FROM club;
x varchar2(30);
BEGIN
  FOR j IN vcur LOOP
    x := j.name||' No Members';
    IF j.members.exists(1) THEN -- exists
    IF sub <= j.members.last THEN -- last
      x := j.name||' '||j.members(sub);
        -- access array element
    ELSE
      x := j.name||' Less than '||sub||' members';
    END IF;
    END IF;
    dbms_output.put_line(x);
  END LOOP;
END vs3;
```

Now:

```
exec vs3(1)
```

Gives:

```
NY No Members
VA Beryl
MD Beryl
AL Brenda
FL Gen
```

And,

```
exec vs3(2)
```

Gives:

```
NY No Members
VA Fred
MD Fred
AL Richard
FL John
```

And,

```
exec vs3(3)
```

Gives:

```
NY No Members
VA Less than 3 members
MD Less than 3 members
AL Less than 3 members
FL Steph
```

And,

```
exec vs3(4)
```

Gives:

```
NY No Members
VA Less than 4 members
MD Less than 4 members
AL Less than 4 members
FL JJ
```

The COUNT Function

The COUNT function returns the number of members in a VARRAY. As with PL/SQL that uses other VARRAY functions (above), if the possibility that members could be null is ignored, then the following procedure will give an error:

```
CREATE OR REPLACE PROCEDURE vartest
/* cr_vartest - program to test access of VARRAYs */
/* June 24, 2005 - R. Earp  */
IS
CURSOR fcur IS
  SELECT members FROM club;
BEGIN
  FOR j IN fcur LOOP
    dbms_output.put_list(j.members.count);
  END LOOP;  /* end for j in fcur loop */
END vartest;

SQL> exec vartest
BEGIN vartest; END;
```

Will give the following error message:

```
*
ERROR at line 1:
ORA-06531: Reference to uninitialized collection
ORA-06512: at "xxxxxxx.VARTEST", line 9
ORA-06512: at line 1
```

Therefore, the EXISTS clause must be added:

```
CREATE OR REPLACE PROCEDURE vartest
/* cr_vartest - program to test access of VARRAYs */
/* June 24, 2005 - R. Earp  */
IS
CURSOR fcur IS
  SELECT members FROM club;
BEGIN
  FOR j IN fcur LOOP
    IF j.members.exists(1) THEN
      dbms_output.put_line(j.name||' has '||
          j.members.count||' members');
```

```
      END IF;
    END LOOP;  /* end for j in fcur loop */
END vartest;
```

Now:

```
SQL> exec vartest
```

Will give:

```
VA has 2 members
MD has 2 members
AL has 2 members
FL has 4 members
```

LAST and COUNT give the same result for VARRAYs.

FIRST and LAST Used in a Loop

The functions FIRST and LAST may be used to set the upper and lower limit of a for-loop to access members of the array one at a time in PL/SQL.

```
CREATE OR REPLACE PROCEDURE vartest1
/* vartest1 - program to test access of VARRAYs */
/* July 6, 2005 - R. Earp */
IS
CURSOR fcur IS
  SELECT name, members FROM club;
BEGIN
  FOR j IN fcur LOOP
    dbms_output.put_line('For the '||j.name||' club ...');
      IF j.members.exists(1) THEN
        FOR k IN j.members.first..j.members.last LOOP
          dbms_output.put_line('** '||j.members(k));
        END LOOP;
      ELSE
        dbms_output.put_line('**  There are no
            members on file');
      END IF;
```

```
  END LOOP;  /* end for j in fcur loop */
END vartest1;
```

Again, note the necessity of the "IF j.members.exists(1)" clause.

Now:

```
exec vartest1
```

Will give:

```
For the NY club ...
**  There are no members on file
For the VA club ...
**  Beryl
**  Fred
For the MD club ...
**  Beryl
**  Fred
For the AL club ...
**  Brenda
**  Richard
For the FL club ...
**  Gen
**  John
**  Steph
**  JJ
```

Creating User-defined Functions for VARRAYs

As we have seen before, MEMBER FUNCTIONs can be added to an object creation. In this example we will use a MEMBER FUNCTION to find a given element of our VARRAY:

```
CREATE OR REPLACE TYPE members_type2_obj as object
  (members_type2 mem_type,
MEMBER FUNCTION member_function (sub integer) RETURN
    varchar2)
```

Also as we saw before, creating a TYPE with a member function requires us to create a TYPE BODY to define the function's action. The action here is to return a value from the VARRAY given its element number:

```
CREATE OR REPLACE TYPE BODY members_type2_obj AS
  MEMBER FUNCTION member_function (sub integer) RETURN
      varchar2
  IS
  BEGIN
    RETURN members_type2(sub);
  END member_function;
END; /* end of body definition */
```

Now that we have defined a TYPE and a TYPE BODY, we can create a table containing a column of our defined type:

```
CREATE TABLE club2 (location VARCHAR2(20),
    members members_type2_obj)
```

Refer to the CREATE TYPE code at the top of the previous page: Since "members_type2" uses TYPE "mem_type", we recall the description of mem_type for the VARRAY:

```
DESC mem_type
```

is mem_type VARRAY(10) OF VARCHAR2(15).

Here is the description of the table, Club2, that we just created:

```
DESC club2
```

Giving:

Name	Null?	Type
LOCATION		VARCHAR2(20)
MEMBERS		MEMBERS_TYPE2_OBJ

Now that we have a table, we insert values into it:

```
INSERT INTO club2 (location, members) VALUES ('MS',
  members_type2_obj(mem_type('Alice','Brenda','Beryl')))
INSERT INTO club2 (location, members) VALUES
  ('GA',members_type2_obj(mem_type('MJ','Daphne')))
```

Notice in the INSERT that we have to use the constructor for the TYPE in Club2, which is members_type2_obj, and members_type2_obj in turn requires we use the constructor of the defined TYPE it contains, mem_type.

```
SELECT *
FROM club2
```

Gives:

```
LOCATION
--------------------
MEMBERS(MEMBERS_TYPE2)
-----------------------------------------------------------
MS
MEMBERS_TYPE2_OBJ(MEM_TYPE('Alice', 'Brenda', 'Beryl'))

GA
MEMBERS_TYPE2_OBJ(MEM_TYPE('MJ', 'Daphne'))
```

SELECTing individual columns without the "element-getter" function works fine:

```
SELECT c.location, c.members
FROM club2 c
```

Gives:

```
LOCATION
--------------------
MEMBERS(MEMBERS_TYPE2)
-----------------------------------------------------------
MS
MEMBERS_TYPE2_OBJ(MEM_TYPE('Alice', 'Brenda', 'Beryl'))

GA
MEMBERS_TYPE2_OBJ(MEM_TYPE('MJ', 'Daphne'))
```

But we may now use a more straightforward command directly in SQL to get a specific member of the VARRAY:

```
SELECT c.location, c.members.member_function(2) third_member
FROM club2 c
```

Giving:

```
LOCATION              THIRD_MEMBER
--------------------  --------------------
MS                    Brenda
GA                    Daphne
```

Now for a problem. Consider this query:

```
SELECT c.location, c.members.member_function(3) third_member
FROM club2 c
SQL> /
```

which gives the following error message:

```
ERROR:
ORA-06533: Subscript beyond count
ORA-06512: at "RICHARD.MEMBERS_TYPE2_OBJ", line 5
ORA-06512: at line 1
```

This error occurs because we have not dealt with the possibility of "no element" for a particular subscript. Therefore, we need to modify the member_function function within mem_type2 to return null if the requested subscript is greater than the number of items in the array. It is the programmer's responsibility to ensure that errors like the above do not occur.

```
CREATE OR REPLACE TYPE BODY members_type2_obj AS
  MEMBER FUNCTION member_function (sub integer) RETURN
      varchar2
  IS
  BEGIN
    IF sub <= members_type2.last THEN
      RETURN members_type2(sub);
    ELSE
      RETURN 'Not that many members';
    END IF;
  END member_function;
END; /* end of body definition */
```

To verify that our error-proofing worked, we rerun the error-prone query, and we get element 2 or a message:

```
SELECT c.location,
  c.members.member_function(3) third_member
FROM club2 c
```

Gives:

```
LOCATION              THIRD_MEMBER
-------------------   --------------------------------
MS                    Beryl
GA                    Not that many members
```

Nested Tables

Having created objects (classes) of composite types and VARRAYs, we will now create tables that contain other tables — *nested tables*. Many of the same principles and syntax we have seen earlier will apply. Suppose we want to create tabular information in a row and treat the tabular information as we would treat a column. For example, suppose we have a table of employees: EMP (empno, ename, ejob), keyed on employee-number (empno).

Now suppose we wanted to add dependents to the EMP table. In a relational database we would not do this because relational theory demands that we normalize. In a relational database, a dependent table would be created and a foreign key would be placed in it referencing the appropriate employee. Look at the following table definitions:

```
EMP (empno, ename, ejob)
DEPENDENT (dname, dgender, dbday, EMP.empno)
```

In the relational case, the concatenated dname + EMP.empno would form the key of the DEPENDENT. To retrieve dependent information, an equi-join of EMP and DEPENDENT would occur on EMP.empno and DEPENDENT.EMP.empno.

But suppose that normalization is less interesting to the user than the ability to retrieve dependent information directly from the EMP table without resorting to a join. There might be several reasons for this. For example, perceived performance enhancement could be deemed more important than the ability to query or handle dependents directly and independently. Such a dependent table may be so small that another normalized table to hold its contents might be undesirable. Some users might want to take advantage of the privacy of the embedded dependent table. (It is granted that most relational database folks will find this paragraph distasteful.)

This non-normalized table could be realized in Oracle 8 and later and would be referred to as a nested table. To create the nested table, we first create a class of dependents:

```
CREATE TYPE dependent_object AS OBJECT
  (dname VARCHAR2(20), dgender CHAR(1), dbday DATE)
```

Then, a table framework is created for our dependents:

```
CREATE TYPE dependent_object_table AS TABLE OF dependent_object
```

Now, we can create a table of employees with a nested dependent object:

```
CREATE TABLE emp (empno NUMBER(5),
  ename VARCHAR2(20),
  ejob VARCHAR2(20),
  dep_in_emp dependent_object_table)
NESTED TABLE dep_in_emp STORE AS dep_emp_table
```

Note that we:

1. Define the dependent_object object.

2. Use dependent_object in a "CREATE TYPE .. as table of" statement creating the dependent_object_table.

3. Create the host table, EMP, which contains the nested table. Also, in EMP, we have a column name for our nested table, dep_in_emp, and we have an internal name for the nested table, dep_emp_table.

```
DESC emp
```

Gives:

Name	Null?	Type
EMPNO		NUMBER(5)
ENAME		VARCHAR2(20)
EJOB		VARCHAR2(20)
DEP_IN_EMP		DEPENDENT_OBJECT_TABLE

```
DESC dependent_object_table
```

Gives:

dependent_object_table TABLE OF DEPENDENT_OBJECT

Name	Null?	Type
DNAME		VARCHAR2(20)
DGENDER		CHAR(1)
DBDAY		DATE

Now insert the following into EMP:

```
INSERT INTO emp VALUES(100, 'Smith', 'Programmer',
  dependent_object_table(dependent_object('David',
  'M',to_date('10/10/1997','dd/mm/yyyy')),
  dependent_object('Katie','F',to_date('22/12/2002',
```

```
  'dd/mm/yyyy')), dependent_object('Chrissy','F',
  to_date('31/5/2004','dd/mm/yyyy'))
))
INSERT INTO emp VALUES(100, 'Jones', 'Engineer',
  dependent_object_table(dependent_object('Lindsey','F',
  to_date('10/5/1997','dd/mm/yyyy')),dependent_object
  ('Chloe','F',to_date('22/12/2002','dd/mm/yyyy'))
))
```

And,

```
SELECT *
FROM emp
```

Gives:

```
    EMPNO ENAME                    EJOB
---------- -------------------- --------------------
DEP_IN_EMP(DNAME, DGENDER, DBDAY)
-------------------------------------------------------------
      100 Smith                Programmer
DEPENDENT_OBJECT_TABLE(DEPENDENT_OBJECT('David', 'M',
'10-OCT-97'), DEPENDENT_OBJECT('Katie', 'F', '22-DEC-02'),
DEPENDENT_OBJECT('Chrissy', 'F', '31-MAY-04'))

      100 Jones                Engineer
DEPENDENT_OBJECT_TABLE(DEPENDENT_OBJECT('Lindsey', 'F',
'10-MAY-97'), DEPENDENT_OBJECT('Chloe', 'F', '22-DEC-02'))
```

Unlike what we did before, the content of the table of objects cannot be accessed directly:

```
SELECT * FROM dependent_object_table
```

Gives the following error message:

```
SELECT * FROM dependent_object_table
              *
ERROR at line 1:
ORA-04044: procedure, function, package, or type is not allowed
here
```

And,

```
SELECT * FROM dep_emp_table
```

Gives the following error message:

```
SELECT * FROM dep_emp_table
              *
ERROR at line 1:
ORA-22812: cannot reference nested table column's storage
table.
```

We can use the TABLE function and access the nested data through table EMP:

```
SELECT VALUE(x) FROM
TABLE(SELECT dep_in_emp
FROM emp
WHERE ename = 'Jones') x
```

Giving:

```
VALUE(X)(DNAME, DGENDER, DBDAY)
-----------------------------------------------
DEPENDENT_OBJECT('Lindsey', 'F', '10-MAY-97')
DEPENDENT_OBJECT('Chloe', 'F', '22-DEC-02')
```

In this case, we are referring to a single row of the EMP table. We have to make the TABLE subquery refer to only one row. If we leave off the filter in the subquery, we are asking Oracle to return all the nested tables from EMP, and the TABLE function does not work like that.

```
SELECT VALUE(x) FROM
TABLE(SELECT dep_in_emp
FROM emp
-- WHERE ename = 'Jones'
) x
SQL> /
```

Gives the following error message:

```
table(SELECT dep_in_emp FROM emp
            *
ERROR at line 2:
ORA-01427: single-row subquery returns more than one row
```

Also, substituting COLUMN_VALUE for the aliased VALUE function will not work:

```
SELECT COLUMN_VALUE -- value(x)
FROM
table(SELECT dep_in_emp FROM emp
WHERE ename = 'Jones'
) x
SQL> /
```

Gives the following error message:

```
SELECT COLUMN_VALUE -- value(x)
       *
ERROR at line 1:
ORA-00904: "COLUMN_VALUE": invalid identifier
```

We can get individual values from the nested table like this:

```
SELECT VALUE(x).dname FROM
TABLE(SELECT dep_in_emp FROM emp
WHERE ename = 'Jones') x
```

Giving:

```
VALUE(X).DNAME
--------------------
Lindsey
Chloe
```

As before, we can use the aliased base table, EMP, in the WHERE clause:

```
SELECT *
FROM emp e
WHERE 'Chloe' IN
(SELECT dname
FROM TABLE(e.dep_in_emp))
```

Giving:

```
     EMPNO ENAME                     EJOB
---------- -------------------- --------------------
DEP_IN_EMP(DNAME, DGENDER, DBDAY)
------------------------------------------------------------
       100 Jones                     Engineer
DEPENDENT_OBJECT_TABLE(DEPENDENT_OBJECT('Lindsey', 'F',
'10-MAY-97'), DEPENDENT_OBJECT('Chloe', 'F', '22-DEC-02'))
```

Here, note the use of the alias from the outer query in the inner one. Of course, subsets of columns may be had in this same fashion (you don't have to use "SELECT * ...").

Further, a Cartesian-like join is also possible between the parent table and the virtual table created with the TABLE function:

```
SELECT *
FROM emp e, TABLE(e.dep_in_emp)
```

Giving:

```
    EMPNO ENAME                    EJOB
---------- -------------------- --------------------
DEP_IN_EMP(DNAME, DGENDER, DBDAY)
-------------------------------------------------------------
DNAME                 D DBDAY
-------------------- - ---------
       100 Smith                 Programmer
DEPENDENT_OBJECT_TABLE(DEPENDENT_OBJECT('David', 'M',
'10-OCT-97'), DEPENDENT_OBJECT('Katie', 'F', '22-DEC-02'),
DEPENDENT_OBJECT('Chrissy', 'F', '31-MAY-04'))
David                 M 10-OCT-97

       100 Smith                 Programmer
DEPENDENT_OBJECT_TABLE(DEPENDENT_OBJECT('David', 'M',
'10-OCT-97'), DEPENDENT_OBJECT('Katie', 'F', '22-DEC-02'),
DEPENDENT_OBJECT('Chrissy', 'F', '31-MAY-04'))
Katie                 F 22-DEC-02

       100 Smith                 Programmer
DEPENDENT_OBJECT_TABLE(DEPENDENT_OBJECT('David', 'M',
'10-OCT-97'), DEPENDENT_OBJECT('Katie', 'F', '22-DEC-02'),
DEPENDENT_OBJECT('Chrissy', 'F', '31-MAY-04'))
Chrissy               F 31-MAY-04

       100 Jones                 Engineer
DEPENDENT_OBJECT_TABLE(DEPENDENT_OBJECT('Lindsey', 'F',
'10-MAY-97'), DEPENDENT_OBJECT('Chloe', 'F', '22-DEC-02'))
Lindsey               F 10-MAY-97

       100 Jones                 Engineer
DEPENDENT_OBJECT_TABLE(DEPENDENT_OBJECT('Lindsey', 'F',
'10-MAY-97'), DEPENDENT_OBJECT('Chloe', 'F', '22-DEC-02'))
Chloe                 F 22-DEC-02
```

Here, since there is no column in the dep_in_emp part of the EMP table, there is no equi-join possibility — the dependents all belong to that employee. So, when a row is retrieved from EMP, the statement brings along

331

all of the dependents with the employee. Since we have joined a real table with a virtual table using the TABLE function, we can then filter based on the contents of either:

```
SELECT *
FROM emp e, TABLE(e.dep_in_emp) f
WHERE e.ename = 'Smith'
```

Giving:

```
    EMPNO ENAME                      EJOB
---------- -------------------- --------------------
DEP_IN_EMP(DNAME, DGENDER, DBDAY)
--------------------------------------------------------------
DNAME                D DBDAY
-------------------- - ---------
       100 Smith                     Programmer
DEPENDENT_OBJECT_TABLE(DEPENDENT_OBJECT('David', 'M',
'10-OCT-97'), DEPENDENT_OBJECT('Katie', 'F', '22-DEC-02'),
DEPENDENT_OBJECT('Chrissy', 'F', '31-MAY-04'))
David                M 10-OCT-97

       100 Smith                     Programmer
DEPENDENT_OBJECT_TABLE(DEPENDENT_OBJECT('David', 'M',
'10-OCT-97'), DEPENDENT_OBJECT('Katie', 'F', '22-DEC-02'),
DEPENDENT_OBJECT('Chrissy', 'F', '31-MAY-04'))
Katie                F 22-DEC-02

       100 Smith                     Programmer
DEPENDENT_OBJECT_TABLE(DEPENDENT_OBJECT('David', 'M',
'10-OCT-97'), DEPENDENT_OBJECT('Katie', 'F', '22-DEC-02'),
DEPENDENT_OBJECT('Chrissy', 'F', '31-MAY-04'))
Chrissy              F 31-MAY-04
```

And,

```
SELECT *
FROM emp e, TABLE(e.dep_in_emp) f
WHERE f.dname = 'Katie'
```

Gives:

```
     EMPNO ENAME                  EJOB
---------- -------------------- --------------------
DEP_IN_EMP(DNAME, DGENDER, DBDAY)
------------------------------------------------------------
DNAME                 D DBDAY
-------------------- - ---------
       100 Smith                 Programmer
DEPENDENT_OBJECT_TABLE(DEPENDENT_OBJECT('David', 'M',
'10-OCT-97'), DEPENDENT_OBJECT('Katie', 'F', '22-DEC-02'),
DEPENDENT_OBJECT('Chrissy', 'F', '31-MAY-04'))
Katie                 F 22-DEC-02
```

We may UPDATE, DELETE, and INSERT into our nested table as we introduced earlier:

```
UPDATE TABLE(SELECT e.dep_in_emp FROM emp e
WHERE e.ename = 'Smith') g
SET g.dname = 'Daphne'
WHERE g.dname = 'David'
```

Now,

```
SELECT *
FROM emp e, TABLE(e.dep_in_emp) f
WHERE f.dname = 'Daphne'
```

Gives:

```
     EMPNO ENAME                  EJOB
---------- -------------------- --------------------
DEP_IN_EMP(DNAME, DGENDER, DBDAY)
------------------------------------------------------------
DNAME                 D DBDAY
-------------------- - ---------
       100 Smith                 Programmer
DEPENDENT_OBJECT_TABLE(DEPENDENT_OBJECT('Daphne', 'M',
'10-OCT-97'), DEPENDENT_OBJECT('Katie', 'F', '22-DEC-02'),
DEPENDENT_OBJECT('Chrissy', 'F', '31-MAY-04'))
Daphne                M 10-OCT-97
```

INSERT INTO nested tables may be handled similarly using the virtual TABLE:

```
INSERT INTO TABLE(SELECT e.dep_in_emp e
FROM emp e
WHERE e.ename = 'Smith')
VALUES ('Roxy','F',to_date('10/10/1992','mm/dd/yyyy'))
```

Now,

```
SELECT *
FROM emp
WHERE ename = 'Smith'
```

Gives:

```
    EMPNO ENAME                      EJOB
---------- -------------------- --------------------
DEP_IN_EMP(DNAME, DGENDER, DBDAY)
-------------------------------------------------------------
      100 Smith                     Programmer
DEPENDENT_OBJECT_TABLE(DEPENDENT_OBJECT('David', 'M',
'10-OCT-97'), DEPENDENT_OBJECT('Katie', 'F', '22-DEC-02'),
DEPENDENT_OBJECT('Chrissy', 'F', '31-MAY-04'),
DEPENDENT_OBJECT('Roxy', 'F', '10-OCT-92'))
```

Summary

In this chapter, we have shown how to create and use objects — actually classes in the object-oriented sense. Objects may consist of simple composite constructions, VARRAYs, or nested tables. Like object-oriented classes, our objects may also contain member functions. Unlike true object-oriented programming, functions may be created externally to manipulate data within the objects.

References

A website from Stanford that is entitled "Object-Relational Features of Oracle," authored by J. Ullman as part of notes for the book *Database Systems: The Complete Book (DS:CB)*, by Hector Garcia-Molina, Jeff Ullman, and Jennifer Widom, and class notes for teachers using that book: http://216.239.41.104/search?q=cache:KjbWS2AKd QUJ:www-db.stanford.edu/~ullman/fcdb/oracle/ or-objects.html+MEMBER+FUNCTION+ oRACLE&hl=en.

Feuerstein, S., *Oracle PL/SQL*, O'Reilly & Associates, Sebastopol, CA, 1997, p. 539, 670.

Klaene, Michael, "Oracle Programming with PL/SQL Collections," at http://www.developer.com/db/ article.php/10920_3379271_1.

Chapter 9

SQL and XML

The chapter opens a door and looks inside the world of XML and SQL with some examples of how transformation is performed. This new addition to Oracle provides a way to handle situations where data may be exchanged and manipulated via XML. In some shops XML is used extensively by data gatherers who may in turn want a more direct path to SQL and Oracle. If the new XML-SQL bridge is not used, then the alternative would be for the XML users to create a separate data storage for the XML data that would be more commonly handled by SQL and its associated utility functions. There are many facets to this new world, and what is common and popular today may well be passé tomorrow. This chapter is not intended to be exhaustive in terms of SQL-XML, but rather to illustrate ideas of how these two powerful entities may be combined.

What Is XML?

XML is an abbreviation for Extensible Markup Language. A "markup language" is a means of describing data. The common web markup language is HTML (Hypertext Markup Language). HTML uses tags to surround data items where the tags describe the data contents. HTML is used by web browsers to describe how data is to look when it is output to a computer screen. A web browser (Microsoft's Explorer, Netscape, etc.) is a program that uses a text document with HTML tags as input and outputs the text data according to the HTML tags. As an example, if a text document contains a tag for **bolding** data, the word "Hello" could be surrounded by a "b" tag:

```
<b>Hello</b>
```

The <b> is an opening tag and the </b> is a closing tag. Most but not all HTML tags have opening and closing counterparts.

 Note: This is a very brief description of XML and is not intended to be complete. The focus here is to introduce XML to those who are unfamiliar with the language, and to show how SQL handles this standard data exchange format.

XML resembles HTML, but its purpose and form are quite different. Where HTML is used to describe an output, XML is used to describe data as data. XML is used as a standard means of exchanging data over the Internet. In HTML, tags are standard. For example, <b> is an opening tag for bolding, </u> is a closing tag for underlining, <h2> is an opening tag for a header of relative size 2. In XML, tags are user-defined. Tags in XML are meant to be descriptive. With no prompting of what the following XML document is supposed to represent, can you guess its purpose?

```
<?xml version="1.0" encoding="ISO-8859-1"?>
<!DOCTYPE chemical SYSTEM "myfirst.dtd">
<chemical>
   <name>Oxygen</name>
   <symbol>O</symbol>
   <name>Hydrogen</name>
   <symbol>H</symbol>
   <name>Beryllium</name>
   <symbol>Be</symbol>
</chemical>
```

It sort of looks like HTML with some leading "header" information and tags that look like HTML, but the tags are more expressive. If you guessed that this document describes the names and symbols of some chemicals you would be correct. Ignoring the two header lines for a minute, note that there are user-defined opening and closing tags that describe the data that is contained in them. The names and symbols of some chemicals are enclosed within an outer chemical-tag "wrapper":

```
<chemical>...</chemical>
```

The point of this tagging is to allow a receiver of the data to know what the XML represents. In this document, <chemical> is said to be the root document and the <name> and <symbol> lines are children. XML is always arranged hierarchically, and references to XML documents often use the parent-child terminology.

The tags in an XML document are called XML elements.

An XML element is everything from (including) the element's start tag to (including) the element's end tag. An element can have element content, mixed content, simple content, or empty content. An element can also have attributes.[1]

Although a construction consisting of elements within elements is usually preferred, an element-with-attributes version of the previous example would look like this:

```
<chemical name = "Oxygen">
  <symbol>O</symbol>
</chemical>
<chemical name = "Hydrogen">
  <symbol>H</symbol>
</chemical>
<chemical name = "Beryllium">
  <symbol>Be</symbol>
</chemical>
```

There are some problems with using attributes in XML.

Some of the problems with using attributes are:

▼ attributes cannot contain multiple values (child elements can)

▼ attributes are not easily expandable (for future changes)

▼ attributes cannot describe structures (child elements can)

▼ attributes are more difficult to manipulate by program code

▼ attribute values are not easy to test against a Document Type Definition (DTD) — [which is

---

1   Gennick, Jonathan, "SQL in, XML out." http://www.oracle.com/technology/oramag/oracle/03-may/o33xml.html.

used to define the legal elements of an XML document]

▼ If you use attributes as containers for data, you end up with documents that are difficult to read and maintain. Try to use elements to describe data. Use attributes only to provide information that is not relevant to the data.[1]

Now let's look back at our example:

```
<?xml version="1.0" encoding="ISO-8859-1"?>
<!DOCTYPE chemical SYSTEM "myfirst.dtd">
<chemical>
   <name>Oxygen</name>
   <symbol>O</symbol>
   <name>Hydrogen</name>
   <symbol>H</symbol>
   <name>Beryllium</name>
   <symbol>Be</symbol>
</chemical>
```

The first two lines are called header lines. The first header line is a standard line that describes the version of XML and the standard for encoding data. The second line describes an accompanying document, myfirst.dtd, that describes how the data in an XML file is supposed to look. A DTD (Document Type Definition) describes what is legal and what is not legal in the XML file. When working with XML, the scenario is to first define a DTD, then put data into an XML file according to the pattern described in the DTD. If person A wanted to transmit some data to person B via XML, then the two should have a common DTD to tell one another what the data is supposed to look like. Person A would generate an XML file that conformed to the DTD that it references in header line 2 of the XML file. In addition to conforming to XML syntax, a document that also conforms to its DTD is said to be *well formed.* The DTD, myfirst.dtd, looks like this:

```
<!ELEMENT chemical (name, symbol*)>
<!ELEMENT name (#PCDATA)>
<!ELEMENT symbol (#PCDATA)>
```

The DTD says that we will have some chemicals (chemical) consisting of names and symbols (name, symbol). PCDATA stands for "parsed character data." The * sign following the word "symbol" in the first line means that the child element message can occur zero or more times inside the chemical element.[2]

Displaying XML in a Browser

XML is designed to transfer data in a standard fashion. Displaying XML data in a browser requires something other than a DTD because the browser is looking for something like HTML — a language that tells the browser how to display the XML. Stylesheets (CSS files), XSL (Extensible Stylesheet Language), JavaScript, and XML Data Islands can be used to format an XML file in a browser. CSS stylesheets are considered old fashioned and less stylish than XSL-type stylesheets; however, many people are familiar with style sheets and use them. JavaScript is yet another way to display XML, as is the use of a Data Island (binding XML to an HTML construct like a table). Each of these languages has its own tutorial

---

2   This wording is adapted from the DTD link from the web tutorial on DTDs at http://www.w3schools.com/dtd/default.asp.

which is available through the original XML tutorial on the web from W3CSchools.[3]

Note: W3C is an abbreviation for the World Wide Web Consortium. The purpose of this organization is to promote standards in web tools and applications. The W3C may be explored at its website: http://www.w3.org/.

Below is an example of an XML document with a references stylesheet.

The XML document:

```
<?xml version="1.0" encoding="ISO-8859-1"?>
<?xml-stylesheet type="text/css" href="chemical.css"?>
<chemical>
<name>Oxygen</name>
<symbol>O</symbol>
</chemical>
```

And, chemical.css looks like this:

```
chemical
{
background-color: #ffffff;
width: 100%;
}
name
{
display: block;
margin-bottom: 30pt;
margin-left: 0;
}
symbol
```

---

3   An excellent reference for learning XML may be found at a website about W3C entities: http://www.w3schools.com/xml/default.asp. This page has hyperlinks to other pages describing associated components of XML (DTDs, CSSs, XSL, etc.).

```
{
color: #FF0000;
font-size: 15pt;
}
```

XSL is far more complicated than the above CSS stylesheet. XSL is so complicated and picky about syntax that tools are most often used to create XSL documents.[4]

SQL to XML

As of Oracle version 9, Oracle's SQL contained functions that allow SQL programmers to generate and accept XML. XML may be generated in result sets from native types in tables using new functions. Tables that may contain xmltypes and functions are provided that can be used to receive and store XML directly. Each of these capabilities will be demonstrated.

Generating XML from "Ordinary" Tables

Suppose we have the following table in our SQL account, where:

```
DESC chemical
```

---

[4] A common tool that links, verifies, and coordinates all of the XML family of files is Altova. Check the Altova website at http://www.altova.com/training.html for more details on this tool.

Gives:

Name	Null?	Type
NAME		VARCHAR2(20)
SYMBOL		VARCHAR2(2)
FORM		VARCHAR2(20)

And:

```
SELECT *
FROM chemical
```

Gives:

NAME	SY	FORM
Mercury	Hg	liquid
Neon	Ne	gas
Iron	Fe	solid
Oxygen	O	gas
Beryllium	Be	solid

Now suppose we wanted to share our data with someone else and we wanted to generate an XML file as a result set. Oracle provides a function, XMLElement, that transforms data into XML format. The function takes two arguments — the tag name and the data. Consider this example:

```
SELECT xmlelement("Name",name), xmlelement("Symbol",symbol),
  xmlelement("Form", form)
FROM chemical
```

This gives:

```
XMLELEMENT("NAME",NAME)
------------------------------------------------------------------
XMLELEMENT("SYMBOL",SYMBOL)
------------------------------------------------------------------
XMLELEMENT("FORM",FORM)
------------------------------------------------------------------
<Name>Mercury</Name>
<Symbol>Hg</Symbol>
<Form>liquid</Form>

<Name>Neon</Name>
<Symbol>Ne</Symbol>
<Form>gas</Form>

<Name>Iron</Name>
<Symbol>Fe</Symbol>
<Form>solid</Form>

<Name>Oxygen</Name>
<Symbol>O</Symbol>
<Form>gas</Form>

<Name>Beryllium</Name>
<Symbol>Be</Symbol>
<Form>solid</Form>
```

To turn this into useful XML, a header could be manually put onto the stored result set ("stored" perhaps by spooling) and a wrapper tag would have to be provided. An example of a wrapper tag could be:

```
<chemical>...</chemical>
```

with the final result (without illustrating a DTD) looking like this:

```
<?xml version="1.0" encoding="ISO-8859-1"?>
<chemical>
<Name>Mercury</Name>
```

```
<Symbol>Hg</Symbol>
<Form>liquid</Form>
<Name>Neon</Name>
<Symbol>Ne</Symbol>
<Form>gas</Form>
<Name>Iron</Name>
<Symbol>Fe</Symbol>
<Form>solid</Form>
<Name>Oxygen</Name>
<Symbol>O</Symbol>
<Form>gas</Form>
<Name>Beryllium</Name>
<Symbol>Be</Symbol>
<Form>solid</Form>
</chemical>
```

Other ways of converting SQL tables into XML formats include using the functions XMLAttribute and XMLForest.[5]

XML to SQL

Creating a SQL structure from an XML document may be done by converting the XML document to a flat file of some kind. If the data to be converted consists of a series of XML files, then the files would have to be either concatenated first and a wrapper applied, or they would have to be dealt with individually. Processing out the XML tags from a concatenated flat file can take place in a variety of ways. For small XML files, a word processor could be used to edit out the tags with Edit/Replace. For larger concatenated XML files, a text file with the tags intact could be created and the tags could subsequently be removed using

---

5 See the Oracle Technology Network website at: http://www.oracle.com/technology/oramag/oracle/03-may/o33xml_l3.html.

REPLACE functions against a sqlloaded text table. It is important to include a sequence number if sqlload is used because, as expected, the order of the original data will be lost when the table is created. There are a variety of ways to bridge the gap between XML and SQL; this section will deal with how to go directly from XML to SQL by using xmltypes in a SQL table.

To directly create a SQL accessible table from an XML document, we first define a table with an XMLTYPE. We will begin by using character string literals and then try to use some actual XML data. First, a table is created with an XML data type:

```
CREATE TABLE testxml (id NUMBER(3), dt SYS.XMLTYPE)
```

XMLTYPE has built-in functions to allow us to manipulate the data values being placed into the column defined as SYS.XMLTYPE. Data may be inserted into the table using the sys.xmltype.createxml procedure like this:

```
INSERT INTO testxml VALUES(111,
sys.xmltype.createxml(
'<?xml version="1.0"?>
<customer>
<name>Joe Smith</name>
<title>Mathematician</title>
</customer>'))
SQL> /
```

Which will give:

```
1 row created.
```

The column of XMLTYPE is a CLOB. To display XMLTYPEs with SELECT statements, we need to first set a relatively large value for the parameter LONG. If this parameter is not set and the display of the XMLTYPE is longer than 80 characters (the default for LONG), then the output result set is truncated. For example:

```
SET LONG 2000
SELECT *
FROM testxml
```

Will generate:

```
        ID
----------
DT
------------------------------------------------------------

       111
<?xml version="1.0"?>
<customer>
<name>Joe Smith</name>
<title>Mathematician</title>
</customer>'))
```

This loading process may be performed using an anonymous PL/SQL script like the following one.

The anonymous PL/SQL script, loadx1.sql, is created as a text file in the host:

```
DECLARE
  x VARCHAR2(1000);
BEGIN
INSERT INTO testxml VALUES (222,
sys.xmltype.createxml(
'<?xml version="1.0"?>
<customer>
  <name>Tom Jones</name>
  <title>Plumber</title>
</customer>'));
end;
/
```

and then executed by:

```
SQL> @loadx1
```

This gives:

```
PL/SQL procedure successfully completed.
```

Now, to get the updated table:

```
SELECT *
FROM testxml
```

Gives:

```
        ID
----------
DT
-----------------------------------------------

       111
<?xml version="1.0"?>
<customer>
<name>Joe Smith</name>
<title>Mathematician</title>
</customer>

       222
<?xml version="1.0"?>

        ID
----------
DT
-----------------------------------------------

<customer>
  <name>Tom Jones</name>
  <title>Plumber</title>
</customer>
```

Since the XMLTYPE is a CLOB, we can add some flexibility to the load procedure by defining a CLOB and using the CLOB in the insert statement within the anonymous PL/SQL block:

```
DECLARE
  x clob;
BEGIN
 x := '<?xml version="1.0"?>
 <customer>
  <name>Chuck Charles</name>
  <title>Golfer</title>
 </customer>';
INSERT INTO testxml VALUES (123,
 sys.xmltype.createxml(x)
  );
end;
/
```

Then,

```
SELECT *
FROM testxml
```

Will give:

```
        ID
----------
DT
-------------------------------------------------

       111
<?xml version="1.0"?>
<customer>
<name>Joe Smith</name>
<title>Mathematician</title>
</customer>

       222
<?xml version="1.0"?>
```

```
          ID
----------
DT
----------------------------------------------
<customer>
  <name>Tom Jones</name>
  <title>Plumber</title>
</customer>

         123
<?xml version="1.0"?>
 <customer>
  <name>Chuck Charles</name>

          ID
----------
DT
----------------------------------------------

  <title>Golfer</title>
 </customer>
```

A function is provided to see the CLOB values. It looks like this:

```
SELECT t.dt.getclobval()
FROM testxml t
WHERE ROWNUM < 2
```

Which gives:

```
T.DT.GETCLOBVAL()
------------------------------------------------
<?xml version="1.0"?>
<customer>
<name>Joe Smith</name>
<title>Mathematician</title>
</customer>
```

The table alias in the above SQL statement is necessary to make it work. Although it would seem that a statement like "SELECT dt.getclobval() FROM testxml" ought to work, it will produce an "invalid identifier" error.

We may use the function GETCLOBVAL to extract information from the table as a string like this:

```
SELECT *
FROM testxml t
WHERE t.dt.getclobval() LIKE '%Golf%'
```

Which would give:

```
        ID
----------
DT
-----------------------------------------------

       123
<?xml version="1.0"?>
 <customer>
  <name>Chuck Charles</name>
  <title>Golfer</title>
 </customer>
```

Handling the column dt of XMLTYPE just as one would handle a simple string also works, as shown by the query below:

```
SELECT *
FROM testxml t
WHERE t.dt LIKE '%Golf%'
SQL> /
```

This gives:

```
         ID
----------
DT
------------------------------------------------

        123
<?xml version="1.0"?>
 <customer>
  <name>Chuck Charles</name>
  <title>Golfer</title>
 </customer>
```

Individual fields from the XMLTYPE'd column may be found using the EXTRACTVALUE function like this:

```
SELECT EXTRACTVALUE(dt,'//name')
FROM testxml
```

Giving:

```
EXTRACTVALUE(DT,'//NAME')
------------------------------------------------
Joe Smith
Tom Jones
Chuck Charles
```

EXTRACTVALUE is an Oracle function that uses an XPath expression, '//name'. XPath is a language that is used to access XML document parts.[6] The double slashes in the tag-name, '//name', finds "name" anywhere in the document.

The purpose of this chapter was to introduce and bridge XML and SQL with some examples. XML and associated topics like XPath, style sheets (CSS files), XSL (Extensible Stylesheet Language), JavaScript,

---

6 XPath is another study apart from SQL. A good reference for XPath syntax may be found at the website at http://www.w3.org/TR/xpath.

and XML Data Islands are all interesting studies in their own right. We hope that by presenting these examples, if one needs to further bridge the XML/SQL gap, then that process is smoothed somewhat. Very much in this area depends on how the XML producer generates and uses data as well as how well the creator follows their DTD to generate well-formed XML.

References

http://www.oracle.com/technology/oramag/oracle/03-may/o33xml.html contains an article about Oracle called "SQL in, XML out," by Jonathan Gennick.

Information about DTDs can be found in the web tutorial on DTDs at http://www.w3schools.com/dtd/default.asp.

An excellent reference for learning XML may be found at a website about W3C entities: http://www.w3schools.com/xml/default.asp. This page has hyperlinks to other pages describing associated components of XML (DTDs, CSSs, XSL, etc.).

A common tool that links, verifies, and coordinates all of the XML family of files is Altova. Check the Altova website at http://www.altova.com/training.html for more details on this tool.

See the Oracle Technology Network website at: http://www.oracle.com/technology/oramag/oracle/03-may/o33xml_l3.html.

XPath is another study apart from SQL. A good reference for XPath syntax may be found at the website at http://www.w3.org/TR/xpath.

Appendix A

String Functions

ASCII

This function gives the ASCII value of the first character of a string. The general format for this function is:

```
ASCII(string)
```

For example, the query:

```
SELECT ASCII('first') FROM dual
```

Will give:

```
ASCII('FIRST')
---------------
            102
```

CONCAT

This function concatenates two strings. The general format for this function is:

```
CONCAT(string1, string2)
```

For example, the query:

```
SELECT CONCAT('A ', 'concatenation') FROM dual
```

Will give:

```
CONCAT('A','CON
---------------
A concatenation
```

INITCAP

This function changes the first (initial) letter of a word (string) or series of words into uppercase. The general format for this function is:

```
INITCAP(string)
```

For example, the query:

```
SELECT INITCAP('capitals') FROM dual
```

Will give:

```
INITCAP(
--------
Capitals
```

INSTR

This function returns the location (beginning) of a pattern in a given string. The general format for this function is:

```
INSTR(string, pattern-to-find)
```

For example, the query:

```
SELECT INSTR('Pattern', 'tt') FROM dual
```

Will give:

```
INSTR('PATTERN','TT')
---------------------
                    3
```

LENGTH

This function returns the length of a string. The general format for this function is:

```
LENGTH(string)
```

For example, the query:

```
SELECT LENGTH('gives_length_of_word') FROM dual
```

Will give:

```
LENGTH('GIVES_LENGTH_OF_WORD')
------------------------------
                            20
```

LOWER

This function converts every letter of a string to lower-case. The general format for this function is:

```
LOWER(string)
```

For example, the query:

```
SELECT LOWER('PUTS IN LOWERCASE') FROM dual
```

Will give:

```
LOWER('PUTSINLOWER
------------------
puts in lowercase
```

LPAD

This function makes a string a certain length by adding (padding) a specified set of characters to the left of the original string. LPAD stands for "left pad." The general format for this function is:

```
LPAD(string, length_to_make_string,
  what_to_add_to_left_of_string)
```

For example, the query:

```
SELECT LPAD('Column', 15, '.') FROM dual
```

Will give:

```
LPAD('COLUMN',1
---------------
.........Column
```

LTRIM

This function removes a set of characters from the left of a string. LTRIM stands for "left trim." The general format for this function is:

```
LTRIM(string, characters_to_remove)
```

For example, the query:

```
SELECT LTRIM('...Mitho', '.') FROM dual
```

Will give:

```
LTRIM
-----
Mitho
```

REGEXP_INSTR

This function returns the location (beginning) of a pattern in a given string. REGEXP_INSTR extends the regular INSTR string function by allowing searches of regular expressions. The simplest form of this function is:

```
REGEXP_INSTR(source_string, pattern_to_find)
```

This part works like the INSTR function.

The general format for the REGEXP_INSTR function with all the options is:

```
REGEXP_INSTR(source_string, pattern_to_find [, position,
    occurrence, return_option, match_parameter])
```

source_string is the string in which you wish to search for the pattern.

pattern_to_find is the pattern that you wish to search for in a string.

position indicates where to start searching in *source_string*.

occurrence indicates which occurrence of the *pattern_to_find* (in the *source_string*) you wish to search for. For example, which occurrence of "si" do you want to extract from the source string "Mississippi".

return_option can be 0 or 1. If *return_option* is 0, Oracle returns the first character of the occurrence (this is the default); if *return_option* is 1, Oracle returns the position of the character following the occurrence.

match_parameter allows you to further customize your search.

▼ "i" in *match_parameter* can be used for case-insensitive matching

▼ "c" in *match_parameter* can be used for case-sensitive matching

▼ "n" in *match_parameter* allows the period to match the new line character

▼ "m" in *match_parameter* allows for more than one line in *source_string*

For example, the query:

```
SELECT REGEXP_INSTR('Mississippi', 'si', 1,2,0,'i') FROM dual
```

Will give:

```
REGEXP_INSTR('MISSISSIPPI','SI',1,2,0,'I')
-------------------------------------------
                                          7
```

The general format for the REGEXP_SUBSTR function with all the options is:

```
REGEXP_SUBSTR(source_string, pattern_to_find [, position,
  occurrence, match_parameter])
```

For example, the query:

```
SELECT REGEXP_SUBSTR('Mississippi', 'si', 1, 2, 'i') FROM dual
```

Will give:

```
RE
--
si
```

REPLACE

This function returns a string in which every occurrence of the *pattern_to_find* has been replaced with *pattern_to_replace_by*. The general format for this function is:

```
REPLACE(source_string, pattern_to_find, pattern_to_replace_by)
```

For example, the query:

```
SELECT REPLACE('Mississippi', 'pi', 'PI') FROM dual
```

Will give:

```
REPLACE('MI
-----------
MississipPI
```

RPAD

This function makes a string a certain length by adding (padding) a specified set of characters to the right of the original string. RPAD stands for "right pad." The general format for this function is:

```
RPAD(string, length_to_make_string,
  what_to_add_to_right_of_string)
```

For example, the query:

```
SELECT RPAD('Letters', 20, '.') FROM dual
```

Will give:

```
RPAD('LETTERS',20,'.
--------------------
Letters.............
```

RTRIM

This function removes a set of characters from the right of a string. RTRIM stands for "right trim." The general format for this function is:

```
RTRIM(string, characters_to_remove)
```

For example, the query:

```
SELECT RTRIM('Computers', 's') FROM dual
```

Will give:

```
RTRIM('C
--------
Computer
```

SOUNDEX

This function converts a string to a code value. Words with similar sounds will have a similar code value, so you can use SOUNDEX to compare words that are spelled slightly differently but sound basically the same. The general format for this function is:

```
SOUNDEX(string)
```

For example, the query:

```
SELECT SOUNDEX('Time') FROM dual
```

Will give:

```
SOUN
----
T500
```

String||String

This function concatenates two strings. The general format for this function is:

```
String||String
```

For example, the query:

```
SELECT 'This' || ' is '|| 'a' || ' concatenation' FROM dual
```

Will give:

```
'THIS'||'IS'||'A'||'CON
-----------------------
This is a concatenation
```

SUBSTR

This function allows you to retrieve a portion of the string. The general format for this function is:

```
SUBSTR(string, start_at_position, number_of_characters_
  to_retrieve)
```

For example, the query:

```
SELECT SUBSTR('Mississippi', 5, 3) FROM dual
```

Will give:

```
SUB
---
iss
```

TRANSLATE

This function replaces a string character by character. Where REPLACE looks for a whole string pattern and replaces the whole string pattern with another string pattern, TRANSLATE will only match characters (by character) within the string pattern and replace the string character by character. The general format for this function is:

```
TRANSLATE(string, characters_to_find, characters_to_replace_by)
```

For example, the query:

```
SELECT TRANSLATE('Mississippi', 's','S') FROM dual
```

Will give:

```
TRANSLATE('
-----------
MiSSiSSippi
```

TRIM

This function removes a set of characters from both sides of a string. The general format for this function is:

```
TRIM ([{leading_characters | trailing_characters | both}
[trim_character]) |
    trim_character} FROM | source_string)
```

For example, the query:

```
SELECT TRIM(trailing 's' from 'Cars') FROM dual
```

Will give:

```
TRI
---
Car
```

UPPER

This function converts every letter in a string to upper-case. The general format for this function is:

```
UPPER(string)
```

For example, the query:

```
SELECT UPPER('makes the string into big letters') FROM dual
```

Will give:

```
UPPER('MAKESTHESTRINGINTOBIGLETTE
---------------------------------
MAKES THE STRING INTO BIG LETTERS
```

VSIZE

This function returns the storage size of a string in Oracle. The general format for this function is:

```
VSIZE(string)
```

For example, the query:

```
SELECT VSIZE('Returns the storage size of a string') FROM dual
```

Will give:

```
VSIZE('RETURNSTHESTORAGESIZEOFASTRING')
------------------------------------------
                                        36
```

Appendix B

Statistical Functions

The following dataset (table), Stat_test, is used for all the query examples in this appendix:

```
         Y          X
---------- ----------
         2          1
         7          2
         9          3
        12          4
        15          5
        17          6
        19          7
        20          8
        21          9
        21         10
        23         11
        24         12
```

AVG

This function returns the average or mean of a group of numbers. The general format for this function is:

```
AVG(expr)
```

For example, the query:

```
SELECT AVG(y) FROM stat_test
```

Will give:

```
   AVG(Y)
----------
15.8333333
```

CORR

This function calculates the correlation coefficient of a set of paired observations. The CORR function returns a number between −1 and 1. The general format for this function is:

```
CORR(expr1, expr2)
```

For example, the query:

```
SELECT CORR(y, x) FROM stat_test
```

Will give:

```
CORR(Y,X)
----------
.964703605
```

CORR_K

This function calculates a rank correlation. It is a non-parametric procedure. The following options are available for the CORR_K function.

For the coefficient:

```
CORR_K(expr1, expr2, 'COEFFICIENT')
```

For significance level of one-sided test:

```
CORR_K(expr1, expr2, 'ONE_SIDED_SIG')
```

For significance level of two-sided test:

```
CORR_K(expr1, expr2, 'TWO_SIDED_SIG')
```

CORR_S

This function also calculates a rank correlation. It is also a non-parametric procedure. The following options are available for the CORR_S function.

For the coefficient:

```
CORR_S(expr1, expr2, 'COEFFICIENT')
```

For significance level of one-sided test:

```
CORR_S(expr1, expr2, 'ONE_SIDED_SIG')
```

For significance level of two-sided test:

```
CORR_S(expr1, expr2, 'TWO_SIDED_SIG')
```

COVAR_POP

This function returns a population covariance between expr1 and expr2. The general format of the COVAR_POP function is:

```
COVAR_POP(expr1, expr2)
```

For example, the query:

```
SELECT COVAR_POP(y, x) FROM stat_test
```

Will give:

```
COVAR_POP(Y,X)
--------------
    22.1666667
```

COVAR_SAMP

This function returns a sample covariance between *expr1* and *expr2*, and the general format is:

```
COVAR_SAMP(expr1, expr2)
```

For example, the query:

```
SELECT COVAR_SAMP(y, x) FROM stat_test
```

Will give:

```
COVAR_SAMP(Y,X)
--------------
    24.1818182
```

CUME_DIST

This function calculates the cumulative probability of a value for a given set of observations. It ranges from 0 to 1. The general format for the CUME_DIST function is:

```
CUME_DIST(expr [, expr] ...) WITHIN GROUP
(ORDER BY
expr [DESC | ASC] [ NULLS {FIRST | LAST }]
[, expr [DESC | ASC] [NULLS {FIRST |LAST }]] ...)
```

MEDIAN

This function returns the median from a group of numbers. The general format for this function is:

```
MEDIAN(expr1)
```

For example, the query,

```
SELECT MEDIAN(y) from stat_test
```

Will give:

```
MEDIAN(Y)
----------
        18
```

PERCENTILE_CONT

This function takes a probability value (between 0 and 1) and returns a percentile value (for a continuous distribution). The general format for this function is:

```
PERCENTILE_CONT (expr) WITHIN GROUP (ORDER BY expr [DESC |
    ASC]) OVER (query_partition_clause)]
```

PERCENTILE_DISC

This function takes a probability value (between 0 and 1) and returns an approximate percentile value (for a discrete distribution). The general format for this function is:

```
PERCENTILE_DISC (expr) WITHIN GROUP (ORDER BY expr [DESC |
    ASC]) OVER (query_partition_clause)]
```

REGR

This linear regression function gives a least square regression line to a set of pairs of numbers. The following options are available for the REGR function.

For the estimated slope of the line:

```
REGR_SLOPE(expr1, expr2)
```

For example, the query:

```
SELECT REGR_SLOPE(y, x) FROM stat_test
```

Will give:

```
REGR_SLOPE(Y,X)
----------------
      1.86013986
```

For the y-intercept of the line:

```
REGR_INTERCEPT(expr1, expr2)
```

For example, the query:

```
SELECT REGR_INTERCEPT(y, x) FROM stat_test
```

Will give:

```
REGR_INTERCEPT(Y,X)
-------------------
         3.74242424
```

For the number of observations:

```
REGR_COUNT(expr1, expr2)
```

For example, the query:

```
SELECT REGR_COUNT(y, x) FROM stat_test
```

Will give:

```
REGR_COUNT(Y,X)
----------------
              12
```

For the coefficient of determination (R-square):

```
REGR_R2(expr1, expr2)
```

For example, the query:

```
SELECT REGR_R2(y, x) FROM REARP.stat_test
```

Will give:

```
REGR_R2(Y,X)
-------------
 .930653046
```

For average value of independent (x) variables:

```
REGR_AVGX(expr1, expr2)
```

For example, the query:

```
SELECT REGR_AVGX(y, x) FROM stat_test
```

Will give:

```
REGR_AVGX(Y,X)
---------------
           6.5
```

For average value of dependent (y) variables:

```
REGR_AVGY(expr1, expr2)
```

For example, the query:

```
SELECT REGR_AVGY(y, x) FROM stat_test
```

Will give:

```
REGR_AVGY(Y,X)
---------------
    15.8333333
```

For sum of squares x:

```
REGR_SXX(expr1, expr2)
```

For example, the query:

```
SELECT REGR_SXX(y, x) FROM stat_test
```

Will give:

```
REGR_SXX(Y,X)
-------------
       143
```

For sum of squares y:

```
REGR_SYY(expr1, expr2)
```

For example, the query:

```
SELECT REGR_SYY(y, x) FROM stat_test
```

Will give:

```
REGR_SYY(Y,X)
-------------
   531.666667
```

For sum of cross-product xy:

```
REGR_SXY(expr1, expr2)
```

For example, the query:

```
SELECT REGR_SXY(y, x) FROM stat_test
```

Will give:

```
REGR_SXY(Y,X)
-------------
          266
```

STATS_BINOMIAL_TEST

This function tests the binomial success probability of a given value. The following options are available for the STATS_BINOMIAL TEST function.

For one-sided probability or less:

```
STATS_BINOMIAL_TEST(expr1, expr2, p, 'ONE_SIDED_PROB_OR_LESS')
```

For one-sided probability or more:

```
STATS_BINOMIAL_TEST(expr1, expr2, p, 'ONE_SIDED_PROB_OR_MORE')
```

For two-sided probability:

```
STATS_BINOMIAL_TEST(expr1, expr2, p, 'TWO_SIDED_PROB')
```

For exact probability:

```
STATS_BINOMIAL_TEST(expr1, expr2, p, 'EXACT_PROB')
```

STATS_CROSSTAB

This function takes in two nominal values and returns a value based on the third argument. The following options are available for this function.

For chi-square value:

```
STATS_CROSSTAB(expr1, expr2, 'CHISQ_OBS')
```

For chi-square significance level:

```
STATS_CROSSTAB(expr1, expr2, 'CHISQ_SIG')
```

For chi-square degrees of freedom:

```
STATS_CROSSTAB(expr1, expr2, 'CHISQ_DF')
```

For other related test statistics:

```
STATS_CROSSTAB(expr1, expr2, 'PHI_COEFFICIENT')
STATS_CROSSTAB(expr1, expr2, 'CRAMERS_V')
STATS_CROSSTAB(expr1, expr2, 'CONT_COEFFICIENT')
STATS_CROSSTAB(expr1, expr2, 'COHENS_K')
```

STATS_F_TEST

This function tests the equality of two population variances. The resulting f value is the ratio of one sample variance to the other sample variance. Values very different from 1 usually indicate significant differences between the two variances. The following options are available in the STATS_F_TEST function.

For the test statistic value:

```
STATS_F_TEST(expr1, expr2, 'STATISTIC')
```

For degrees of freedom:

```
STATS_F_TEST(expr1, expr2, 'DF_NUM')
STATS_F_TEST(expr1, expr2, 'DF_DEN')
```

For significance level of one-sided test:

```
STATS_F_TEST(expr1, expr2, 'ONE_SIDED_SIG')
```

For significance level of two-sided test:

```
STATS_F_TEST(expr1, expr2, 'TWO_SIDED_SIG')
```

STATS_KS_TEST

This is a non-parametric test. This Kolmogorov-Smirnov function compares two samples to test whether the populations have the same distribution. The following options are available in the STATS_KS_TEST function.

For the test statistic:

```
STATS_KS_TEST(expr1, expr2, 'STATISTIC')
```

For the significance level:

```
STATS_KS_TEST(expr1, expr2, 'SIG')
```

STATS_MODE

This function returns the mode of a set of numbers.

```
STATS_MODE(expr)
```

For example, the query:

```
SELECT STATS_MODE(y) FROM stat_test
```

Will give:

```
STATS_MODE(Y)
-------------
          21
```

STATS_MW_TEST

The Mann-Whitney test is a non-parametric test that compares two independent samples to test whether two populations are identical against the alternative hypothesis that the two populations are different. The following options are available in the STATS_MW_TEST.

For the test statistic:

```
STATS_MW_TEST(expr1, expr2, 'STATISTIC')
```

For another equivalent test statistic:

```
STATS_MW_TEST(expr1, expr2, 'U_STATISTIC')
```

For significance level for one-sided test:

```
STATS_MW_TEST(expr1, expr2, 'ONE_SIDED_SIG')
```

For significance level for two-sided test:

```
STATS_MW_TEST(expr1, expr2, 'TWO_SIDED_SIG')
```

STATS_ONE_WAY_ANOVA

STATS_ONE_WAY_ANOVA tests the equality of several means. The test statistics is based on F statistic, which is obtained using the following options. The following options are available in the STATS_ONE_WAY_ANOVA function.

For between sum of squares (SS):

```
STATS_ONE_WAY_ANOVA(expr1, expr2,'SUM_SQUARES_BETWEEN')
```

For within sum of squares (SS):

`STATS_ONE_WAY_ANOVA(expr1, expr2, 'SUM_SQUARES_WITHIN')`

For between degrees of freedom (DF):

`STATS_ONE_WAY_ANOVA(expr1, expr2, 'DF_BETWEEN')`

For within degrees of freedom (DF):

`STATS_ONE_WAY_ANOVA(expr1, expr2, 'DF_WITHIN')`

For mean square (MS) between:

`STATS_ONE_WAY_ANOVA(expr1, expr2, 'MEAN_SQUARES_BETWEEN')`

For mean square (MS) within:

`STATS_ONE_WAY_ANOVA(expr1, expr2, 'SUM_SQUARES_WITHIN')`

For F statistic:

`STATS_ONE_WAY_ANOVA(expr1, expr2, 'F_RATIO')`

For significance level:

`STATS_ONE_WAY_ANOVA(expr1, expr2, 'SIG')`

STATS_T_TEST_INDEP

This function is used when one compares the means of two independent populations with the same population variance. This *t*-test returns one number. The following options are available in the STATS_T_TEST_INDEP function.

For the test statistic value:

```
STATS_T_TEST_INDEP(expr1, expr2, 'STATISTIC')
```

For degrees of freedom (DF):

```
STATS_T_TEST_INDEP(expr1, expr2, 'DF')
```

For one-tailed significance level:

```
STATS_T_TEST_INDEP(expr1, expr2, 'ONE_SIDED_SIG')
```

For two-tailed significance level:

```
STATS_T_TEST_INDEP(expr1, expr2, 'TWO_SIDED_SIG')
```

STATS_T_TEST_INDEPU

This is another *t*-test of two independent groups with unequal population variances. This *t*-test function returns one number. The following options are available in the STATS_T_TEST_INDEPU function.

For the test statistic value:

```
STATS_T_TEST_INDEPU(expr1, expr2, 'STATISTIC')
```

For degrees of freedom (DF):

```
STATS_T_TEST_INDEPU(expr1, expr2, 'DF')
```

For one-tailed significance level:

```
STATS_T_TEST_INDEPU(expr1, expr2, 'ONE_SIDED_SIG')
```

For two-tailed significance level:

```
STATS_T_TEST_INDEPU(expr1, expr2, 'TWO_SIDED_SIG')
```

STATS_T_TEST_ONE

This function tests the mean of a population when the population variance is unknown. This one-sample *t*-test returns one number. The following options are available in the STATS_T_TEST_ONE function.

For the test statistic value:

```
STATS_T_TEST_ONE(expr1, expr2, 'STATISTIC')
```

For degrees of freedom (DF):

```
STATS_T_TEST_ONE(expr1, expr2, 'DF')
```

For one-tailed significance level:

```
STATS_T_TEST_ONE(expr1, expr2, 'ONE_SIDED_SIG')
```

For two-tailed significance level:

```
STATS_T_TEST_ONE(expr1, expr2, 'TWO_SIDED_SIG')
```

STATS_T_TEST_PAIRED

This function is used when two paired samples are dependent. This paired *t*-test returns one number. The following options are available in the STATS_T_TEST_PAIRED function.

For the test statistic value:

```
STATS_T_TEST_PAIRED(expr1, expr2, 'STATISTIC')
```

For degrees of freedom (DF):

```
STATS_T_TEST_PAIRED(expr1, expr2, 'DF')
```

For one-tailed significance level:

```
STATS_T_TEST_PAIRED(expr1, expr2, 'ONE_SIDED_SIG')
```

For two-tailed significance level:

```
STATS_T_TEST_PAIRED(expr1, expr2, 'TWO_SIDED_SIG')
```

STATS_WSR_TEST

This is a non-parametric test called the Wilcoxon Signed Ranks test, which tests whether medians of two populations are significantly different. The following options are available in the STATS_WSR_TEST function.

For the test statistic value:

```
STATS_WSR_TEST(expr1, expr2, 'STATISTIC')
```

For example, the query:

```
SELECT STATS_WSR_TEST(y, x, 'STATISTIC') FROM stat_test
```

Will give:

```
STATS_WSR_TEST(Y,X,'STATISTIC')
--------------------------------
                      -3.0844258
```

For one-tailed significance level:

```
STATS_WSR_TEST(expr1, expr2, 'ONE_SIDED_SIG')
```

For example, the query:

```
SELECT STATS_WSR_TEST(y, x, 'ONE_SIDED_SIG') FROM stat_test
```

Will give:

```
STATS_WSR_TEST(Y,X,'ONE_SIDED_SIG')
------------------------------------
                          .001019727
```

For two-tailed significance level:

```
STATS_WSR_TEST(expr1, expr2, 'TWO_SIDED_SIG')
```

For example, the query:

```
SELECT STATS_WSR_TEST(y, x, 'TWO_SIDED_SIG') FROM stat_test
```

Will give:

```
STATS_WSR_TEST(Y,X,'TWO_SIDED_SIG')
------------------------------------
                          .002039454
```

STDDEV

This function returns the standard deviation value. The general format for this function is:

```
STDDEV([DISTINCT | ALL] value) [OVER (analytic_clause)]
```

For example, the query:

```
SELECT STDDEV(y) FROM stat_test
```

Will give:

```
STDDEV(Y)
----------
6.95221787
```

STDDEV_POP

This function computes the population standard deviation and gives the square root of the population variance. The general format for this function is:

```
STDDEV_POP(expr) [OVER(analytic_clause)]
```

For example, the query:

```
SELECT STDDEV_POP(y) FROM stat_test
```

Will give:

```
STDDEV_POP(Y)
-------------
   6.65624185
```

STDDEV_SAMP

This function computes the cumulative sample standard deviation. It gives the square root of the sample variance. The general format for this function is:

```
STDDEV_SAMP(expr) [OVER(analytic_clause)]
```

For example, the query:

```
SELECT STDDEV_SAMP(y) FROM stat_test
```

Will give:

```
STDDEV_SAMP(Y)
--------------
    6.95221787
```

VAR_POP

This function calculates the population variance. The general format for this function is:

```
VAR_POP(expr)
```

For example, the query:

```
SELECT VAR_POP(y) FROM stat_test
```

Will give:

```
VAR_POP(Y)
----------
44.3055556
```

VAR_SAMP

This function calculates the sample variance. The general format for this function is:

```
VAR_SAMP(expr)
```

For example, the query:

```
SELECT VAR_SAMP(y) FROM stat_test
```

Will give:

```
VAR_SAMP(Y)
-----------
48.3333333
```

VARIANCE

This function gives the variance of all values of a group of rows. The general format for this function is:

```
VARIANCE([DISTINCT |ALL] expr)
```

For example, the query:

```
SELECT VARIANCE (DISTINCT(y)) FROM stat_test
```

Will give:

```
VARIANCE(DISTINCT(Y))
---------------------
          50.2545455
```

Index

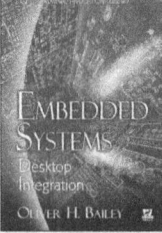

www.ingramcontent.com/pod-product-compliance
Lightning Source LLC
Chambersburg PA
CBHW060630211225
37093CB00001B/13